# GO SLOW TO GO FAST

# GO SLOW TO GO FAST

## —PLANNING TO EXECUTION—

*Tools to Disrupt Incumbent Strategy and Behavior*
*to WIN your Competitive Landscape*

## DAMIAN D. "SKIPPER" PITTS

New York

# GO SLOW TO GO FAST
## —PLANNING TO EXECUTION—
*Tools to Disrupt Incumbent Strategy and Behavior to WIN your Competitive Landscape*

© 2016 **DAMIAN D. "SKIPPER" PITTS**.

Published in New York, New York, by Morgan James Publishing. Morgan James and The Entrepreneurial Publisher are trademarks of Morgan James, LLC. www.MorganJamesPublishing.com

The Morgan James Speakers Group can bring authors to your live event. For more information or to book an event visit The Morgan James Speakers Group at www.TheMorganJamesSpeakersGroup.com.

A **free** eBook edition is available with the purchase of this print book.

CLEARLY PRINT YOUR NAME ABOVE IN UPPER CASE

**Instructions to claim your free eBook edition:**
1. Download the BitLit app for Android or iOS
2. Write your name in **UPPER CASE** on the line
3. Use the BitLit app to submit a photo
4. Download your eBook to any device

ISBN 978-1-63047-596-3 paperback
ISBN 978-1-63047-597-0 eBook
Library of Congress Control Number:
2015903231

**Cover Design by:**
Rachel Lopez
www.r2cdesign.com

**Interior Design by:**
Bonnie Bushman
bonnie@caboodlegraphics.com

In an effort to support local communities and raise awareness and funds, Morgan James Publishing donates a percentage of all book sales for the life of each book to Habitat for Humanity Peninsula and Greater Williamsburg.

Get involved today, visit
www.MorganJamesBuilds.com

**Habitat**
for Humanity®
Peninsula and
Greater Williamsburg
Building Partner

# Table of Contents

# What's Ahead In
## *Go Slow To Go Fast?*

When I started to write *Go Slow to Go Fast,* I had in my mind to offer a step-wise procedural approach for people to responsibly act on and learn to preemptively use the tools designed to avoid risk, lead out from crises before they happen and go beyond best practices using Next-Level Practice Decisions (NLPDs) transforms into Next-Level Practices (NLPs). What I ended up with was more than what I expected. The end result now enables decision-makers with reliable "real-time" data, tools and resources to begin using preemptive strategies to solve complex problems and challenges.

Go Slow to Go Fast strategy has one mission: to support operational readiness requirements with effective, transparent, cross-functional processes that informs risk-balanced decisions to be made about operating in competitive environments. It is the initial component in the Crisis

Leadership curriculum that provides a comprehensive viewpoint about the readiness and behavioral positioning of an organization's culture. The system's approach is designed to help leaders build, measure, learn, execute and report on process improvements within a supporting infrastructure. More importantly, Go Slow to Go Fast is a strategy that improves efficiencies using effective time on mission to focus on and deliver qualitative outcomes including:

- **Enterprise-Wide Early Adoption Strategies**

Asset usage to maximize and expand resources.

- **Complete Vision: Three-dimensional Future Outlook**

Past Behaviors (the future), Present Status (the event horizon), and Tomorrow's Requirements (the Future Picture).

- **Step-wise Process Improvement to unpack Performance-Driven Execution**

"Gemba Walking" to identify how to Better *your* Best!

A copy of the **Go Slow to Go Fast slide deck presentation** that supports this book is available at: http://bit.ly/GS2GFSlidedeck, along with **the Leadership GPS System**: http://bit.ly/leadershipgpssystem that is discussed in full detail throughout the book.

In the end, Go Slow to Go Fast strategy ensures the right organization is positioned with the right configuration, in the right place, at the right time, with the expected readiness to respond to tomorrow's requirements today. Not to be undone by Big-bang Disruption (fast moving paradigms that devastate entire product lines virtually overnight), Go Slow to Go Fast strategy also provides a preemptive configuration to conduct operations with positive organizational behaviors and systems to win over incumbent thinking in all kinds of environments: establishing high performance-driven execution techniques, outcomes and trends others will look to follow. Go Slow to Go Fast strategy is focused, disciplined and transforming. It shows the differences between the traditional "bell curve" known as "managing the probable" and the value in today's use of the "shark fin" known as "leading the possible" to empower decision-makers with usable, actionable and reliable information to use NOW for impacting the Future Picture.

## A 21st Century Parable

*Go Slow to Go Fast* can be considered the first book in a series of stories that explains how to use the strategy of *'Big-bang disruption' (considered modern day Aesop fables)* to your advantage, where each story concludes with a lesson learned, and then follows with an illustrative approach for users to achieve high performance-driven execution in today's world. It explains why preemptive actions focused on changing behaviors, attitudes and thinking are important to transform every aspect of a leaders' and organizations' Centers of Gravity (CoGs), known as the "Five Rings:" Leadership (decision-makers), Process (strategies and tactics), Infrastructure (organizations and emerging markets), Populations (people) and Action Units (customers and vendors)—fast and with deliberate action. A preemptive change to these five rings ultimately increases revenue, marketshare and most importantly, differentiation. And in doing so, they provide the direct actions used to create a new 'way to play' in the innovation sandbox to **start users on the path of becoming a potential "Grey Rhino"** to begin setting new trends others will seek to follow in an increasingly competitive environment and world.

The opposite approach is also critically important. A Grey Rhino is a dangerously hard animal to spot in the South African bush. It is normally obscured by the surrounding vegetation and by the time they're visible, they're most likely already storming toward you, leaving little chance to react. A leader's role today must be focused on both respecting the Grey Rhino as well as helping their people and organization understand the sounds in the marketplace of the rustling leaves or cracking twigs of an approaching challenge (or opportunity) before it's upon them. To do that, they must focus on the segments of the environment that matter most to make sure the tools and resources available are fit for the real purpose they may need to face at one time or another. This book essentially has ten (10) stories in it with lessons that will lead you to change your approach and lens of leadership to respond more favorably, responsibly and effectively making your decisions incredibly hard to combat, hence the metaphor of the dangerous Grey Rhino.

Think of the concept of Big-bang Disruptors that resemble Grey Rhinos obscure in today's marketplace noise and vegetation. They often come out of nowhere fast and don't look like what you would expect. They're developers set on inventions using low-cost experiments with existing technologies to see what new products they can dream up. Once launched, these innovations don't adhere to conventional strategic paths or normal patterns of market adoption. That makes them incredibly hard to combat. And for this reason, I suggest that a leader today must *not* be afraid to Go Slow to Go Fast to remain relevant. The marketplace is NOT fair, so get over it and get used to it. It will be what you make it after slowing down to perfectly align your future with extraordinary outcomes from your own decisions, products and services. Like the Grey Rhino, a leader or organization will either disrupt or be disrupted!

**Who Goes Slow Goes Far... Who Goes Fast Dies!**
There's an old Sicilian proverb that says *"Chi va Piano va Lontano... Chi va Forte va alla Morte!"* This is a statement that my friend's Italian grandmother would say to her while growing up. People today can glean

much wisdom from this edgy statement to lead their own lives, and the organizations they are members, to meet tomorrow's requirements today. *"Who goes slow goes far... Who goes fast dies,"* the meaning of the proverb offers wisdom that will still be dismissed by some of you today because who wants to slow down? Slowing down may result in missing out on future opportunities, or could it also mean that missed possibilities will stop being missed? As I continue to offer instruction to leaders about the importance of looking at life through a different set of lenses to see the world as it can become versus the way it is, we continue to see life and our competitive landscapes slowly morphing into powerful objectives to be conquered.

The slow morphing, *Chi va Piano va Lontano,* allows your objectives to stimulate your mind, provoke thought and plant those needed seeds to evolve, grow and be open to changing your behavior towards the future. You see, this morphing goes beyond "best practices" to offer "Next-Level Practices (NLPs)," allowing you and your trusted "what-if" thinkers to consider what others have yet to consider; "why not?"

So in essence, *Chi va Piano va Lontano* as a Next-Level Practice (NLP) will lead to optimizing your thinking, allowing you to *Think Above the Bar* to attain *Breakthrough Achievable Results.* I would suggest that you consider adopting it for further consideration and use in your role as a leader and across your organization. The resulting factors are Right-time Decision-making that facilitates step-wise choices to avoid risk by leading out from crises *before* they happen—doing more by carrying less.

*Chi va Piano va Lontano* also builds solid foundations that will allow you to do the right things to get the right things done. This alone offers a disruptive approach to the way things have and continue to be done today that has also led us into the crisis in leadership we're currently experiencing. What's most important is how it differentiates from best-practices: yesterday's news that is no longer relevant today. You can never regain the time (or effort) that was lost, so why continue to do what continues to be done that has yet to deliver the results you are seeking? This is, without any doubt, another definition of foolish insanity. Trying a different approach is no longer taboo in the creative and digital age of the 21st century; likewise, it is very welcomed and highly needed.

Understanding the value of slowing things down to go faster by making better decisions and choices about the future, *Chi va Piano va Lontano,* offers you a significant edge over your rivals and competitors. It will ultimately create the change that is needed or in some cases, the change that is long overdue to lead you into a world of innovation; disruptive innovation. Disruptive innovation helps to create new opportunities of value that will eventually guide your paths to disrupt existing conditions, business markets and value networks.

The opposite effect and traditional approach, *Chi va Forte va alla Morte…* dies a slow death. However you figure it, to lead or become a laggard, choices must be made. You're either going to disrupt or unfortunately get disrupted! These are the only two choices that now wait for your decision. Choose wisely because your future depends on it; for tomorrow, you won't be able to get the time and effort back from your choices today.

—**Damian D. "Skipper" Pitts**

# Who Can Learn From This Book?

This book is for you if you are a leader at any level in an organization that is undergoing any form of transformation, specifically a *lean* transformation. It brings a much different viewpoint and perspective on what the future can become by moving from "managing the probable" to "leading the possible." It will help address challenges in a fundamentally different way.

Rather than simply disaggregating existing complexities into pieces your teams may find more tractable, I believe that by learning to integrate the Go Slow to Go Fast: Planning to Execution processes, starting with a Lean Leadership Thinking model, you'll be able to broaden your range of interventions by learning to break out of familiar patterns using a whole different approach.

It will also help you expand your options, experiment in low-risk ways and realize potentially out-sized payoffs using a unique integration of "Next-Gen" practices for change through decision-making skills designed to transform the organization's culture to improve outcomes using positive organizational behaviors.

The book offers a defined "Next-Gen" change approach that teaches the *how* in "execution excellence" with the methodologies and associated tools that gives leaders and organizations the ability to experience high performance-driven execution. It will advance the associated team's skills (supervisors to the CEO) using process development, improvement and problem solving techniques. What's important to understand before taking this journey is one where people need to understand that eighty-percent (80%) of their effort is behavioral while only twenty-percent (20%) relates to the tools used when striving to develop a culture of continuous improvement.

This book provides tangible takeaways for everyone involved and together with your team, you'll be able to go beyond "best practices" using "Next-Level Practices" to make real-time, high pressure decisions that transform reflexive reaction into a purposeful response. This will definitely position you, your leaders and the organization to change a few simple habits of mind that we'll discuss later in the upcoming pages.

The book will also help you to understand what happened to the last change assignment you worked on that didn't produce the expected results you were hoping to achieve. Perhaps you're someone who is simply exploring a different approach to realize improvements to your levels of performance. Either way, this book will help.

By the end, you will need to make some decisions and consider how using some of the strategies may be able to help you guide your path forward to make fast, deliberate "Next-Gen" change. It's all about moving to the next level, achieving "execution excellence" along the way and becoming lean in the process to remain relevant.

Whoever you are, I welcome you to the start of a new journey. But, before you begin, I want you to learn a new term that explains *"how to lead by example."* The term is *Ductus Exemplo* and derives from the Latin vernacular, adopted across the Go Slow to Go Fast strategy, and used by us who teach it for you to learn. So, are you ready? Let's go!

# Acknowledgements

I am very appreciative to many people who have supported this body of work over the years, helping with feedback in my developing the project and the current university course. I will try to acknowledge them here and apologize for those I miss. Friends, students, clients, colleagues and most of all, Guy Dunn, Annagjid Payne and Temple University, who have all provided enormous encouragement and support along the way to my completing this book. My colleagues on our Go Slow to Go Fast journey have been incredibly important in helping to develop and refine much that is covered in this book. Kare Anderson (helped me with the title), Susan Guiher, Lori Ruff, Bob Bowden, Deepshikha Singh, Jonathan Treacy and Wade Brockington all contributed to what is known as the strategies and concepts outlined in this book.

I learned a lot about improving my consulting techniques around leadership from my N2Growth colleagues, namely John Baldoni, Mike Myatt and John Childress and am thankful they shared their knowledge and perspectives with me.

I have had some terrific executive clients while developing and testing the concepts and tools. Among them are Darnell Thomas, Jean Oursler, Louis Rodriguez, Renee Brown and Sandra Jones.

Jerry Miller had read an early draft of the manuscript and provided helpful critique to make the book more readable and meaningful. I appreciate his willingness to take the time to provide such encouragement and honest feedback, regardless of how tough it may have been to swallow, to make this project better.

The National Precast Concrete Association (NPA) gave me access to a wider professional audience with the good fortune of putting Go Slow to Go Fast on an international stage at the 2014 NCPA Annual Conference in Montreal, Canada. This event gave vehicles for reaching a much larger audience that I wouldn't have had otherwise. I am thankful to Kathy Ritsmon and my colleague Maria Concetta Cilluffo, both of whom provided a significant delivery platform for this project.

The SoundViewPro organization took a chance on the basis of a presentation and online course featuring the project in 2014 and provided support, encouragement and a live webinar audience during the development process. Ursula Sharp, Jen Parmer, Andrew Clancy, Javier Ortiz and the entire SVP team provided invaluable resources for the project that I am so very thankful.

Finally, I want to acknowledge and thank David Hancock for taking a chance on accepting to become my publisher for this body of work. And most of all, I want to thank my primary editor, my wife Nina Marie for all of the long weekends and even longer nights teaching me that no matter what, everyone needs someone to look over what I might believe is already great, but can be so much better! She will never know just how amazing I now know it was to put up with me throughout the course of developing this project. I am forever grateful.

"Chi va Piano va Lontano... Chi va Forte va alla Morte!"
*Who Goes Slow Goes Far... Who Goes Fast Dies!*

# PART I

# DISCOVER THE BENEFITS OF GOING SLOW

# 1

# INTRODUCTION
## *Take a Walk on the Gemba Side of Things*

---

This is a story that explains the importance of making better decisions using unconventional wisdom to drive results. The title Go Slow to Go Fast: Planning to Execution simply identifies reasons not to slow things down, but to position yourself to make better or improved decisions to greatly impact the Future Picture. Go Slow to Go Fast explains how using the best adopted skills and practices to focus on rapid growth with long-term success creates the art of the pivot to transform incumbent thinking and the actions that come from it. By learning from those who've done it before, anyone can increase their chances of successfully giving their businesses and organizations a much needed shot of adrenaline.

To achieve increased productivity, strategic advantage and profitability, high value-creating businesses can consistently turn to

Go Slow to Go Fast strategy concepts for solutions. At some point in time, deep and disruptive change will show itself as with the financial crises in 2008 across the globe. Be it for our civilizations, our societies, our communities, our businesses and organizations, our leadership capabilities, our teams, our systems, organizational behaviors, processes or even within our family structures. And most often it is like being hit in the forehead with a 2x4 because it is both unavoidable and ultimately inevitable. The only question to consider is "did I see it coming?" Or, "what was I doing to be caught off guard once again?"

It doesn't matter how old or how young you are in life and in business, one thing is for certain, everything in life has a finite shelf life and an expiration date. Some call it father time and whatever the name you have for it, one thing is for sure, it cannot be avoided when the time comes that it's your turn to face the outcomes. These are just a starting point when considering the art of the pivot to transform incumbent thinking and the outcomes that will follow. The 'art of the pivot' is simply about making the right shifts at the right time to remain relevant in leadership, strategy, implementation and execution that is truly authentic to impact how your world should be while moving away from the problems and challenges that define how your world and ecosystem is currently. For this to actually happen, some serious decisions must be made and acted upon to experience real change. From this point forward in the upcoming pages, this text takes you on a journey that offers a strategic approach to deal with the new age of Big-bang disruption using practical insights and tools. It explains the importance of becoming a Big-bang Disruptor, one of those people that introduce, from out of nowhere, new disciplines, processes, products and services in ways that cause heart ache to others who just don't see them coming. They don't look like traditional competitors and they don't behave as incumbents.

Instead, they are *the* 'disruptors' who look at past and present behavior to think about what hasn't been considered. They use low-cost experiments with existing technologies to see what new products they can dream up and when they hit, their innovations don't adhere to conventional strategic paths or normal patterns of market adoption. That makes them incredibly hard to combat. They understand that one of two things are sure to happen; you either disrupt or you're going to be disrupted!

Today, it doesn't matter if you one of the giants of industry or simply a community organizer working to build healthy communities, Big-bang Disruption is here and it's here to stay. Everyone with an idea to do something is vulnerable to big bangs. In essence, it mostly causes change without any early warning signs. Leaders who adopt this perspective keep everyone else tired from sleepless nights wondering "what's coming next"—and this is essentially the new 'way to play' in life's innovation sandbox—for leadership and organizational design. When you finally make-up your mind to become a Big-bang Disruptor, the resulting factor will be "Lean Leadership Thinking" that will go on to accelerate your growth using lean principles and unconventional wisdom. Since 2009, I've been researching and teaching the essence of Go Slow to Go Fast strategy concepts in the executive education environment to business professionals and I must say, over the years, we've made huge strides in developing and perfecting their uses with significant outcomes. They have impacted not only how we think, but also how others think about our business approach to the marketplace with our products and services.

The focus has been specific to understanding performance-driven execution and achieving results that are different from the norms. The integration of Lean Leadership principles offers a step-wise approach for examining partnerships adopted from lean production systems to gain improved operational effectiveness while lowering costs. The Go Slow to Go Fast approach refers to this as a "performance-driven thinking" wave to understand how relationships differ, but influences momentum in an entirely new direction. This new direction will work to achieve improved outcomes and differentiation. It can then be used to advance thinking, processes and systems to offer improvements after both identifying and understanding the expectations of consumers to meet their needs with greater value and better solutions.

Here are the six essential principles in the Go Slow to Go Fast approach:

✓ **PRINCIPLE ONE**: Think Above the Bar—address and solve the customer's challenges and problems FAST, and complete the first time.

✓ **PRINCIPLE TWO**: Understand Performance-Driven Execution—eliminate all forms of waste to ensure the customer's time/efforts are maximized and go beyond incumbent thinking.

✓ **PRINCIPLE THREE**: Discover the Benefits of Going Slow— make decisions to do the right things to get the right things done.

✓ **PRINCIPLE FOUR**: Gemba Walking is Important.

✓ **PRINCIPLE FIVE**: Utilize the Rule of Three—Leadership Triplicity™—differentiation is more valuable when delivered in sequence with impact.

✓ **PRINCIPLE SIX**: Explore the Opportunities of Going Fast— build what the customer wants and needs (MVP), while delivering what they need and want (MVA) using "Next-Gen" practices.

In order for leaders and organizations to achieve these five (5) essential principles, they must have confidence in their content, value, experiences and product capabilities. The baseline essence of value creation is the successful matching and synchronization of customer wants with business process capabilities. Intuitively, everything done in business should be systems-oriented and designed to create a value-centric platform via some process of transforming inputs into improved outputs. The problem is that traditional measures to achieve the right content, value, experiences and product capabilities in terms of overall productivity is no longer functioning effectively because change is introduced with enormous fluidity, always in motion at a pace that's unforgiving. The days are long past to just own your content, value, experiences and product capabilities. Today's requirement is one where you must now own the platform your content, value, experiences and product capabilities reside. They must provide a vision of what the future can become, carefully illustrating the opportunities to be had once the people fully understand the problems or challenges from the start.

Doing this allows everyone to be able to fully articulate the hero's journey on the flip side of the coin with better options, while delivering the right content, value, experiences and product capabilities at the right time and for the right reasons. How is it that the essential linkage between widely understood productivity processes and effective performance execution is in such productivity disarray? Regardless of the core problem or reason, a door of significant opportunity is open to transition from "performance-driven thinking" to "performance-driven execution" in organizations that practice *future-focused* applications and processes.

The long-term solution to ineffective productivity can be summarized in a single concept—the consistent elimination of outdated thinking, processes and waste. Waste is essentially any process activity that fails to add value—customer value—that as previously noted, is being progressively "lean" defined. The generally accepted origin of lean solution thinking was popularized in publications describing the Toyota Production System. Lean has three principles that anyone can learn to apply within their existing systems to improve outcomes—build, measure and learn. Together, they offer an increase in thinking capacity to identify ways to build better ideas, measure product performance, and utilize the data to learn how to improve the lifecycle of the outcomes.

These examples form what has become known as the Minimum Viable Product (MVP), whereas the outcomes from the process—the product—delivers improved and better results. Using the Go Slow to Go Fast approach, the process goes on to eliminate, raise, reduce and create performance factors to ensure the end product is as close to perfect as possible, allowing it to remain agile to pivot when needed on a minutes' notice without causing harm in the process.

The pivoting perspective allows performance-driven thinking to bridge the gaps between planning and execution. Not being able to do so creates unwanted challenges that will ultimately harm the product in the long-term. Visualize the constraints of outdated thinking to produce effective results and you'll see the challenges in performance improvements and the approaches taken to realize better outcomes.

This creates opportunities for a lack of effective communications, the continued use of "best practices," poor leadership acumen, ineffective organizational behaviors, inadequate team building maneuvers, poor organizational design and efficacy efforts and more. What's important to realize here is the continued use of "best practices." When the Go Slow to Go Fast process integrates with *lean* principles to form "Lean Leadership practices," capabilities increase allowing leaders and organizations to *go beyond best practices* using Next-Level Practice Decisions (NLPDs) that transform into Next-Level Practices (NLPs) to expose and subsequently eliminate unwanted defects and waste. There are two factors in Lean Leadership that hinders the organizations from achieving viable long-term lean solutions:

1. Inertia, i.e. resistance to change
2. Ignorance, i.e. lack of knowledge in learning what you don't know you don't know about adapting to a better meaning with greater purpose.

In summary, much has been written about the use of lean principles to achieve productivity gains, yet relatively little overall improvement has been achieved in the area of "performance-driven execution:" foundation building using KWAPs (Key Words And Phrases) for effective communications and GODOs (the things to "Go and Do") to eventually become contagious beyond the contact sport of leadership by learning how to do the right things at all times, over and over again—to achieve mastery! Performance-Driven Execution is the ability to strategically and flawlessly execute a grand strategy; doing the right things to get the right things done, while facilitating the lessons learned to ensure people are able to avoid risk, lead out from crises before they happen and take systems beyond *best practices* to impact the Future Picture.

Evidence shows that the average leader today continue to spend the majority of h/her time in unproductive and wasteful non-productive leadership activities, whereby Minimum Viable Products (MVPs) are missed on far too many occasions. Insanity has been defined as continuing to do something that is not working. Customers have grown to expect "Next-Gen" products and services, with performance results that far exceed the norms to overcome the demands placed on them and their organizations by the constant pace of change.

Something new, something different and something influential must be offered to doing business using an approach to become properly aligned with today's market demands and tomorrow's expectations. Sustainable productivity gains will only be achieved through initiatives that drive the continuous and systematic removal of waste. They must be specifically designed to help leadership and productivity processes work smarter, work faster, and work stronger to do it right the first time.

The Lean Leadership approach using a Go Slow to Go Fast perspective is the right activity to realize a "Next-Gen" solution is the way to ensure people are doing the right things to get the right things done (Better *their* Best), while introducing better solutions with better products into the marketplace. Now is the right time and the upcoming pages will not only provide the tools for achieving better, they will also show you how.

### Build. Measure. Learn.

These three words are the pathway to a successful "whatever you desire" when they're allowed to meet at the intersection of disruption and innovation. They configure an application within a well crafted methodology across the business industry known as *lean*. They offer a window of empowerment for bringing ideas into vision and visions into realities that go on to change how people see things differently in the future.

So, one could ask how three words can hold so much power to allow people, systems and things to become something new and better with so much fluidity? Arriving at the answer to this question is the very reason why the combination of the three words can also cause for alarm if they are not allowed to work together, in sequence, to result a new beginning or in some cases, a new tomorrow. These three words are the reasons why others like me have been able to save a promising career as an educator and consultant while teaching others the *how* to also be empowered by the "Build-Measure-Learn" formulation that I had to learn in a hurry after the world's economic and financial collapse between 2007-2010.

What's amazing now as I look back on the past to learn from the many lessons is how the power of these three words came into my life to identify a much different perspective to a numerical value that really cannot be used to empower anything else. I began my exploration of understanding disruptive innovation in 2010 after watching the residue from the financial collapse that caused so many businesses to downsize or close their doors, even with some of the country's thriving start-ups.

I too was hurt after being fortunate to grow my business, *The Bison Group® Corporation,* to $12.5M dollars in annual revenue (2005-2008), only to turn the lights down after placing an out-of-business sign on the door. Vowing to never have to revisit that experience again, I realized that a new normal was upon us and the unwelcomed sleeping giant who had just eaten all in its path could one day show itself again. Only the next time, I would not only be prepared, I wanted to make sure that others would also be ready on the day of its return.

Understanding the devastating effects of hyper-change with no allure for those who aren't prepared, 2010 was the year that changed what a complete transformation must look like to avoid being disrupted. My passion for developing the Go Slow to Go Fast strategy and approach began in 2010 after gleaning insight into what a successful company and organizational transformation must look and feel like once completed with successful and sustainable outcomes. I learned the power that follows the application of the Rule of Three.

Using GE's transformation under CEO Jack Welch as a model, Lean Methodology and a little constructive criticism from a few client's, I gleaned from my failures and my many lessons about how to explain what a successful transformation should look like when done the right way because I really didn't have any choice in the matter. GE's transformation using Six Sigma and a strong leadership formula from everyone across the organization made it the company it is today. Welch made the transformation program one of his personal corporate goals to be a Six Sigma company by 2000 in only few short years. He led from the front and ensured GE attained its Six Sigma goals within a strongly held and stipulated period of time.

The following six essential insights were gleaned from GE's successful transformation that I needed to learn to use as my guiding precepts. These same precepts are today, a significant part of my leadership model using Go Slow to Go Fast strategy concepts for leaders to learn and use every day. Consider them a roadmap to inspire change across environments and to help others lead change from a proven and credible platform:

## 1. Declare a Process Transformation is Required

Senior leadership, whether it's in a mature organization or a start-up, must declare (and mean), that a change is required in order to continue striving for success and remain on the right track, while making success their reality within a predetermined period of time. This means that "Continuous Integration" (CI) of disruptive tools and resources must become a cultural process to change incumbent thinking, acting and doing to realize something new. To do so, the organization must establish what is known as a "Work-Out" plan that will open the existing culture to ideas from everyone and everywhere. The resulting learning environment must prepare the ground for process transformation to occur.

## 2. Establish the Strategy Forward

Next, the plan must be decided upon based on internal capabilities, but not without ensuring that everyone understands what it means to *Think Above the Bar* to attain *Breakthrough Achievable Results*. This essentially means that 'incumbent thinking must be dismissed' to allow leaders to rethink policy to establish targets over continuing to set goals. **TARGETs** is an acronym that's defines as: Take Action Right-now Giving Everyone Timely-value. Targets have one purpose and only one purpose; to be hit versus the opposite when people are behaving in ways that allow them to continue to establish goals. In the 21st Century, goals represent the residue from the 19th and 20th centuries; strategies that no longer have a place in today's world because *goals* are opportunities for excuses allowing people to say "well, I tried but…"

Targets are established to be hit at all times. Fundamentally, to *Think Above the Bar,* Targets are created as experiential outcomes from everyone's efforts to raise the bar in performance for everyone to strive towards extraordinary results. Credit for the implementation of a new "Strategy Forward" must have the DNA of all leadership personnel who must make it their overarching policy to attain process transformation *targets* within a 30-60-90 day timeline. This will provide the steps to begin formulating the way forward over the next two-three (2-3) years. Training is critical while working to ensure people are doing the right things to get the right things done with discipline, attention-to-detail, objectivity and steadfastness.

### 3. Train While Working—GODOs (Tacit Knowledge)

The assigned program implementation across the organization must start with a heavy emphasis on training the workforce for data-based problem analysis; problem-predicting while problem-solving. Leadership must require all exempt employees to undertake a multi-day training initiative that encapsulates a significant amount of hours within the design of the plan. This is important for participants to learn the required nomenclature and methodologies, in order to create a change platform and complete a real project within the first three to six (3-6) months. Employees completing the initial steps in the plan must go through follow-up training to reinforce the newly acquired skills to ensure they are ready to **"go and do" (the GODOs)** all that is required to be successful.

### 4. Develop Master Discipline Trainers (MDTs)—Mentoring

A critical part of any training is mentoring. The success story of any triumphant finish with winning strategies across its process transformations would not be possible without a reliable and strong system of mentoring programs. Full-time program specialists that have demonstrated how to successfully integrate program requirements must lead the process in the plan.

Known as **"Master Discipline Trainers" (MDTs)**, these individuals must train and mentor key process employees to bring them into the MDT level. Employees selected to become MDTs must undergo a minimum four-months of training using applied program tools and resources *at work* under the guidance of the Master Discipline Trainer/ mentor. When successful, the organization will be positioned to soon deploy full-time Master Discipline teams to implement projects throughout the organization using "Continuous Integration" (CI) as the mantra for moving forward. Part time project leaders or employees who also complete the steps in the plan along with the program training can be placed on projects to become **"Guiding Partners."**

## 5. Achieve a State of Crisis Leadership & Performance-Driven Execution™

Leadership is the fabric woven throughout everything that offers value to an entire ecosystem. When leadership is true to the overall mission, nothing can stop the force that drives momentum from that energy. An organization's approach to process transformation and disruptive innovation must be grounded within the fabric of leadership. Its experience in the implementation of a process transformation plan must show that the best of training and mentoring efforts would crumble without effective leadership.

Leadership must support the plan and its initiatives, not just with the necessary financial resources, but also through securing vital commitment from both the senior teams and the workforce. One of the things that can be done is to do what Welch did at GE; link promotions and bonuses to quality improvement. Welch made sure that forty-five percent (45%) of each top management bonus depended on the successful implementation of program objectives (targets) with a minimum requirement for the promotion of all other employees (e.g., becoming Guiding Partners).

Leaders must commit to ensuring a hands-on approach is taken to the plan, leading from the "front-middle-rear," and in the trenches with the teams to ensure that everyone is doing the right things to get the right things done for the organization to remain on a successful path of completing its necessary tasks on-time; Continuous Integration (CI). Here are a few things that leaders must also do:

✓ **Make time, to take the time, to make time** for program success; there are **no silver bullets!** No one thing will guarantee success without the proper guidance and attendance of leadership.

✓ **Spend time in program training sessions** to personally answer questions for all participants undergoing training.

✓ Engage **unannounced surprised visits** to program review sessions.

✓ **Get the hands dirty;** make workplace and work-floor visits to make first hand observations of Continuous Integration (CI) in the workplace.

✓ **Request weekly summary reports and monthly reviews** from Master Discipline Trainers (MDTs) and Master Discipline teams.

In the 21st Century, leadership alone is not enough, more is required. Programs today engaging in a plan of process transformation require more for the overall mission to win success, fast, with impact to the Future Picture. Crisis Leadership & Performance-Driven Execution™ takes leadership, discipline and program rigor to a new level of performance to ensure all people involved are equipped to Better *their* Best. It means letting go of the past, moving away from incumbent thinking, acting, behaving and doing something new to realize what the future can become. It means that the plan for process transformation must be focused on avoiding risk, leading out from crises before they happen and going beyond *best practices.*

To achieve this and more, the plan must adapt and use Next-Level Practice Decisions (NLPDs) to *eliminate* outdated thinking, *raise* performance above the norms, *reduce* deficiencies below the norms, and *create* what has yet to be considered (organizationally and across the industry) using Next-Level Practices (NLPs). This is what Crisis Leadership & Performance-Driven Execution™ is all about, the overarching plan and parent to Go Slow to Go Fast strategy. It's the difference between leading and following; setting the trends that others follow (leading the possible) versus following the trends that others set (managing the probable).

### 6. Focus Implementation on Flawless Execution

One major reason for achieving a success story after gleaning from the five previous essential insights for successful transformation is the focused approach toward implementation and flawless execution to finish with finesse. GE's three time-tested implementation approach; "Show Me the Money," "Everybody Plays" and "Specific Techniques" offered the inspiration for me to create a key application, strategy and resource for the Go Slow to Go Fast strategy approach known as "Leadership Triplicity™".

Leadership Triplicity™ is defined as having three things that must happen, in parallel, for people to understand, learn and do *something* to impact the Future Picture. Why three things? Simply because people can remember things in three's easily without having to venture to far into the "VUCA" world around them. VUCA is an acronym for Volatility, Uncertainty, Complexity and Ambiguity. These have influenced the actions of all people, *the tenets of sort for decision-making*, in the world after recovering from the 2007-2010 global events, and now in our newly discovered hyper-speed 21st Century world. VUCA needs to be heavily considered when making high speed/high stress decisions in real-time for successful outcomes.

VUCA also plays a significant part in *focused implementation for flawless execution,* specifically when it comes to the application of

"Disruptive Innovation" (an innovation that helps to create a new market or value network that eventually disrupts incumbent markets and value networks to ultimately displace an earlier advancement). It also plays a role in "Big-bang Disruption" (known as a "Worst Nightmare" in situations, this is a phenomena whereby entire product lines and whole markets—the organization—are devastated overnight by a new comer who is not only set on beating incumbents, they actually do it without ever being seen before they are realized Big-bang Disruptors are known as the "Grey Rhinos").

The point of view of Leadership Triplicity™ keeps both forms of disruption at the forefront of everything it sets out to accomplish, becoming its own form of both disruptions by using the perspectives to remain cognizant of situational awareness and leadership as it evolves with the changing environment. Keeping a focus on the bottom-line with a need to cut costs in a competitive price-sensitive marketplace without ever loosing quality, allows a plan of transformation to remain engaged on its "Strategy Canvas:" to Eliminate things that are outdated, to Raise factors and performance above their norms, to Reduce factors, deficiencies and performance levels below their norms, and to Create what has yet to be considered by others, as seen earlier in the Crisis Leadership & Performance-Driven Execution™ essential insight. The Strategy Canvas focuses on removing defects in the workplace, in products and in services, while improving productivity and performance.

The Strategy Canvas can be considered when building a coalition of forces to affect the "Centers of Gravity" (CoGs), where the following is influenced:

✓  Leadership (decision-makers),
✓  Processes (strategies and tactics),
✓  Infrastructure (the organization and emerging markets),

✓ Populations (people), and

✓ Action Units (customers and vendors).

Leaders must be able to align all of the moving parts in a plan to allow each Center of Gravity to participate in the organization's process transformation plans, initiatives and outcomes. This approach ensures that the organization's initiatives are fully compliant and invested in doing the right things to get the right things done by cultivating plan initiatives to align them with business objectives (Targets) through available tools and resources such as developing a Strategy Map and establishing a "Leadership GPS System" to name a few. The successful application of the six essential insights created the guiding precepts in what is now known as the Lean Leadership model using Go Slow to Go Fast strategy concepts. Together, they focus on improving organizational efficacy, creating a "can-do" attitude.

Application of a plan of transformation using the six essential insights brings a marked culture change in the attitude of leadership personnel toward quality, translating it into dramatically faster "Go to Market Strategies," process transformations that greatly improves the opportunity to achieve "Minimum Viable Products" (MVP) reliability. The basics of a good strategy plan help leaders learn how to disrupt incumbent thinking and behavior to win their competitive environments while keeping three (3) things in mind:

✓ **Everyone has data and a reason to change.** The key is to use and leverage the data to compel others to think, act and behave the way leaders would like them to around their products, services and abilities to shape how their overall ecosystem (society) behaves after they put their data to work for their benefit. This means differentiation.

✓ **Every ecosystem is made up of five rings** to be influenced known as their Centers of Gravity (CoGs): Leadership (decision-makers), Processes (strategies and tactics), Infrastructure (organizations and emerging markets), Populations (people), and Action Units (customers and vendors). They must affect (influence) and shape all five rings—internally and externally—to shape how society behaves around their products, services, teams and organizations.

✓ **The Five Rings MUST Become their own Minimum Viable Product (MVP).** This means that they must become a newer version of themselves that allow their teams to collect the maximum amount of validated learning about their Centers of Gravity (CoGs) with the least amount of effort. In other terms, their investment must greatly outweigh the applied risk to maximize potential and optimize outcomes to shape how society behaves around their products and services, and across their entire ecosystem.

In the long-term, the Six Sigma effort at GE contributed $700 million in corporate benefits in 1997, just two years into the program. From a small beginning to improving product quality by reducing defects at the workplace, the scope of their program has expanded over the years, and today's Six Sigma's customer focused, data driven philosophy defines how GE and others still work.

To be the best, you must be willing to be inspired to follow and learn from the best. Best is tough to do, let alone to be, but these essential insights increases a leader's chances of achieve "best-in-class" "Next-Gen" outcomes, and even extraordinary results to get the training moving down the tracks. Without fail, a program such as the Lean Leadership model using Go Slow to Go Fast strategy concepts carries with it this series of cardinal rules known as the six essential insights for all leaders to adapt their initiatives to experience better outcomes. In the end, the strategy ultimately:

✓ Defines value with nimbleness and agility.
✓ Maps process transformation and value streams.
✓ Creates momentum and flow towards a better meaning.
✓ Establishes push-pull maneuvers using a defined tactical approach.
✓ Pursues quality and perfection to establish a high level of performance-driven execution.

Exceeding business objectives using process transformation has never been so critical as it is now in the 21st Century. The new age of doing business and leading effective teams (and organizations) that perform *Above the Bar* to attain extraordinary outcomes on a continuous basis is now upon us. It's all about improving organizational efficacy and the efforts from these essential insights that will help anyone glean significant financial and process transformation reward in a short, decisive timeframe when applied correctly, including greater quality within the threads (fabric) of leadership. Waiting to change only changes the amount of time it will take to start alleviating the pains of incumbent thinking that ultimately causes more challenges and problems.

Making the right decision *to make the time, to take the time, to make time, as so decisively spoken by my friend and colleague Jonathan T. "Tracer" Treacy, MajGen, USAF (Ret)*, and to seize life's little presence-heightening opportunities through the expressed capabilities of achieved "differentiation," will most likely contribute the enduring benefits leaders are truly striving to attain with higher value in the future.

## Why I am Starting this Book Teaching the Model?

So far, I've been focusing on describing the Lean Leadership model using Go Slow to Go Fast strategy concepts that basically leads to the development of a Minimum Viable Product (MVP) with an unfair advantage of applying the Go Slow to Go Fast process to bridge the gaps between planning and execution. I start off with laying the foundation for the totality of the empowered model and strategy to help you learn why this concept exists and what it can do if applied correctly. The Go Slow to Go Fast strategy offers the Next-Level Practices (NLPs) that will be introduced in later chapters, but for now, here's the Lean Leadership model with the MVP approach and principles in motion. It is known as our own "Gemba Walk:"

Diagram 1. Gemba Walking: LEAN Leadership Model, MVP Approach and Principles-in-Motion™

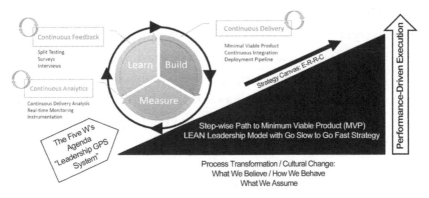

Using Go Slow to Go Fast strategy concepts, we refer to this as taking a "gemba walk." We'll address this concept shortly, but to summarize it here, it comes down to transitioning your choices into decisions on performance and improvement using different perspectives around Lean Leadership to get things done—better! It's all about becoming more rigorous to improve decisions.

First and foremost, we need the gemba walk because it thoroughly represents behavioral rigor and looks at how individuals, teams, organizations and institutions actually behave to accurately describe real-time realities. The gemba walk is a concept of lean, but when you combine it with Go Slow to Go Fast strategy concepts, it eliminates opportunities to confuse beautiful models with messy reality causing all to greatly suffer in the end.

When we confuse beautiful models with messy reality, we all suffer. Leading up to the financial crisis of 2008, for example, many policy makers deluded themselves into thinking that markets could regulate themselves (like today with some leaders who believe problems in their organizations will fix themselves), while regulators remained blissfully unaware of the business models and structures that had developed in the financial sector over time. These are oversights that just have no reason today to ever happen again, hence the reason to take a gemba walk.

The concept of *lean* originated from the manufacturing sector and the big world of business, specifically in the automobile industry. The whole concept derived from the Toyota Motor Corporation and basically promotes the concept of delivering value to your customers in the most efficient manner while eliminating waste in the process. A summation of taking a gemba walk using the rigor of the Lean Leadership model offers a defined meaning and behavioral interpretation for the way forward:

✓ Starting a simple, yet influential process (Leadership GPS System).

✓ Knowing that there's always room to improve; remaining agile (MVP).

✓ Improving constantly within the "pivot" based on valuable feedback (Strategy Canvas).

This behavioral work is far more promising than a traditional approach to identifying an improvement process. It also helps the users to learn more and more about behavioral biases and the way individuals really make decisions in their own rights. Now, all we need is for more leaders to understand the importance of using behavioral and evolutionary actions to get their teams to step up and show us how organizations can make better decisions—in their ability to pivot to remain relevant—to understand why they can expect improvements in their decisions versus sticking with wrong or even outdated behaviors. The more we know about organizational behavior that can actually help, the better the outcomes we can achieve.

Using this approach, the perspective drives the engine using a much different concept from the traditional way of leading a change program. This approach introduces a change platform that both facilitates and influences extraordinary greatness in every part of the business and leadership functions. It applies an "efficient customer-driven" approach while projecting momentum up the slope according to the feedback from *relevant information* instead of relying on pure intuition.

A simplified version here means that you must:

- ✓ Identify a clear Leadership GPS System (Five Ws).
- ✓ Build a Minimum Viable Product (MVP).
- ✓ Find out if people will pay money for it (MVA).
- ✓ Use feedback from those buyers to rapidly evolve the product into something better that will sell in the broader market (Strategy Canvas).

The scary thing about applying the Lean Leadership model using Go Slow to Go Fast strategy concepts for some is that their perceived product offering just truly (sometimes) don't really exist, and they just watch for buyer intention by using small "test-fail" experiments (mostly on the web) to identify what worked and what did not. This allows them to "pivot" on the good, erase the bad, and go to market to deliver on what the customer stated the real need is while using their final release as the solution to the problem. The challenge with this approach comes when you don't have the product or offering figured out concisely with value to move on a customer's "YES" immediately after it is received.

Despite the scariness, the Lean Leadership model using Go Slow to Go Fast strategy concepts work exceptionally well in the context of things and relates well to business on ALL operational levels. That's because the only way to know what people will buy *"is for them to actually buy it,"* or to fully understand "where the value is buried, you need to first know where to dig." And, you don't want to sink huge resources into something that doesn't sell or have value. It's great to finally see this movement becoming mainstream in different areas outside of manufacturing. All of the business concepts launched by me and my organization since 2010 have been developed according to Lean Leadership principles.

And now that the Go Slow to Go Fast strategy has been developed using the MVP approach before integrating into the system, we don't move without having either of them present. With each new line of business (and there's been many), we initially built a minimum viable product (mostly service oriented), and then we rapidly evolved newer and better versions based on customer feedback—and I must say, you need to have tough skin to embark on this type of journey because the feedback can be rough or outright brutal. Learning from our own experiences, there's another major difference in our approach now. We recently initiated another step in the process at the beginning by building and identifying the right audience using the *Minimum Viable Audience (MVA)* concept. This concept allows us to codify the right people with the right challenges to meet the needs of our internal capabilities to solve their immediate challenges and problems.

The MVA is how we identified and found our scalable business model to actually become a "real" company and organization. Serving the audience with valuable free content in the executive education space, our laboratory before launching, revealed significant insights into the problems and desires not currently being met in the broader context and marketplace. Enough, in fact, for our team to make our MVPs more "viable" from the start than we would have been able to otherwise. This led to better initial sales momentum, higher customer satisfaction, and ultimately more profits down the line.

Using this adapted process, we haven't launched a product or service that hasn't been successful since 2012 and for that reason, I strongly advocate that you start first by building a *Minimum Viable Audience (MVA)*. Have you asked yourself "what's a Minimum Viable Audience (MVA)?" As alluded to earlier, a *Minimum Viable Audience* (MVA) helps with finding out what a targeted segment is willing to buy to solve a real need from potential significant shifts in the sector or marketplace in order to remain relevant and stay ahead of the industry shifts (e.g., similar to the behavioral shifts across the law enforcement communities with body-worn technology, etc).

But without fail, today's systems allow for you to have a close eye on digital media and content marketing that affects what you're doing, as they both offer significant value when trying to identify and understand the relevance or capability factor. This will allow you to be able to deliver on the specific needs of the MVAs, thanks to the power of agile content marketing.

You'll know that you have a *Minimum Viable Audience* (MVA) when:

✓ You're receiving enough feedback from existing customer comments, emails, social networks and social media news sites in order to adapt and evolve your MVP to better serve the audience.

✓ You're growing your audience organically thanks to solutions provided to existing client needs and you begin to see them sharing testimonials across the social media platforms singing your praises. We call this valuable earned media that's priceless!

✓ You're gaining enough insight into what the audience needs to solve their problems or satisfy their desires beyond the free education you've been providing.

As you can figure, the first two aspects of an MVA feeds the third. So let's look at some of the specific benefits of starting with an audience rather than going straight to development of a product or service:

## 1. Gemba Walking

As seen in diagram 1, gemba walking is a management practice that's designed to allow leaders to grasp the situation at hand before taking action. It should take place where value is created. Value is always created to flow horizontally, yet organizations are organized vertically and "therein lies the problem!" How do you take a gemba walk? You select a value stream, gather all the decision-makers (leaders and managers) from all the vertical functions that touch the value stream and walk together for the sole purpose of impacting each of the Centers of Gravity (CoGs). "If we all took a walk together, we wouldn't have to talk;" this of course is a modest suggestion (eliminate the reason for long-winded meetings).

During the walk, everyone *must* focus the conversation by asking about the purpose of the value stream and its process, and talk to one another along the value stream. There are no substitutes for face time. Ideally, CEOs and COOs *must* participate in a daily or weekly gemba walk, as well as value-stream leaders.

Realistically, it typically falls to whoever is taking responsibility for the value stream, as well as others whose roles directly touch the value stream. And when do such walks occur? Basically before commencing a lean transformation! There is only one response to this question. Ultimately, it should occur as often as necessary to grasp situational awareness to ensure people are doing the right things to get the right things done. "The gemba walk is the best way to truly grasp the situation so that great lean things can happen—Lean Leadership using Go Slow to Go Fast strategy." It is a practice you learn by doing and learn from practicing the strategy and process. The diagram explains the steps in a gemba walk using the Lean Leadership model and Go Slow to Go Fast strategy concepts to deliver a different perspective for getting things done—better!

## 2. Serving to Receive Market Research from the Audience

Experience has allowed me to realize the value of giving time to teach using the Freemium model to increase value while gathering market research in my development process.

The Freemium model was first introduced in 2009 with the release of author Chris Anderson's book "FREE." The concept is still around today and can be used to create significant value to validate internal value for the organization's product or service offering. Now, many would argue that this concept goes against all conventional thinking because at the end of the day, there's no real benefit from it and it also exhausts time and resources.

Clearly in its basic form, the business model of Freemium was meant to tell the users that basic features of a certain product or service are given for free and later, should the user wish to explore the higher aspects of the same product or get additional benefits, it would come at a cost as stated in advance. The inherent understanding is that the free version of the product is offered in exchange for examining the product or for its limited use. That would be the quid pro quo.

Emma Butin, a social media blogger from Israel explained the Freemium concept this way; "… *The problem is that Free or Freemium is no longer perceived as really free. We live in an era where companies want much more in return for providing us a free product. In today's world, a free use of product is understood as "free of cash payment," not free from other payments. We do pay for "Free," but with other means; with information for example, often valued much higher than a cash payment. When companies offer a product at a "freemium," they're hitching a ride on the use of the word "Free." They expect users have the product for assessment purposes. But user's basic conscious understanding is that they pay for "free." Alas, the problem of Freemium/Premium is rooted when companies use the word "freemium." By doing so, they inadvertently ask users to change their acquired belief of the word 'Free.'"*

Although she may be right, I have been doing the Freemium model and concept since starting my research back in 2009, but I refer to it as the Premium concept. Why? Simply because for me, I didn't want anything in return for giving my intellectual property away other than the learning reward to test my hypothesis, formulations and context of the content. The resulting response from my respondents after learning that my intentions were to add value to them and in return, they would add value to me, was all the intellectual compensation I needed to take my product to market.

My service to my audience provided a premium return on the time spent developing my MVP and taking it to market. Using this perspective, Freemium became my greatest freely accessible market research environment that if I would have had to pay, I wouldn't have been able to afford. Let me be very clear with this final statement on the concept; it only works when all parties are transparent up front with the understanding about what is actually happening. And, it won't work in the first place if you are not already qualified and experienced with the right "know-how" to add value to the audience. Otherwise, you are only hurting people by experimenting and delivering poor information or value. The key with the Freemium concept is to turn it into a Premium for all parties by adding significant value in the long-term.

## 3. Create a Better Product FAST!

Whenever you launch a new product or service, you must be prepared to accept the outcomes regardless of circumstances. In no way shape or form can you expect the outcomes to be spot-on-perfect. Even armed with better insight thanks to the audience when using the Freemium/ Premium concept, you won't get everything just right. Plus, once a sufficient number of people interact with your new product or service, they'll do and think of things that you've never even considered. Serving as a U.S Marine, we had a saying that everyone fully understood; "all best laid plans change at first contact with the enemy." This is a good thing. One key point of the approach to achieving a Minimum Viable Product (MVP) is that early adopters of something new are more forgiving, and more willing to provide feedback, than customers that come along later. In my humbling experience, this is absolutely true.

However, no one is more forgiving than an early-adopting *fan*. People who already know, like, and trust you due in large part of the value and quality provided to them are the best initial customers you'll ever have. The key is to be very explicit about the situation. We always launch a new product or service at our very best price, on our very best terms and at our very best timing. And then we tell them exactly why: "this outstanding product or service will help you to Better *your* Best, and we're the only company that does or offer it. We're the best at it and that's why we created it for you, our customer." And by the way, we're in the process of doing this very same thing again right now with our next MVA to solve one of our many national crises across the law enforcement community. What we're learning is that our audience is quickly realizing the value and this service has the ability to attract outside opportunities beyond our initial expectations.

Although I would like to stick to providing three benefits of starting with an audience rather than going straight to development of a product or service, I cannot forget to offer this final one as a bonus; "Waste it,

Forget it!" This benefit is all about Lean Leadership because it focuses on eliminating waste that will happen as soon as you begin to strive for the end result, the MVP. On our team, we call this "Target Fixation on the Important."

"Target Fixation on the Important" basically means that you don't want to leave anything out that may be critically important to the customer. The only problem with this (as we also found out) concept is that you'll find yourself inundating the customer with far too much information causing for "VUCA" (Volatility, Uncertainty, Complexity and Ambiguity) to creep in like water. Anywhere water wants to go, it will go. For you, this may mean that no matter what you try to do to avoid *"Target Fixation on the Important,"* it will creep in at different points and your MVP will no longer be an MVP. Explore the benefits of hiring an outside professional to review your MVP and allow them the opportunity to improve on your ideas and stop you from releasing a long-winded brochure filled with unneeded information (it happened to us). Spend much of your time making sure that "Target Fixation on the Important" doesn't find its way into your initiative, allowing your MVP to remain an actual MVP.

Start with an audience, and let them reveal what they want. At that point, you'll be in a much better position to determine how much money and resources you'll need to deliver it to them. You'll also have better leverage in negotiating your valuation once the MVP is ready for launch in the marketplace. You may even find that you're wasting much more than you intended.

### Allow Your Efforts to Drive Performance-Driven Execution to Achieve "Execution Excellence"

The fundamental activity of driving towards achieving a Minimum Viable Product (MVP) is to turn ideas into products, measure how your Centers of Gravity (CoGs) respond, and then learn whether to pivot or persevere. All successful MVP processes should be geared to accelerate that feedback loop. This is a core function of the Lean Leadership model using Go Slow to Go Fast strategy concepts and the Build-Measure-Learn loop that is critical when figuring out the problem that needs to be solved to begin the process of learning as quickly as possible.

Once the MVP is established, the leadership team and all stakeholders are required to flush the engines using the Strategy Canvas to eliminate waste and outdated thinking, raise performance above the norms to improve outcomes, reduce any lasting deficiencies below the new norms, and consider what has yet to be considered in order to create new possibilities and opportunities.

These will most likely involve measurements and learning, and must also integrate the ancillary procedures (avoid VUCA, apply the new change language seen later in the text), and actionable metrics that can demonstrate cause and effect questions.

The idea of allowing your efforts to drive performance-driven execution is to work smarter, not harder. Doing this well will allow your product to have customers before the launch happens. The efforts being applied to the process must also utilize an investigative development method called the "Five W's Agenda" that asks the simple questions to study and solve challenges and problems along the way.

This agenda establishes your Leadership GPS System to ensure you are always doing the right things to get the right things done. When this process of measuring and learning is done correctly, it will be clear that a process is either moving the drivers of the business model or not. If not, it is a sign that it is time to pivot or make a structural course correction to test a new fundamental hypothesis about the product, strategy and engine for growth. This is where the Strategy Canvas adds value.

The Lean Leadership model using Go Slow to Go Fast strategy, concept, process and methodology (it's all of these things and more) has as a premise that every idea is a grand experiment that attempts to answer a question. The question is not "Can this idea/product/plan of transformation be built?" Instead, the questions are "Should this idea/product/plan of transformation be built?" and "Can we build a sustainable business around this set of ideas/products/plans for transformations and services?" This experiment is more than just theoretical inquiry; it is a first product outcome in the preemptive status.

If it is successful, it allows a team to get started with a great campaign: enlisting early adopters, adding the right people and talent to each further experiment or iteration, and eventually starting to build (or rebuild) the product. By the time that product is ready to be distributed widely, it will already have established order over potential chaos within the deployment to ensure customers are willing to accept the value it offers with credible outcomes. It will have solved real problems and offer detailed specifications for what needs to be built.

There are twelve points to consider when driving performance-driven execution from your MVP. Their design is focused on eliminating confusion from the process. The lack of a tailored management process has led many a start-up to experience conditions of extreme uncertainty, leading to the process to unfortunately go down a path of abandonment. They take the approach of Nike to "just do it" that avoids all forms of management and process. For this reason, the Italian adage is offered: *"Chi va Piano va Lontano," "Chi va Forte va alla Morte!" ("who goes slow goes far…" but "who goes fast dies!").* The best advice I can offer is to slow things down and as you well know up to this point, "slow" only means to make better or improved decisions. It's all about testing a vision continuously to create guiding precepts and cardinal rules to Better *your* Best. Go Slow to Go Fast isn't simply about spending less money. It is not just about failing fast, failing cheap.

It's about putting a process and a methodology around the development of a product to ensure the product is a good one that offers value before launching into the sea of people who needs what it now offers—solutions. With the solutions, the process that ensures its success will offer methods that can teach you how to drive an idea with the proper steering, when to turn and when to persevere and grow a business around the idea with maximum acceleration.

Here's the 12 Considerations When Driving Performance-Driven Execution:

1. The process must bridge the gaps between planning and execution: MVP/MVA.
2. Capability building must be (and remain) a top priority.
3. Effective and timely metrics are always required and must be continuous.
4. Metrics must impact the "Five Rings;" Centers of Gravity (CoGs).
5. Qualitative and quantitative metrics must be present.
6. Reference successfully applied case studies to your current realities and situations (e.g., UBER, Apple, NYPD, etc).
7. The Language of Performance-Driven Execution (change language) must be applied in the process (coming up).
8. Identify your coalition of forces to maximize opportunities within your Centers of Gravity (CoGs).
9. Ensure lessons learned are teachable and actionable to cause others to Think Above the Bar.
10. Use your Strategy Mapping feature (coming up) to identify gaps in performance.
11. Establish "agile" rules for governance; follow the rules and guiding precepts (seen earlier).
12. Understand your "Future Picture," "Event Horizon," and your "Future" perspectives—the three-dimensional window.

Keep these considerations in mind, so that when senior leaders become more confident about a program's contribution to business performance, they can start thinking, as they assess their strategic choices, about potential capability gaps and become better able to estimate the potential value of filling them. This statement simply clarifies the reasons why "better is not always better, better is not always best, but better best or to Better *your* Best" is the right choice in any process.

## A Stepwise Path to Better *Your* Best

Organizational Behavior (OB) is the study of the way people interact within groups or teams. Normally this study is applied in an attempt to create more efficient business organizations. The central idea of the study of organizational behavior is that a scientific approach can be applied to the management of people who are selected to work on tasks to achieve an objective. Organizational behavior theories are used for human resource purposes to maximize the output from individuals, groups and teams. So as you can see, it plays a critical importance in the Lean Leadership model using Go Slow to Go Fast strategy concepts.

Using the focus of Leadership Triplicity™ where three things must happen, in parallel, for people to understand, learn and do *something* to impact the Future Picture, organizational behavior is a critical element in the Lean Leadership model using Go Slow to Go Fast strategy concepts. Namely, it requires three things to occur to successfully bring successful ideas and products to market:

✓ Managing the Probable
✓ Habits of the Mind
✓ Leading the Possible

The following table explains each of the three organizational behaviors to complement the *12 Considerations When Driving Performance-Driven*

*Execution.* They provide additional reference and areas of research to help improve project performance, increase project satisfaction, promote innovation and encourage leadership to move beyond best practices.

In order to achieve the desired results within the Lean Leadership model using Go Slow to Go Fast strategy concepts, leaders may adopt different tactics, including reorganizing groups, modifying project benefit structures or changing the way performance is evaluated to ensure the MVP is delivered on time regardless of circumstances (internally or externally).

Table 1. Three Organizational Behaviors to Drive Performance-Driven Execution (PDE)

| Managing the Probable: the "Future" | Habits of the Mind: the "Event Horizon" | Leading the Possible: the "Future Picture" |
|---|---|---|
| When facing challenges, most people typically fall back on their familiar standard operating procedures: provides assurance of predictability. | Ask different questions; refer to your "Strategy Canvas:" Eliminate- Raise-Reduce-Create. Take multiple perspectives. See Systems: develop 'safe-to-fail' experiments to nudge existing systems in a better direction. | Broaden your range of interventions by breaking away from your familiar behaviors, habits and patterns using a whole new approach to expand your options. Experiment in low risk ways, and realize potentially out-sized payoffs: "move beyond the check-box" mentality. |

In order to change incumbent thinking, behaving and performing, these three organizational behaviors must also be present and considered. "Managing the Probable" (the "Future," your compass heading) *must* pass through the "Habits of the Mind" (the "Event Horizon," your bridge between planning and execution) to achieve "Leading the Possible" (the "Future Picture," your expected future state prior to arriving to it) when executing the Lean Leadership model using Go Slow to Go Fast strategy concepts. There will always be leadership implications along the way, specifically in *Habits of the Mind* residency. The most critical of the implications is Organizational Efficacy (OE). This is not a term that most leaders today have become comfortable talking about within their organizations or teams. It's not because they don't understand what it means or the affects that it will have on their systems. The main reason, *in most cases,* stem from the vacuum of leadership their enterprises are experiencing within the emerging leader ranks.

This void is causing the traits of successful organizational practices to arrive late, or not at all, at the intersection of environmental confidence to deal with the demands, challenges, stresses and opportunities that cause the gaps in overall performance that ultimately lead to inadequate outcomes. At its core, OE simulates the aggregate confidence levels across an organization's culture, starting with the people, their sense of mission, purpose, effectiveness and resilience that relates to an overall "can do" attitude and approach to doing the right things to get the right things done. Organizational Efficacy in the 21st Century does not resemble its own reflection from a short 15 years ago at the start of the century.

Today, OE is faced with the hyper-speed of change that leaders must face on a daily basis. They must be prepared to answer four essential questions—the Strategy Canvas—to lead their teams and organizations down a step-wise path of successful practices unlike ever before.

This leadership implication will ensure that the MVP process is poised to prepare leaders to avoid risk, lead out from crises before they happen, and go beyond *best practices* using Next-Level Practice Decisions (NLPDs). These decisions will start to transform incumbent thinking to ultimately realize the results that stem from Next-Level Practices (NLPs) to lead and change the competitive landscape.

## The Lean Leadership Model Using Go Slow To Go Fast Strategy: "Utilizing The Strategy Mapping Feature"

As we begin to wrap-up the introduction to the Lean Leadership model using Go Slow to Go Fast strategy concepts, and before we deep dive into the Next-Level Practices (NLPs) that go beyond "best practices," it is important for me to say that however new the concepts are in this book to some, they are proven. Executives around the world are striving to measure the impact of training and employee-learning programs on the performance of business. In doing more research while developing the Lean Leadership model using Go Slow to Go Fast strategy concepts, the team and I took a look at the respondents of a 2014 McKinsey survey.

Half of the respondents stated that they see organizational capability (efficacy) building as one of their top strategic priorities, but many stated their companies could do better. When respondents were asked about their companies' biggest challenge with training programs, their response fell in-line with the overall thinking across the globe with "a lack of effective metrics" as a growing concern. The 2014 survey analyzed the attitudes and experiences of more than 1,400 executives in all the main regions of the world that followed in a similar study on organizational capability building conducted in 2010.

Only this time, roughly one-quarter of the respondents described their organizations' capability-building programs as "very effective." Slightly over half said that they were "somewhat effective." A preoccupation with metrics was one of the most striking changes between the two surveys: in 2014, a greater number of respondents said the lack of credible metrics was a business challenge. Almost one-fifth said that their organizations did not attempt to measure the impact of training and learning programs at all; only thirteen-percent (13%) responded that their organizations tried to quantify the *financial* return on their learning or training investments. These findings support the need to learn how to apply and utilize the Lean Leadership model using Go Slow to Go Fast strategy concepts to identify ways to differentiate from incumbent thinking.

It was once said, "Leaders practice repetitively until they can't get things wrong." The upcoming information outlines the basic steps leaders can use to develop a promising change platform to make change happen, matter and stick using the Lean Leadership model using Go Slow to Go Fast strategy concepts. Accordingly, the approach taken with outlining the change platform marries into the perspective of Leadership Triplicity™, whereas you'll see how three things need to happen, in parallel, for people to understand, learn and do *something* (achieve the "MVP" in this case) to impact the Future Picture.

Essentially, this information describes the "Strategy Mapping" feature that both supports a successful implementation plan with defined strategies and processes. The feature also provide an effective series of metrics known as "Measures of Merit" to support the "gemba walking" concept that goes on to alleviate growing concerns when driving performance-driven execution in the face of VUCA: Volatility, Uncertainty, Complexity and Ambiguity. The "gemba walking" concept takes on another important perspective in the "rule of three." In the concept of the rule of three, the Go Slow to Go Fast strategy concept using Lean Leadership Thinking applies the rule using what is known as "Leadership Triplicity™." Using the Leadership Triplicity™ perspective, decision-makers can inspire their users to only focus on three *things* within the Strategy Mapping feature. These three things include:

1. The ability to establish Six Essential Insights.
2. Go Slow to Go Fast strategy concepts.
3. The ability to leverage your Data to define what the future can become.

These concepts are used to empower the applications within the Lean Leadership model using Go Slow to Go Fast strategy concepts (a change platform with positive organizational behaviors to bring cultural transformations, MVPs and MVAs into reality):

## I. Establish Six Essential Insights (your Cardinal Rules).

1. Declare a Process Transformation is Required.
2. Establish your Strategy-Forward.
3. Train While Working—GODOs (Tacit Knowledge).
4. Develop Master Discipline Trainers (MDTs)—Mentoring.
5. Achieve a State of Crisis Leadership & Performance-Driven Execution™.
6. Focus Implementation on Flawless Execution—the Art of the Debrief.

## II. Go Slow to Go Fast (Bridge the Gap Between Planning and Execution)

✓ Build a Case for Change (?!). The symbols require you to ask a question and then to act on the answer by adding value for accountability purposes.

✓ Become Contagious Beyond the Game: Speak the Language of Performance-Driven Execution™ (Novo, Distinctio, Cretum/ Cresco, Socius, OrgSx and Exitus/Exigo)

✓ Avoid the Poker's Bluff (Internal Capabilities vs. Actual Outcomes)
✓ Create an Opportunity Statement
✓ Impact using your Centers of Gravity: Leadership (decision-makers), Processes (strategies/tactics), Infrastructure (organization/emerging markets), Populations (people), Action Units (customers/vendors)—the **"Five Rings"**

### III. Leverage your Data (It's ALL about the Data): Gemba Walking!
✓ **Work Step 1.** Establish your Leadership GPS System™
✓ **Work Step 2.** Achieve your MVP: Build IDEAS- Measure Product- Learn from Data
✓ **Work Step 3.** Establish your Strategy Canvas: Eliminate-Raise-Reduce-Create

Remember, you must not forget to apply the "Four Phases of Innovation" (with metrics: Qualitative, Quantitative, Vanity, Lagging, Leading and Exploratory) at each intersection of the Leadership Triplicity™ to achieve "Correlation" and "Causality" when going through the following four phases to optimize outcomes and results:

✓ **Phase 1. Initial Diffusion: Systematic Innovation**—new systems/processes that are far reaching.
✓ **Phase 2. Fast (Early) Growth: Radical Innovation**—new products/services to cause an eventual departure from the normal (expected) trajectory.
✓ **Phase 3. Fast (Late) Growth: Incremental Innovation**—realize your "Bandwagon Effect"
✓ **Phase 4. Maturity: New Specifics & Know-how's:** Go-to-Market Strategies (OrgSx: the "Pearl Effect")

## Leaders Know the Nomenclature is Different Between Strategy, Implementation and Execution

I read an article that shared the difference in nomenclature between three important behaviors that every leader should learn. The article did a wonderful job identifying the great differences between strategy, implementation and execution, and how the wrong word choice when dealing with each of them can either provide a great service to all involved or an even greater disservice. In my experiences, when leaders don't have a good grasp and understanding on the differences between the three, the actions from their decisions ultimately erodes, if not corrupts the minds of those people who are entrusted to lead.

This reminds me of that saying that we've all heard in our careers at some point; "knowledge is power." I must say that knowledge is not power when it is used in the wrong manner. Knowledge is only power when it is used within the context of making the best decisions possible to influence better outcomes or to provide improvements to a process or processes to change situations for the better. Ask yourself these three questions:

1.  How meticulous are you and your team about word choice as it relates to strategy, implementation and execution?
2.  Are you one of those leaders who don't know the differences between them?
3.  Are you someone who understands the critical importance of deciding the power of your own and your organization's destiny by choosing the right words to make better decisions to get the right things done?

The three questions carry significant implications in the Lean Leadership model using Go Slow to Go Fast strategy concepts, and you need to understand what they are before moving forward with strategy, implementation and execution. "To lead the future that you want, you must first have a clear vision that is useful and a compelling image of an available Future Picture for others to see, understand and be willing to do."

This cannot be realized without having an understanding between the management concepts in strategy, implementation and execution to allow people to be and feel empowered. **Empowerment can be defined as the creation of an environment in which people at all levels feel they have a voice in the matter and a real influence over standards of quality, service and effectiveness within their areas of responsibility.**

It is a strategy and philosophy that enables people to make decisions about leading the possible in the future versus managing the probable in the now—a pass through of habits in the mind. In organizations where this learning style has yet to catch on to become the natural behavior over the adaptive behavior, it will be a difficult change to embrace. But, for those organizations who are close or willing to make the changes, efforts to learn new adaptive approaches will cause success in the long-term. This is why Lean leadership using Go Slow to Go Fast strategy concepts was developed; to empower people when helping them to understand the differences between the strategy, implementation and execution in Lean enterprise thinking.

There are meaningful distinctions when people are empowered with knowing and understanding the differences between strategy, implementation, and execution in business. Ignoring, blurring or getting them wrong will create and impeded operations moving forward with the proper momentum needed to resolve issues. It simply creates sloppy thinking, deciding and doing across each operating level and will easily seep into the customer user experience.

Most experts who are familiar with using Lean enterprise thinking as a strategy in organizations will most likely make statements to the effect of "…. the major obstacle in getting organizations to onboard lean thinking is their inability to trust the overall culture and to really give up a certain level of control in order to give people the power to implement their own ideas in areas that will allow their expertise to show and be respected as experts in their area…." This way of thinking fails at understanding the real definition of what and how "strategy" empowers people and ultimately, organizations.

As the term is understood, strategy consists of two categories: organizational strategy and business unit strategy. Organizational strategy consists of CEOs and top executives making just three basic choices:

1. What should be the capabilities that distinguish the organization?
2. What should be the organization's comparative advantage in adding value to its individual businesses and the user experience?
3. What business should the organization be in to provide value?

These are the fundamental choices that organizational strategy comprises and they should frame and guide all the decisions the organization's top leadership, decision-makers and executives to make every day, including how they run daily operations, what they buy, what markets they enter, how they identify emerging markets for growth, and how they measure success, and so on.

For a business unit strategy, there are also three key decisions that cannot be delegated by its leader. They are different, but no less fundamental:

1. Who is the Minimum Viable Audience (MVA) that defines our target market?

2. What should be the value proposition that differentiates our products and services with the customers in those target markets?
3. What should be the capabilities that make our business better than any other in delivering that value proposition?

These are the choices that a business strategy comprises and they should drive the decisions a business unit's leadership team, functions, and staff make every day, including pricing, R&D, where to manufacture and many more. Organizations that support empowered people with an understanding of strategy definitely posses some common characteristics:

✓ There are few management layers in the organization.
✓ Wide spans of agile control (allowing people to be flexible in their creativity) exist with relative responsibilities and accountabilities.
✓ A process-based organization structure is established as opposed to a purely functional based structure.
✓ Leadership stands fervently behind people allowing them to be and feel empowered.

This brings us to implementation. Implementing a strategy consists of all the decisions and activities required to turn the two sets of strategic choices just described into reality. If the organization has the capabilities, enterprise advantage and business portfolio it wants after using Lean thinking to go beyond the "Go-no-Go" point, its strategy is implemented. If the unit has the customers after using the MVA proposition to add value, along with the skills it has chosen that are disciplined to uphold the rigors to follow, its strategy is also fully implemented.

Of course, almost by definition, a strategy can never actually be fully implemented because everything that you necessarily assumed when formulating it: customer constructs, technology, regulations, competitors and so on, is in a constant state of flux. CEOs and their business unit leaders must continuously evolve their strategies (i.e., those fundamental choices listed above) if they are to remain relevant and competitive.

And if that's the case, there will always be gaps between planning and execution about where the organization is with its capabilities and what their strategies call for. Closing that gap is "implementation." Thus, strategy and implementation are running almost continuously in parallel rather than in sequence, and must remain always in motion to deal with the changes in the operating environment. Organizations that support empowered people with an understanding of implementation definitely posses some common characteristics:

✓ People understand the importance of "Gap Analysis" with the importance of using bench marking tools such as the Strategy Canvas, Six Sigma's DMAIC, the Balanced Scorecard, etc to close those gaps.

✓ There are mechanisms (hives) in place to create a surge around change.

✓ Agile environments are important across the culture to inspire cultural change.

✓ Leadership stands fervently behind people allowing them to use "low-risk" experiments to broaden the organization's range of interventions by breaking out of familiar patterns using a whole new approach to expand options. This empowers people to strive to experience potentially out-sized payoffs to move beyond the check-in-the-box mentality and lead into the possible.

With strategy and implementation outlined to show what they are and how they empower people and decision-makers, what, then, is execution? I've been talking about execution my entire life. As a United States Marine, I had the pleasure of learning about execution at a very young age by one of the finest organizations on the planet known by all for its ability to execute, both flawlessly and strategically. I tell folks all of the time; "don't speak of execution as a wise strategy if it is not two dimensional: flawless and strategic." One allows you to finish with finesse and the latter allows you to make every action matter and link to another behavior to increase value within the outcomes.

I define execution as the decisions and activities you undertake in order to turn your implemented strategy into commercial success using the two dimensional perspective. To achieve "execution excellence" is to realize the best possible results a strategy and its implementation will allow. It's the difference between "managing the probable" and "leading the possible" that passes through the "habits of the mind" to experience an ultimate transformation.

To understand what this means, let's say that a non-profit organization decides to operate as a for-profit business with the defining organizational behaviors used to generate significant revenues as a strategic choice (as I defined above). Once the organization establishes its new strategy and has gone as far as to institutionalize it across the enterprise, that "strategy" (or that part of its strategy) is implemented.

Now, they must do things such as establish target objectives and plans for the new enterprise, establish the right incentives, create a purpose-driven mission statement, and other such things that leaders do to get results from their companies. They must also ensure that the organizational behaviors are poised to impact both group and individual performance and activity within the organization. They make sure that internal and external perspectives are the two drivers of performance-driven execution, and are used to guide positive organizational behavior

(MVP and MVA) to achieve organizational efficacy at the highest levels by and for the organization. Those are all activities needed to produce results within the context of an implemented strategy. This is execution.

Strategy, implementation and execution are three empowerment determinants that successful leaders and organizations use within their daily operating nomenclatures. They determine the results in outputs both at the organizational and business unit levels, but cannot achieve their designed effects without having leadership and performance-driven execution present.

The results are incredibly difficult to achieve if the differentiators are not fully understood before going into any one of them. When we see an organization or business unit producing poor results over multiple years, no one can say for sure whether it's due to poor strategy, implementation, or execution. But in my experience, it's very difficult to implement a poor strategy well and doubly difficult to produce excellent results with a poor strategy that's being poorly implemented—and of course, having a great organizational or business strategy is no guarantee of achieving great results either; you still have to implement and execute well.

I refer to people doing the implementation concept well as them being able to *"Think Above the Bar"* to attain *"Breakthrough Achievable Results;"* a concept that still today, most leaders and organizations continue to get wrong without fail.

Understanding strategy, implementation and execution increases success in all things and without them, high levels of trust will always be in jeopardy. Having a high level of trust within the workforce, those who know best how to improve the operation, will feel more confident in their abilities when they all know that everyone fully understands the differences in strategy, implementation and execution. Lean thinking helps, but not without people being and feeling they are empowered to do the right things to get the right things done to help the situation improve with impact to the Future Picture.

Once the three are understood, eliminating waste with continuous improvement and integration will become a way of thinking to be truly successful. The trick is to leverage one's self though the talents of everyone involved by following the tenets in *The Leadership Challenge* authored by James Kouzes and Barry Z. Posner, with their *Five Practices of Exemplary Leadership®: Model the Way, Inspire a Shared Vision, Challenge the Process, Enable Others to Act, and Encourage the Heart.* These actions will get everyone moving in the same direction using the same amounts of energy towards the same objectives.

Together with understanding the differences between strategy, implementation and execution, people will be empowered in their application of the Lean Leadership model using Go Slow to Go Fast strategy concepts. The distinctions I make above are not between thinking and doing, deciding and acting or planning and producing. All of these kinds of activities are involved in all three of strategy, implementation, and execution.

Does that make strategy, implementation, and execution the same thing? Absolutely not. They each involve very different specific activities, tools, and people. And when business leaders conflate strategy, implementation, and execution, they usually end up with a lot of the success trappings of running a 21st Century organization or business unit: setting goals instead of establishing targets, choosing a change program versus a change platform, making plans over setting initiatives, and not realizing the purpose of the MVP mission, vision, and purpose to achieve the MVA value proposition and statements. These success trappings are mostly due to leaders having very little actual strategy, implementation, or execution experience.

Empowerment is in the hands of the beholders when a full understanding of strategy, implementation, and execution are institutionalized using Lean enterprise thinking. Why? Simply because the best leaders are insatiable learners who have little to no excuses for ever being led astray into the abyss. They establish a process and set the direction for their organizations to follow while allowing the workforce to identify ways to achieve the possible. And, by allowing the workforce to feel and be free to explore, they experience more productive operations and promise. The process of adapting to an empowerment style using Lean enterprise thinking that subjugates high levels of success requires operating with strategy, implementation and execution. There's no better way to achieve this and more than to exercise the applications of the Lean Leadership model using Go Slow to Go Fast strategy concepts responsibly. But be warned; care must be taken to educate and transition all those involved.

Lean enterprise thinking is a difficult transition to make, but is one that can be accomplished. It does take time and having a coach can be a real help. Your coach can come from many different places. For me, in addition to having a few consulting coaches, I'm a serious reader, self motivator, consummate educator and look to be inspired by thought-leaders anywhere I can find one. Ken Favaro, a senior partner in the New York office at the consulting firm Strategy& (formerly Booz & Company) and the global head of its Enterprise Strategy practice, recently talked about strategy, implementation and execution and inspired me to glean insight from him to share some of it in my book. I would encourage you to also become a reader, self motivator and consummate educator, and look to be inspired by other thought-leaders to impact your journey in life.

## Strategy Don't Always Work According To Plan...

What I had to learn like most other leaders have (in most cases, the hard way) is that strategy doesn't work the way we think or believe that it does. The importance of investigating the organizational dynamics offered in this book speaks to a more related issue: when I have my academic hat on, there's a lot of time to spend looking at the way strategic decisions are really created. Often, what we call strategy is less about navigating to a distant functional point in the future than it is on placing strategy under a microscope in a fictional universe where ideas are made and analyzed about the "what-ifs" and allocating resources among competing projects or the people in the scenarios are decoded. In the real world where I have to keep my CEO hat on to keep the ship afloat and out at sea, even our infatuation with innovation integration may have to do more with making sure the organization keeps its focus on customers than it does with launching new products and services. No matter what, strategy acts as a motivating factor within a series of critical moving parts that are disciplined on helping to avoid organizational pathologies.

*Organizational pathology* draws an extended metaphor that the life cycle of an organization is akin to the biological life cycle. Like all living things, organizations will encounter problems and challenges that lead to decline and eventual failure when strategy does not move to overcome the challenges it is designed to resolve.

Go Slow to Go Fast strategy concepts lend purpose to the basic problems and life threatening diseases responsible for an organization's potential failure or even death. The consideration of these issues follows a diagnostic model to be used at any juncture and in any scenario. My argument is one where organizational challenges and problems that lead to failure can be predicted or diagnosed early when the proper tools, resources and people are allowed to be utilized in the right manner.

When doing so, the severity of challenges and problems can be identified and possible remedies can be implemented to avoid escalating crises. At the very least, strategy provides an understanding that is gained from the analysis of why and how decline is able to start in the first place, and on an unfortunate slippery slope. By leveraging behavioral and evolutionary work, we can get a much clearer picture of the organizational reality of strategy and a better understanding of how to add value through cognitive issues (such as the use of the right frameworks and analogies) and a focus on the most relevant parts of the environment; business and non-business alike. And without focusing too much on the negative, we need to understand strategic failure better in order to identify the process that drives it before the turbulence happens.

As these things relate to a leader's own growth to guide h/her organization to greener pastures, I would suggest this information be used and the concept of *lean enterprise thinking* to be adopted. Everyone involved will need to be patient to realize that the organization is learning a new way to operate, but once it is successful with adapting to the strategy, implementation and execution tactics, everyone in the process—essentially the entire organization—will have taken a major step towards to being *lean* and not just talking about becoming a lean enterprise.

Even with all of the things outlined and talked about up to this point, none of it is even possible without first understanding the Go Slow to Go Fast strategy concepts, known as Next-Level Practices (NLPs), in the upcoming pages. Lean enterprise thinking is a great adaption for some and a nightmare for others when they are not prepared to transition. And here's one more thing to consider before getting ready to move in a new direction. According to a recent Harvard Business Review article, think about using the "8-1,800 Rule:"

✓ If you have to solve a challenge or problem, or to make a decision, 8 people should be included in the process.
✓ If you need results and want to brainstorm an idea, 18 people should be included in the process.
✓ And, if you want to rally the troops around something new for the organization, up to 1,800 people should be included in the process.

In the whole thick of things, clearly to rally the troops, you'll definitely need mass. But to brainstorm an idea, solve a challenge or problem, or to make a decision, 8-18 people will do. However, as with anything operating in our fast-paced and changing environment (the new world order of 21st Century technology), leaders and organizations can no longer fail to adapt to change.

The consequences are far too great and will ultimately lead them to becoming laggards—and we all know the rest of the story with these folks regardless of how many people are involved in the process. At the end of the day, the key is to "Lead by Example" (Ductus Exemplo) and take others along the way on your journey to **Better *your* Best! It's always better to have others with you when crossing the finish line because collaboration is the real currency that pays the largest dividends.** Get on your way and learn why you must pivot, *and how to pivot*, the right way using Go Slow to Go Fast to begin transforming your future with impact. If you don't and if you continue to wait, someone else will do it for you. Trust me, they will.

# 2

# What it Means to
# Go Slow to Go Fast

---

*"Time is uncertain for people who wait. Time is sluggish for people who are afraid. Time is long for people who persevere. Time is short for people who celebrate. Time is deliberate for those who rejoice, but for people who see what others don't and do what others won't, time is what they make it to become with lasting memories of extraordinary outcomes."*
— **Damian D. "Skipper" Pitts**

## What it Means to Go Slow to Go Fast

A simple and elaborate approach to doing the right things to get the right things done, Go Slow to Go Fast offers a preemptive methodology and concept used within the context of Crisis

Leadership & Performance-Driven Execution. Before defining it, I must first help you understand the foundations from which it is constructed and introduced. Crisis Leadership & Performance-Driven Execution is a disruptive innovation approach to avoiding risk by leading out from crises before they happen. Imagine having the ability to transform changes in the distant future, let's say ten years from now, but bring them into realization by eliminating five-to-seven years to attain impactful outcomes early. That's what Crisis Leadership & Performance-Driven Execution is all about and the Go Slow to Go Fast strategic approach helps to achieve its target objective. Together, they offer a preemptive and disruptive strategic focus used to guide leadership and strategy decisions to do the right things to get the right things done… essentially, getting more done by carrying less in the long run. So now that the foundation is defined, let's start to unpack the Go Slow to Go Fast strategy. This is a tactical concept used for achieving the objectives using high performance-driven execution. It is the concrete to shore-up the foundation when moving forward using a disciplined approach. It introduces process transformation methodology that transitions the users mind to help in the understanding of the critical importance of slowing things down to improve situational awareness. And to begin, it takes from the old country of Italy and the Sicilian proverb *"Chi va Piano va Lontano… Chi va Forte va alla Morte!"* This translates to mean *"who goes slow goes far, who goes fast dies."*

Why is this important? Simply by slowing things down, leaders are able to see things more clearly, allowing them to be more effective in their communications with others. Decision-making becomes clearer as well allowing them to focus on doing the right things to get the absolute right things done. Instead of focusing on the normal pace of the day (rat race), the focus is on identifying opportunities to learn how to Better *their* Best ensuring momentum remains in their favor to address the challenges and problems before they can fester into bigger issues.

Go Slow to Go Fast also has an underlying purpose; it allows everyone to use their creative juices to develop accurate, disciplined (iterative), and value-added decisions to empower others within the organization. And by empowerment, I mean that everyone is focused on making sure organizational output is significantly poised (disciplined) to eliminate risk, missteps and dysfunctional behaviors that are all too familiar with incumbent behaviors, strategies and outputs.

Go Slow to Go Fast is a behavior that is in itself set on process transformation, and at the same time, it fosters transforming thought-leadership and outright culture change. My work with Wachovia Banks based in Charlotte, NC *(pre the economic downfall) for example,* identified strategic leadership as an institutional learning tool and critical skill for developing a culture that could adapt quickly to change. And as the banking community is known for changing at a snail's pace, this alone was very disruptive thinking back in early 2005.

Teams were able to slow process down without the need for authority from the corporate offices to gain better and real-time understanding of what was actually happening in the branches with the customer base. Emerging leaders were allowed to make process more explicit without changing the "BIGMAC" so to speak. Just the idea of taking a "time-out" to glean greater insight into customer data sets (needs over wants) at the management levels to learn exactly how to deliver on the voice of the consumer became a key performance indicator over time. It wasn't long before the entire culture was set on changing the belief not because it was a top-down decision and process, but because it was the right thing to do from every department. The brand was morphing into an improved people-centric ecosystem whereby everyone had a voice in the way the customer was to be treated. No longer as a banking relationship simply a product-based engagement; making sure the customer was serviced with the right needs for their long-term needs became a critical daily function that was also represented on the profit-loss statement. Happiness became a key performance indicator that leaders throughout the culture were allowed to control. The perspective of Go Slow to Go Fast took root and led to permanent changes in business performance.

With Go Slow to Go Fast strategy in business, there a significant difference between slowing things down to go faster with competitive strategy and the speed that an organization is actually capable of moving. The traditional rat race today with organizations led by leaders who are afraid of losing their competitive edge seems to always want the pace to be go-go-go. But, in a study conducted on 343 business organizations by the Forum Corporation, a global professional services firm, organizations and their leaders who embraced the go-go-go approach to gain an edge over their rivals ended up with lower sales and lower operating profits than those who paused at the right moments to make sure they were still on the right track to achieve their objectives. Even better, those organizations who slowed down improved their bottom lines, on average increased their sales by forty-percent (40%) and their operating profits by fifty-two percent (52%) over a three-year period.

The reason this was the case had nothing to do with luck, speed or business magic in defying the laws of business physics. Instead, it related to thought-leadership and the lens of change. Leaders in better performing organizations thought differently about what "slower" and "faster" meant and this was important. Leaders in the throes of competitive chaos, in most cases, disconnected with reality to believe operational speed (moving quickly) overcomes strategic agility (reducing the time it takes to deliver value). This is a critical mistake that businesses continue to make simply because the two concepts are quite different. Simply increasing the pace of production using the go-go-go conceptual perspective, for example, often leads to decreased value over time, in the form of lower-quality product and service outputs. Likewise, new initiatives that move fast may not deliver any value if the time to slow down to gain a better perspective isn't taken to identify and adjust the true value proposition of the situation or initiative they will be used.

Go Slow to Go Fast strategy identifies the importance of slowing down to boost momentum in the long-run. Leaders who learn the importance of this strategy places themselves and their organizations in a position to *Think Above the Bar* to attain *Breakthrough Achievable Results*. And with this, it is much different from thinking-outside-the-box; raising the bar through thought-leadership simply means to consider going where no others have considered. This means that you're willing to consider and behave using the following direct actions that most people take for granted:

- What factors can we *eliminate* that seem to be outdated?
- What factors can we *reduce* deficiencies below their norms?
- What factors can we *create* that have yet to be considered?
- What factors can we improve upon or *rise* above the norms?

Taking from Blue Ocean Strategy Canvas, these four questions ultimately cause for pause because they inspire challenging direct actions when leaders truly consider ways of achieving a significant edge over the competitive landscape. They represent a leader's ability to take pause and the need to *Think Above the Bar* using strategic agility (reducing the time it takes to deliver value) over the go-go-go theory or concept that stems from operational speed (moving quickly). Go Slow to Go Fast strategy aligns with strategic agility because it creates alignment and makes it a purposeful priority with every stakeholder. Everyone is encouraged to *Think Above the Bar* to encourage creativity from one another with time (not too much) for reflection when the need to act on ideas becomes the requirement to win.

In contrast, not doing so will definitely cause performance to suffer and things like morale issues, lack of collaboration, high deficiency rates and more unwanted turbulence that ultimately leads to chaotic situations later. Ultimately, Go Slow to Go Fast strategy works well when it is allowed to become a functional aspect of a leader's ability to get the organization and environment to focus on doing the right things to get the right things done. Teams that become comfortable taking time to get things right, rather than plow ahead full bore, are more successful in meeting their objectives. That kind of assurance can only be met by understanding the importance of slowing things down to make better decisions to be able to speed things up later. And for this reason, the Sicilian proverb adds value: *"Chi va Piano va Lontano... Chi va Forte va alla Morte!"... "who goes slow goes far, who goes fast dies."*

Are you willing to slow things down? Isn't it time to change your go-go-go perspective to allow you to smell the roses from the value of your efforts? Once you are able to master the Go Slow to Go Fast principle, and teach others how to do the same, you'll be in a better position to master anything you set-out to accomplish. But, beware of the naysayers around you due to bias. Bias is defined as *"prejudice in favor of or against one thing, person or group compared with another, usually in a way considered to be completely unfair."* When introducing new concepts in the world of business, this definition also applies to concepts and ideas and can quickly become the Achilles' heel to stall, slow or diminish any kinds of momentum that may lead up to the introduction.

Here's further evidence to support this case. Another survey by McKinsey Consulting asked executives to rate the outcome of a recent strategic decision at their organizations as either satisfactory or unsatisfactory, while focusing on the role that various biases may have played a part. The survey found that satisfactory outcomes were associated with less bias, thanks to previous and "robust debate, an objective assessment of facts, and a realistic assessment of corporate capabilities." Additionally, the survey also showed that the leaders within the organizations that produced positive outcomes did a better job of forecasting consumer demand and departmental reactions. These folks did a much better job of assessing their own abilities to implement the decisions and execute on them to move agendas further down range within the system. They were also more likely to engage in certain activities that minimize bad decision-making. Some of these include:

- Allowing people with conflicting points of view to openly express their opinions.
- Thoroughly reviewing the business case for the decisions, even when senior executives and other senior leaders strongly supported the decisions.
- Establishing processes and clear lines of communication to ensure that truly innovative ideas reach the right people who can champion the idea throughout the system.

These kinds of behaviors seem counter intuitive. Partly because they contradict the unspoken biases and assumptions that tell us we already know what we need to know. And partly because they bog down the planning process causing for delays in meeting forecasts and objective timelines. As we all know, it takes time to gather and analyze information to make the best decisions in the moment, especially data that we don't want to see or hear. It takes time to listen to everyone's point of view, especially those that would seem to be naysayers. And when people in positions of authority seem to be chomping at the bit to make the decision and move on, it takes time (and courage) to stand up and say, *"I think we need to consider a better 'way to play' or better approach to achieve an even better outcome."*

In today's world, we're all running so fast that pausing to engage in these kinds of processes feels like we're falling behind. But, if we don't take the time to evaluate how we gather information, how we plan to use the information to our advantage, and how we plan to reach conclusions based on that information, we'll most likely end up making decisions that can have disastrous consequences. And this is where *"Chi va Forte va alla Morte"* adds value (who goes fast dies a slow death). Slowing down to go fast starts with actively seeking out information from a variety of sources. Pay attention to trends and events inside your organization and outside your industry. Then look for ways to apply that information to improve internal systems and processes or to add value to customers in new and better ways. The next time you are in a position to introduce a new strategy or set of processes, slow down to go fast; you'll be surprised at how much more effective you'll be in the whole scheme of things.

## A Go Slow to Go Fast Case Study: The Misunderstood Law Firm Executive

Take the situation faced by [1]Lisa Moyer, a brilliant MBA now leading one of the country's top law firms. Managing Partner and CEO Jarred Winston hired Lisa because of her unique set of talents and unbarred approach to introducing innovation into systems mired in traditions and decades of storied promise.

She had an impressive track record of rapidly identifying talented individuals, their causes and organizational impact, and always had above-the-bar approaches for taking them to higher levels of performance. The rub was that most of the people who worked with her felt intimidated by how she seemingly found holes in their ideas, or her tendency to publically suggest ways to "execute" solutions using different ways of achieving the objectives with lower risk and potentially lower cost in less time. While Lisa saw her role as "helping to speed things along," her peers saw her as both creative in her ideas, but an impediment in her approach, so they complained to CEO Winston.

Jarred and Lisa would meet on occasion to discuss things, and she was not at all surprised to learn of the frustrations from her co-workers. She was used to this sort of thing from past employer situations, but was set on making this situation a different outcome from her past experiences. She talked things out with Jarred and explained how she was discouraged with the lack of urgency the firm would exhibit when important decisions were to be made on critical findings for the firm's growth. While Jarred was also encouraged by Lisa's tenacity and drive to ensure the firm remained relevant in the marketplace, he wasn't sure that the discontent from other members in the firm was worth the hassle under his tenure as the firm's youngest CEO.

**Lisa decided to use the Go Slow to Go Fast approach: GO Slow**
**Lisa was urged by her coach to take the following "Go Slow" direct actions over the next 90 days:**

1. Stop offering on-the-spot suggestions and critiques of the plans or performances of other department heads. Instead, listen to what others had to say without adding editorial constructs from her perspective.
2. Privately meet with each cohort and offer a sincere apology for having placed him/her on the spot in past situations. Commit to work cooperatively from this point forward to meet the objectives of all needs.
3. As a key step to rebuilt trust, invest in quality one-on-one time with each team member getting to know them better. Let him/her do most of the talking about the issues most important to them without offering any sort of commentary.
4. In a low key manner, ask others if you could add value to their collective efforts to build their individual practice areas by asking questions to understand the approach further before pouncing. For example, *"Mike, can you please help me see from your perspective what you see as the key issues requiring the fix?"*

5.  When you have an idea or suggestion, go to the team member privately and ask if you can share an idea with them. Never spring an idea on them in open conversations or publically. Ask for their feedback and listen, and in cases where nothing is required, don't offer anything. Even in cases where you could add value, don't. Allow the situation to play itself out for everyone to see how a better approach is warranted.

## How Lisa Got to Go Very Fast!

Once she had re-established trust and built a solid professional relationship with her colleagues and team members, they began seeking her input and feedback on the topics they planned to bring up in the upcoming meeting. Likewise, she began vetting her ideas with them. Because of this preemptive collaboration and approach, when it came time to discuss ideas to grow the firm, an idea's discussion and adoption was often completed in the same session by everyone in the firm.

The bottom line result: within a short eight months, Lisa's peers had all shared examples with CEO Winston of how Lisa helped them to be more effective with their ideas, planning and execution using Next-Level Practices (NLPs) to impact the firm's future. Both the speed and quality of Right-time Decision-making showed promise in the firm's culture and ultimately the bottom line. Happiness became one of the firm's key performance indicators and still today remains a measurement for promise. Are there areas of your career where you could apply the Go Slow to Go Fast Principle?

[1]While the situation described is a real example of Go Slow to Go Fast strategy and concept, Lisa Moyer is not the executive's real name.

# 3

# Understanding
# the Poker's Bluff

*"It doesn't matter what hand you're holding and if you think you can win with it or not. What does matter are the choices you plan to make with the cards you've been dealt and how you plan to act based on the outcomes you're looking to achieve."*
— **Damian D. "Skipper" Pitts**

N ow that you have a good understanding about the Go Slow to Go Fast concept that can be used as a significant strategy in any situation you may be facing, we can move on to tackle a serious issue that mostly goes unaddressed in leadership and business. It is called the Poker's Bluff and talks of the *crisis in leadership* we're experiencing today and will continue to experience if things don't change. It basically stems from people in leadership positions' making promises they cannot actually execute to complete the objectives they are being held accountable. This is a serious problem and continues to be a significant issue in the leadership and management consulting fields. But, to understand this phenomenon fully and how it relates to business, let's take a look at the card game of poker.

A bluff is a bet or raise made with a hand, which is not thought to be a winner. The objective of a bluff is to induce a fold by the opponents who hold the better hands. The size and frequency of a bluff determines its profitability to the bluffer. By extension, the term is often used outside the context of poker as in leadership to describe the act of making promises one cannot execute. Having the pokers bluff in mind as it relates to the behaviors of leadership, strategy and execution, I couldn't help but think about the hallmarks of change—disruption and the use of Go Slow to Go Fast strategy as a means of disrupting incumbent marketplace decisions.

I've come to understand and develop this concept and methodology as a strategic approach that uses two marks or symbols that represent the salient events to follow in the field while learning to avoid risk by leading out from crises before they happen. And with that, everyone should get acquainted with a significant word used throughout the program. The word is "disruption," and it is defined to mean: forceful separation or division into parts.

Although this is the defined meaning based on the dictionary, we use the tern in a different manner. It is used in the context of "disruptive innovation" and as a term to form a function that is applicable to changing existing or incumbent behavior, strategy and outcomes. Mike Myatt, the chairman at the consulting firm N2Grwoth and the author of Hacking Leadership said it this way; *"Leadership exists to disrupt mediocrity."* This way of thinking is one that will both change and impact your decisions on the future and the two marks or symbols play right into the direct actions that lead to leaders like you setting out to disrupt mediocrity.

These two marks define both a question and a consideration that leaders of industry must begin to reflect upon as they continue their journey further into the 21st century. Combined, the two marks or symbols offer significant relevance to the direction, thought-leadership and maneuverability for organizations to be positioned to define executive presence and organizational structure in the world.

These two marks or symbols are "?!" and they begin an unconventional approach to everything or anything going forward, but not before two requirements are met by those individuals who are willing to identify with disruptive change as their means of creating differentiation:

1. As a leader, do you have the intestinal fortitude to use disruptive behavior to transform incumbent strategy and to begin shaping how societies behave around your products and services?!
2. Are you willing to do what is required to disrupt before being disrupted?!

## The Problem

We as a society and a people have lost our way. The very fabric and the foundation that leadership was built upon are stained with an odorous stench from past behavior leading into today's existing conditions (negative events across U.S. law enforcement communities, the U.S. political culture, the threat of terrorism in the Middle East and around the world, etc). Leadership is tired. It is fatigued. It is unmanageable. It is fraught with the peril of outdated Rockstars who dominate the field as broken arrows no longer hitting the correct targets. It is lost and it is clouded in the fog from the depths of the darkness where it now resides.

## Personal Responsibility

Playtime is over and these two questions need to be answered by you. Why use the word playtime? Simply because the world is dealing with a crisis in leadership at every corner, and something needs to happen to change the direction our decisions—your decisions—are forcing things to travel. Yes, it needs to be personal and it needs to remain in your face because it is your responsibility to do something about it.

## Why we MUST think Differently—Think Above the Bar

I remember back just a few short years ago when the price of gasoline skyrocketed above $3 per gallon in the U.S. Everyone was upset, and although the anger fueled much conversation, nothing could be done to change the price of fuel to make it more manageable. At the same time, life as we knew it was changing in front of our eyes with the global economic crisis that would quickly establish a new normal in the new world. Just last week, I was driving down a major U.S. highway and noticed the price of gasoline at $3.19 per gallon.

I quickly glanced at my needle to notice that I had a half of tank of gas and decided to top my tank off. While traveling just at 44mph, I immediately looked for a place to turn around and successfully achieved my objective $24 later with a smile. Not only one mile later, I began to think about how my "perceptive mediocrity" allowed me to quickly become the victim to my own circumstances.

This very statement is what I believe has happened to leadership. Perception changes life circumstances to cause the bar of performance to be lowered at different times and we quickly acclimate to the new normal because of it, while forgetting ever so fashionably the initial disgust and anger that started the change in the first place. I shouldn't have celebrated the $3 price of gasoline, nor should I have been happy with only spending $24. All that I achieved was a celebrated perception of mediocrity and this is precisely the reason that has allowed the current crisis in leadership in the world today to take hold.

## Stop Talking and Lead by Example

So, think about this when you stop for a brief moment to look around at the conditions of your organization. Think for a moment if the two symbols are present in the minds of your leaders. The "?" represents the two questions while the "!" asks *"what the h\*ll are you going to do about it."* I say; *"bury my bones or get out of my way, but you're going to do something because I intend to disrupt and no longer get disrupted."* This is the only way to avoid crises before they happen and take the bull by the horns (literally) to use disruptive behavior and change to—change. The poker's bluff is simply not a strategy to continue in leadership any longer; for tomorrow's sake, you have to play a much better hand today.

# 4

# Next-Level
# Practice Decisions
# (Nlpds)

"*Best practices are the residue carried over from the nineteenth and twentieth century's. Why continue to do what was done yesterday to strive for better results today only to be disappointed with the outcomes in the end. The fault remains with you and no one else. Trying something new allows you to drop the veil to consider 'what can become' versus 'what you already have.' There's another level of 'you' if you follow the rhythms of the heart to go where you have yet to travel.*"

— **Damian D. "Skipper" Pitts**

Next-Level Practice Decisions (NLPDs) are those choices that lead into the direct actions formed from identifying the critical need to change your organization's approach towards the future (even if you are a single owner!). As you plan and act strategically, you will probably find that you need to make needed changes to fit the requirements that are on the horizon. Now is the time to do it.

Next-Level Practice Decisions (NLPDs) is a process that's germane to Go Slow to Go Fast strategy. It keeps the operations of your organization visible to your team (and to you!) by continuing (or starting) to plan and operate in the open allowing everyone involved to have a voice in all matters. Now of course, this would mean that the right people are at the table providing the right capabilities to the organization. This also means that your actions are directly aligned with measuring progress as it occurs to adjust or course correct as needed, and to exit promptly as required. This NLPDs process is defined as **"Interview-Diagnose-Explore-Assess-Strategize"** before modifying to exit.

The NLPDs and process is focused on ideation and transformation. The two salient events, "modify" and "exit" are critical to ensuring the right amounts of energy is focused on the right objectives to meet the right objectives to impact and maximize effort for the organization—to achieve disruption to incumbent behavior and strategy. But, before the NLPDs and process can be put into effect, a prerequisite process must first be achieved. This prerequisite process is known as the OPTIONS process and is important because it allows the decision-making process to go through a series of step-wise procedures to minimize risk while providing significant momentum to the process in the long-run. The OPTIONS process is defined as:

**O**bserve the Situation
**P**ursue a Better Meaning
**T**arget the Future Picture
**I**dentify Opportunities to Innovate
**O**rient, Decide and Execute to WiN
**N**arrate the Story
**S**implify, Show others and Repeat the Process (Rinse/Repeat)

Combined, IDEAS and OPTIONS present the inevitability for change. Within a few short seconds after a decision is made to act after completing the NLPD process, the environment in which the direct actions will take place becomes different from what it was at the time of the decision.

Compounding the challenges or problems that calls for the process to be used is due to your inability as a leader to define the complexities within the operating environment with accuracy.

Although you can reduce the risk inherent in the process transformations being executed upon, you'll need to be sure that your campaign teams, who are responsible for developing and delivering the changes, are capable to act quickly and in parallel. Before using the process and individual constructs, you as the campaign champion (project leader) must accept the necessity for rapid adaptation with exercising on the ability to react appropriately to unexpected events that will occur (definitely) when they are least expected!

Within the constructs of both IDEAS and OPTIONS as individual processes coming together to become a force-multiplier, they will also be disruptive. This form of disruptive change is the kind of change that creates an entirely new operating environment at levels ranging from the macro to the micro. Change, both efficiently qualitative and filled with disruptive innovation, is paramount to progress. The key essential to the process is realizing how the effective changes from NLPDs will stem from the step-wise procedures throughout the entire process itself. The NLPDs process using IDEAS and OPTIONS, in part, accounts for the concepts of time and value; this means simply that value in hand today is worth 10x more than a *maybe* value tomorrow.

## The IDEAS Process

Everything comes down to creative problem solving and IDEAS. *Creative Problem Solving (CPS)* is a proven method for approaching an objective, organizational mission, a problem or a challenge in an imaginative and innovative way. It's a tool that helps people re-define the problems they face, come up with *Breakthrough Achievable Results,* and then take action on the approach for dealing with a situation. At the same time that CPS is a structured direct action, it is also an agile one. When you begin to use and internalize the direct actions from CPS, you'll find them to be cyclical. You begin to see how to move from step to step, and how to jump back and forth between steps. When CPS becomes the core of your performance-driven execution skills, you'll be able to call on them and respond more effectively above the people who don't know how to use them. This, within itself, is a "next-level practice" that carries the fundamentals of CPS, allowing you and your team to be able to adapt the process to every situation you encounter, thereby realizing its full power and increased potential.

The IDEAS process, using CPS direct actions, offers a quick assessment tool to help you strategically execute with defined solutions that are best suited for the situation. This process is one of the salient events used to make sure the Go Slow to Go Fast approach is highly effective and useful when called upon to make an impact in a given situation. Its development is inspired from combined U.S. Marine Corps strategic operations conducted extensively around the world in some of the greatest battlefield conflicts in our history. This means that individually, they've been put to the test and passed. They're highly proven and capable of morphing into a greater force when combined with likewise procedures. And, they've been extrapolated and redefined to help improve the Go Slow to Go Fast strategy and concept to help you Better *your* Best when using the IDEAS process. Significant research has been done to ensure the steps within the IDEAS process offer a complete and validated course of action for solving problems. The result of which are governed by the following 3-rules used to watch-over the entire IDEAS process:

**Rule #1**: Explore the Process.

**Rule #2**: Generate disruptive, innovative and new concepts—Ideate.

**Rule #3**: Prepare for Action—and execute strategically and flawlessly to WiN.

## Rule #1: Explore the Process

Three things must occur in this stage that defines the direct actions from within the "I" (Interview) and the "D" (Diagnose) step-wise procedures:

### 1. Objective Finding: Identify the Target, Understand the Challenge

This is where goals are replaced with targets. Goals are causes for excuses, whereby targets are locked-on and hit (accomplished) with sniper-like reflexes. Goals are a wish; targets are a must. Objective Finding opens the door to using the Creative Problem Solving (CPS) direct actions to avoid dissatisfaction or a desire to act based on false information.

### 2. Fact Finding: Gathering Informed and Accurate Data

Assess and review all the data that pertains to the situation at hand. Who's involved, what's involved, when, where and why it's important. Understand your vantage point (perceptions) and make sure it is what it is! Make a list of the facts and information, as well as the more instinctive hunches, feelings, assumptions and gossip around the situation. In this step, all the data is taken into consideration to review the direct linkage to the objective in order for you to begin to innovate.

### 3. Problem Finding: Clarify the Problem

In this step, explore the facts and data to find all the problems and challenges inherent in the situation, and all the opportunities they represent. This is about making sure you're focusing on the right problems: doing the right things to get the right things done! What's important here is to realize that it is possible to come up with the right answer to the wrong problem. Re-define what you want or what can cause barriers (limitations) to stop or slow your progress.

## Rule #2: Generate disruptive, innovative and new concepts—Ideate

This stage defines the "E" (Explore) and the "A" (Assess) step-wise procedures:

### 4. Idea Finding: Generate Ideas

Generating ideas is much more than brainstorming. During this step, be vigilant about deferring judgment and coming up with wild, outrageous, out-of-the-box ideas. This is where you explore ideas that are possible and plausible solutions (within the existing capabilities of your environment). Be sure that you give your team the best opportunity to execute strategically and flawlessly in order to finish with finesse. The ideas must promote significant profitability and impact to the Future Picture. It's also where you need to stretch to make connections, take risks, and try new combinations to find potentially innovative solutions.

## Rule #3: Prepare for Action— and execute strategically and flawlessly to WiN

This stage defines the "S" (Strategize) step-wise procedure:

### 5. Solution Finding: Select and Strengthen Solutions

First, try to strengthen and improve the best ideas generated. Next, generate the criteria that need to be considered to evaluate the ideas for success. Apply that criteria to the top ideas and decide which are most likely to solve the redefined problem. The best idea needs to meet criteria that make it actionable before it becomes the solution. A creative idea is not really useful if it won't or can't be implemented.

*6. Acceptance Finding: Plan for Action*

In this step, look at who's responsible, what has to be done by when, and what resources are available in order to realize the idea as a full-fledged, activated solution and direct action.

Then engage the **OODA Loop sequence** *(Observe-Orient-Decide-Act)* to make it all come together ensuring your foundation is firmly set before moving. The foundation is your alignment; making sure that everyone involved understands the WHY of the team's actions. Your **FEET** *(KWAP: Flawless Effective Execution that is Targeted/Timely)* must be positioned on solid ground, pointing North Star and in the right direction; moving significant amounts of energy down rage and at the same time for the absolute same reason and purpose!

There's no better way to solve challenges and problems when striving to achieve better outcomes than what has been achieved without having a concise process such as the IDEAS process. Using the process, the CPS direct actions provide a procedural approach that ensures outcomes have a good chance of becoming what the decision-makers and the organizations need versus what they want to have happen. The key to Go Slow to Go Fast strategy is to slow things down in order to avoid risk by leading out from crises before they happen. I suggest that you use and follow the IDEAS process to identify the best solutions to your challenges and problems. The process provides significant opportunities to identify lessons learned to be used in future engagements.

Applying the IDEAS process to a situation—*good or bad*—will definitely change your situational awareness, altitude and perspective, giving a much different vantage point to WiN: think strategically, focus sharply and move quickly… the very essence of Go Slow to Go Fast strategy. Also, keep the three rules in mind to govern your decisions and behaviors accordingly. Following the rules will ensure that your ideas have the best chance of delivering the outcomes you seek without falling into the success traps presented by your wants versus your needs.

To close-out the IDEAS process and CPS direct actions, follow this debriefing sequencing at the start of any situation you face and watch how the magic from your own actions changes the circumstances of your situation using *Next-Level Practice Decisions (NLPDs) (NLPDs)*.

- Interview the Situation…
- Diagnose the WHAT-IF-CONSEQUENCES…
- Explore your Resources (opportunities & threats)…
- Assess the Variables—yours and theirs…
- Strategize to Achieve the Best Results: Use your FEET wisely to finish with finesse!

We're not done yet. Your Next-Level Practice Decisions (NLPDs) are not complete until you've learned to make *better* decisions to preemptively lead you out of needing to use your IDEAS process and CPS direct actions. This is where your OPTIONS process comes into effect to do its part to help you create a different and new 'way to play.' On page 18, the OPTIONS process as a prerequisite is introduced as an important feature in the Next-Level Practice Decisions (NLPDs) sequence. The OPTIONS process gets to the heart of the matter because it allows the course of action in making decisions to go through a series of step-wise procedures designed to minimize risk, while providing significant momentum to the process in the long-run.

The OPTIONS process helps you to make better choices. We must be able to make better decisions in real-time and at the same pace of change as it is happening without fail. Asking the wrong questions for the right situation only results disaster in the end. Having better OPTIONS to ask better questions offer opportunities for better choices to be considered. Neuroscience reveals the things that distort a leader's judgments. Here's how you can keep your own judgment clear when making Next-Level Practice Decisions (NLPDs):

## Observe the Situation

Collect current information from as many sources as practically possible in the shortest amount of time. The essential importance here is to make *"whether or not"* decisions and to quickly realize which decisions make the most sense for the situation you are encountered with. You need to understand the implications the situation will have on your Future Picture and other stakeholders "when you respond" and "how you respond." Closely watch and analyze to understand the actions that led up to the situation happening and what brings you to the moment to engage—known as your *Moment of Truth* in Go Slow to Go Fast strategy. Then, emphatically decide to respond using the voice of your collaborators who will also be influenced by the response in the end.

## Pursue a Better Meaning

Decide if your observation of the situation allowed you to make a decision to pursue a better meaning that align with your original purpose. Every decision made for a situation in life should focus your efforts on improving the idea that allowed you to engage a new path to your success. Your pursuit of excellence must remain in the forefront of everything you setout to accomplish.

Decisions become easier to make when they relate to you improving the expected outcomes from your behaviors; remain constant in your approach to pursue a better meaning. "Incumbents are you and you are the incumbents." This statement essentially means 'don't be upset while sitting in a traffic jam on the highway at the start or end of your day. You are just as much the problem as the other cars also sitting in the same traffic jam. Relax, you'll get to your destination in due time.'

## Target the Future Picture

The Future Picture is how you expect and plan the future to look before arriving there in the distant horizon. It is much different than your future whereby it is only a guide or compass heading to point you where you need to go toward a future state. Then there's your event horizon, that immediate point in time in your far off future right before crossing over into your Future Picture. Your event horizon is your measure of merit to determine for the last time that everything that was supposed to be completed up to that point has been so with excellence. The event horizon is the last gut check before crossing over into the desired state in one's lifetime. This is yet another *Moment of Truth* that should not be taken lightly.

When you set-out to target the Future Picture, you're basically looking at life through a three-dimensional window: the future, the event horizon and the Future Picture. Once you understand how the future state must look, your decisions will be made with a more precise measuring tool to ensure you are doing the right things to get the right things done to accomplish life's ultimate journey—happiness. Every decision must be aligned with the direct actions that will allow you to reach your planned future state—your Future Picture. Otherwise, you shouldn't be doing it in the first place because it won't matter in the end anyway.

## Identify Opportunities to Innovate

Your decisions must make room for you to innovate. And when you innovate, you must set your sights on disrupting incumbent behavior, strategy and outcomes to change the world-view about what *can* become versus what *will* become. Uncommon behaviors deliver radical ideas and even more radical results when they are put into action. The key here is to remove yourself from the norms, making your actions so uncommon, but tested against your existing conditions, that they stipulate edgy unconventional wisdom used to change the world—starting with your own ecosystem. Collaboration is essential when attempting to innovate while the plane is in flight. You can't crash, so make the best decisions to innovate well.

## Orient, Decide and Execute to Win!

Analyze your information and update it to your current reality. Decide how best to respond using the updates and begin to strategically and flawlessly execute to win! Ensure to establish achievable aims; identify your means to act; ensure you have vetted your intelligence; enforce your security (this means that all options have been considered, good, bad and indifferent, before you act); engage your strike like a cobra hunting its prey; and flawlessly execute your exit strategy at the right time as not to stay on mission too long. Determine the course of action and follow through on your decisions.

## Narrate the Story

The story must be told for others to follow with simplicity. Every step in the decision-making process through to the end of the mission must be accounted for and scribed for future use (look it up). Debrief your team on the outcomes, creating a culture of learning that's critical to adapting to a rapidly changing environment and producing opportunities to **Better *your* Best** with the right acumen and skill builders from the events you faced within your **Moments of Truth**.

## Simplify, Show Others and Repeat the Process

The power of simplification is important for people to remember how to execute to win… and how to finish with finesse to teach others. It also allows for effective communications with concise information to occur. Repeating a successful process requires a simplified way of doing. Make your "do" simple or "don't" do at all! So, in essence, the NLPD process is made up of two important constructs:

1. IDEAS: Interview-Diagnose-Explore-Assess-Strategize" before modifying to exit.

2. OPTIONS: making better decisions by doing the right things to get the right things done.

What better way to arrive at a new 'way to play' once you have the right tools at your disposal to offer yourself more, or better, choices in the long-run. Next-Level Practice Decisions (NLPDs) are important in the new world order that basically states only the strong will survive while the rest will perish. I don't know where you are with the whole survive or perish concept, but I hope you've figured it out for yourself. If you haven't this chapter takes away another excuse you have to not arrive at the answer that will benefit you the most. In the end, we all have choices to make. Start making better decisions and you'll have better choices.

More importantly, it's not only about finishing what you've started and leaving a road map for others to also follow. There's also a growing body of research in organizational behavior that looks at the web of relationships within a sector and how economics play in their outcomes: they way that complex production systems emerge, evolve and interact, and how value migrates within and between sectors. Whether you call these webs industry architectures, ecosystems or organizational fields, they're a lens for viewing reality and can show us some very valuable new perspectives, hence the reason for making better choices and teaching others the process for doing the same.

The OPTIONS process is a big set of ideas and have some big implications for competing interests—implications that we're only just beginning to understand. In most cases, making better choices and decisions leads to winning more from your choices. This doesn't just mean finishing first; it means changing the rules of the game to your own advantage—strategic advantage to consider how successful teams have figured out how to redefined the way they interact with one another using the vast amounts of information. OPTIONS allows you to be more inclined to create an ecosystem that collaborates with like-minded people to not only compete, but to achieve an unfair advantage.

# 5

# The Language of Performance-Driven Execution

*"Languages represent our abilities to change and look different in the eyes of the beholder. The second you are able to speak and sound different from your native self, is the second that you have to start a shift of seismic proportions in your life and the lives of others. Learn a new language and make something new happen in your life. You'll wish you had done it sooner."*
**— Damian D. "Skipper" Pitts**

A s we continue on with identifying ways to Go Slow to Go Fast, we just completed the Next-Level Practice Decisions (NLPDs) and how to use them to gain the edge you need and want over your rivals. But, Next-Level Practice Decisions (NLPDs) turn quickly into Next-Level Practices (NLPs) and this is where the fun really begins.

These Next-Level Practices (NLPs) begin with your learning a new language. It then moves into the rule of three with a term in Go Slow to Go Fast strategy known as Leadership Triplicity™. Next, it moves into a Leadership GPS System to help you navigate this new journey you've found yourself on. Then, it goes into what is known as the Four Action Behaviors to provide a step-wise approach that leads to infinite outcomes filled with your newly found key performance indicator; happiness. Next, it illustrates how to properly navigate the obstacles that now lie in your path with Leadership Code Switching abilities— your super powers. And finally, your Next-Level Practices (NLPs) are placed on the table using a preemptive methodology to ensure you are able to never be stopped when you set-out to accomplish the tasks that will lead you to a promised place in your life—high performance-driven execution and extraordinary success. But, none of it is possible without first understanding the importance of learning parallel operations that begins with learning your new language in Go Slow to Go Fast strategy known as the Language of Performance-Driven Execution.

If you're one of those people who are responsible for leading teams, how can you be sure that the work being done throughout the day will innovatively increase impact and productivity to make tomorrow a better place? Or, if you are responsible for managing solopreneur projects, how can you be sure that the work will increase impact and productivity? Isn't that what productivity should be doing? Making the Future Picture (how leaders intend the future to look prior arriving there in the distant future) a well defined place of improvement? These questions are some that leaders everywhere must consider on a more frequent basis with greater purpose in mind if they are *really* focused on providing greater impact across their organizations.

With the millions of publications, blogs and information about business that is readily available today, the inference would be to some that a way forward is readily available. But to the surprise of most leaders today, increasing overall performance has become a complex, and in some cases, a Bermuda Triangle-like mysterious process that continues to baffle even the smartest people in the field of leadership and change.

Accordingly, research has found that most change initiatives are only successful at a fledging rate of 54%, but those companies reporting high engagement levels achieve significantly better results, including 29% higher revenue; they're also 50% more likely to have above-average customer loyalty (internal and external) and are 44% more likely to turn above average profits. Research has also shown that highly engaged workgroups are 50% more productive and 33% more profitable. Their retention rates are 44% higher and customer loyalty is increased 56%. Clearly, engagement matters and the Language of Performance-Driven Execution plays an essential part in all of these things happening and much more *(Source: Leading Organizational Change, Right Management, 2009)*.

Speaking the Language of Performance-Driven Execution clearly reveals the relationships that exist between change, engagement, strategic leadership, strategy execution and strategic alignment. More people today are recognizing the many benefits of becoming bilingual in corporate speak similar to speaking a foreign language: You can increase productivity without having to feel uncomfortable as if you're in a foreign country without having the knowledge of the native language. The language also offers opportunities to be more productive and enticing in today's vast cultural and competitive landscape.

Organizations can immerse themselves in the many cultures that surround them throughout their employees across the environment. Scientific studies have even shown that learning a new language helps to keep memories sharp and naturally enhances overall brain function. The Language of Performance-Driven Execution connects theory with executable action to bridge *good* to empirically-based *greatness* that results *extraordinary* outcomes using applicable acumen to actually make an impact far above what most people believe their reality can become.

The language understands the concept of simplicity because the brain is already wired to speak a new language just as long as it is simple; we just need to activate it to do so. The late Dr. Paul Pimsleur, a Ph.D. and specialist in the field of applied linguistics, devoted his life and career to learning languages and understanding the psychology of language acquisition. He recognized through extensive research that effective communication in any language depends on mastery of a relatively limited number of words. And, trying to learn too many words at first can actually slow the language retention process. However, once this "core vocabulary" is mastered and used consistently, it provides a framework for accelerated language learning.

So, with that said, the Language of Performance-Driven Execution is based on and uses six simple words to support a process transformation initiative and a new 'way to play' to increase organizational behavior and performance.

The combination of these six words, derived from Latin, translates into an executable language leaders can use to overcome the challenges in overall organizational performance. This is the common language used throughout the Go Slow to Go Fast strategic approach that facilitates the direct actions to slow things down and avoid risk by leading out from crises before they happen. The language allows leaders to use a different approach to out maneuver the potential for failure. The Language of Performance-Driven Execution speaks these six words:

1. Novo (to make anew, change)
2. Distinctio (to distinguish, differentiation)
3. Cretum or Cresco (to increase, expand)
4. Socius (to share, association)

5. OrgSx (to get it done, execution)
6. Exitus or Exigo (to finish, exit)

## Novo: Change the Lens of Thought-leadership and the Approach to Professional Development

First, continuing to do today as you did yesterday will not allow you to achieve much tomorrow. Change happens so quickly today that one of two things will occur; you either react and respond to the pace of change or you do what is required to *become the change* that others will require to survive. Novo, the first of the six aspects in the Language of Performance-Driven Execution, understands that reacting or responding keeps you behind the curve. However, becoming the change means that you'll need to change the lens of your thought-leadership and approach to professional development to achieve the simultaneous pursuit of low risk and high output. Organizations like Google and Cirque du Soleil are examples of the Novo approach, so speaking from this aspect in the vernacular shows that it can be achieved.

## Distinctio: Accept a New Way to Play in the Leadership and Innovation Sandbox—Differentiation

This leads us into the second aspect of the vernacular, Distinctio, which leads to the simplicity of distinguished differentiation. Accepting a new way to play in the leadership and innovation sandbox doesn't have to be hard. It simply means a significant change in your thought processes allowing you to be radically different from the norms. Extraordinary greatness today requires us to adopt the story of the fox and the Hedgehog in Jim Collins' outstanding book *Good to Great*.

The story of the hedgehog and the fox talks of how the cunning and brilliant fox grasps the complexity of his natural habitat to catch and eat a hedgehog, spending hours plotting the perfect attack. Meanwhile, the hedgehog, described as simplistic and somewhat drab, goes about its business unaware. When the fox ambushes, the hedgehog rolls himself into a spiny, impenetrable ball. Undeterred, the fox keeps re-strategizing, but the pattern repeats itself over and over. *"The fox knows many things, but the hedgehog knows one big thing,"* the story teaches us in its conclusion.

Change today is the cunning fox while the sandbox represents the hedgehog. With the hedgehog, three simple questions must be answered around leadership purpose by everyone involved in the growth process:

1. What can you be the best in the world at (and equally important—what are you not the best at?)?
2. What drives your economic engines (focus areas)?
3. What are you deeply passionate about (how do you help others and get others to help you contribute)?

Answering these simple questions honestly, facing the brutal facts regardless of circumstance, and you'll begin to see your hedgehog concept emerge as you develop your new way to play in a much different sandbox. The key to speaking this aspect of the vernacular defines how you can use your hedgehog concept to shape how a society behaves from your ability to become so radical that new norms will birth from your behavioral influences.

## Cretum or Cresco: Optimize your Potential for Success—People

The third aspect of the vernacular, Cretum or Cresco, focuses on increasing proficiencies, improving competencies and expanding upon the traits that lead to achieving successful outcomes. This means that to optimize the potential for success, leaders must allow their people to assess their unique and individual proficiencies against a number of different functional, leadership considerations and competency models. By doing this, they'll be able to assess their skills and acumen levels against the norms to identify areas of improvement as they relate to the strategy forward. Optimizing for potential success means that you agree with *the Four Action Behaviors*: Design the Future, Target for Success, Campaign to Win and Finish with Finesse to Better *your* Best—and do the same for others.

Develop creative and relational synergy between *the Four Action Behaviors* and you'll be amazed to see the increase of potential in all the people you influence.

## Socius: Achieve a State of Shared Consciousness and Purpose—Culture

The fourth aspect of the vernacular, Socius, is based on a unique discipline that examines the behaviors individuals bring to the job, the motivators that drive them, the acumen to understand how to do the job, and the individual's ability and potential to provide the competencies required by the job. It reveals specific details in four areas that describe the why, how, what and can of superior performance. As the four core areas define the requirements of any organization, providing a complete system to compare talent to the position and maximize job fit for the people that make up the organization, Socius plays an important part in the language of Performance Driven Execution for everyone to work together towards one common objective. It speaks to the concept known as *Shared Consciousness and Purpose.*

Achieving *Shared Consciousness and Purpose* means adapting individual purpose and awareness of direction into shared awareness and reasoning to become a force-multiplier that ultimately impacts the Future Picture. It also means that an entire culture must understand how to Go Slow to Go Fast to eliminate tension from the valuable techniques used to identify ways of operating with greater success in a fast-paced, rapidly changing environment. Leaders today must contend with high levels of volatility, uncertainty, complexity and ambiguity across their changing competitive landscapes. And, they must constantly reevaluate critical decisions to meet long-term, strategic objectives. To achieve this, five more events known as a Five W's Agenda offer considerations to determine how to bridge the difficult gap between the rational development of strategy and real-life execution:

1.  **WHY** are we doing this? …WHY will it be disruptive as a behavior and action? These questions are the descriptors about your purpose.
2.  **WHO** will be impacted? …WHO will benefit? …WHO will be eliminated? And, WHO will be limited?
3.  **WHAT** are we applying our resources and energy (inertia) against? …WHAT is our compass heading and target (Zulu) time (end point)?
4.  **WHERE** are we going? …WHERE are the gaps in our knowledge and experience for the journey?
5.  **WHEN** do we plan to arrive? …WHEN should we expect the future, the event horizon and the Future Picture? This includes 'descriptive memos' regarding the decisions to achieve the organization's objectives.

With these events and understanding the fourth aspect of the vernacular, Socius, leaders will be able to make better decisions to respond more effectively in their marketplace using shared perspectives, common ownership and responsibility across their organization and culture as the stimulus to achieve extraordinary greatness. The diagram below illustrates the Leadership GPS System:

Diagram 2. The Leadership GPS System

## LEADERSHIP GPS SYSTEM

| GPS COORDINATES | DIRECTIONS |
| --- | --- |
| **COMPETENCE AND CONFIDENCE**<br>Can the leaders take the organization to its objective? Do they truly believe the *purpose* is worth the effort? | **TRUST AND PURPOSE**<br>Has trust been earned due to past behaviors and achievements? Do people believe they are part of something of worth and value? |

 **WHY**
... Are we doing this (purpose)?
... Will it be disruptive as a behavior and action?

 **WHO**
... Will be impacted?
... Will it benefit?
... Will be eliminated?
... Will be limited?

 **WHAT**
... Are we applying our resources and energy (inertia) against?
... Is our compass heading and target (zulu) time?

 **WHERE**
... Are we going?
... Are the gaps in our knowledge and experience for the journey?

 **WHEN**
... Do we plan to arrive?
... Should we expect the future, the event horizon and the Future Picture?

## OrgSx: Launching the Preemptive Strike (the Pearl Affect)

As we move into the most important aspect of the vernacular, OrgSx is ONLY about execution (getting things done), both strategic and flawless. OrgSx, also spoken to mean the OrgSx Paradigm in organizational development (pronounced "Org-Sick"), focuses on organizational strategic execution and takes lessons from the attack at Pearl Harbor by the Japanese in 1941. Launching a preemptive strike across an organizational system operates from the premise of facilitating Design Think to ensure that everyone understands how to use OrgSx as the hedgehog in the language to address and approach problems with a specific methodology.

This part of the language helps leaders to ideate, select and execute solutions. They will be better able to improve their own problem solving processes and take innovation to a higher level. OrgSx is a major construct that leads to *Breakthrough Achievable Results;* an organizational development initiative that permeates the necessary behavioral intelligences throughout an organization or system by ensuring social learning theory becomes the catalyst for significant growth. The OrgSx within the language provides the tactical discipline for all stakeholders to get the right things done and achieve growth or expansion. The aspect of the vernacular is used to create the organization's Grand Strategy. OrgSx establishes several things that must be put into action:

- Development of measurable strategic objectives with a compressed timeline (Future Picture).
- Organizational Behavior "Guidelines" (Guiding Precepts) and strategic principle assessments (Cardinal Rules).
- Identification of needed external and internal systems change (Behavioral Intelligences known as Recon for Risk [internal systems change] and the Pearl Effect concept and strategy [external change across the ecosystem]).

- Resource application points (Centers of Gravity).
- Description of what they must become (Impact Plans).
- Design of campaign plans with compressed timeframes (Parallel Operations).
- Strategic Execution Engagements: (Campaign Operations).
- Identification of Exit Points and Succession Plans (End-game Planning).
- Flawless Execution Engagements: (the Mop-up Grand Strategy).
- End Games and Summaries: Development of follow-on procedures after concluding the Mop-up Grand Strategy (After-Action-Reporting).

OrgSx, in its full vernacular, simply identifies engagement of all organizational resources. As soon as this part of the language is spoken, people who understand how to speak the language understand fully what needs to be done in order to affect real change that will matter and stick. OrgSx represents the making of radical change at specific times (Moments of Truth), and wants the whole organization to be a contributing factor to optimize results while changing outcomes.

## Exitus or Exigo: Finish with Finesse

This brings us to the sixth and last aspect of the vernacular, Exitus or Exigo. Everything that begins must have an end. But, ending well is the ultimate price to pay homage to a well oiled system and change initiative such as the one represented in the Language of Performance-Driven Execution. Exitus or Exigo has an insanely close proximity to cutting-edge practices that adapts traditional business thinking and disciplines to the 21st century creative economy.

When this aspect of the vernacular is spoken and heard by others who also speak the language, everyone knows and understands the importance of combining military-style tactical methodology, *Maneuver Warfare principles,* with Design Think to meet the needs and the context of the challenge or problem head-on in its tracks. They understand the need to use every other aspect of the language to be creative in the generation of insights and solutions, and to use rationality in analyzing and fitting various solutions to the needs of the Future Picture. It basically means that *'we must finish with finesse'* to ensure high performance-driven execution is met at every aspect of a situation. This aspect of the vernacular exposes leaders to a significant performance doctrine; to finish well.

The doctrine is one that defends specifically the event horizon; conceptually that location in time and space where leaders interact with any number of potential threats to change the wills that fight against the behaviors within the Grand Strategy. Exitus or Exigo being spoken means that everyone's actions are beyond reproach because its sole purpose is to protect the various perspectives within the event horizon and nothing more. Defending the event horizon using performance doctrine allows for decision-making to have enough room to realize decisive outcomes from the choices being made when planning, executing and exiting an initiative. The distance to the event horizon is not measured in conventional units of distance; rather it is a proposed reiterative cycle that is expressed as a result of maneuver warfare principles: targeting critical vulnerabilities, boldness, surprise, focus, decentralized decision-making, tempo and combined arms—working together to shape how societies behave.

Exitus or Exigo being spoken and practiced within the organizing envelope of performance doctrine must be focused on reducing any potential for invoking any form of friction or turbulence that can hurt new opportunities and new possibilities within the Future Picture. Actions must be whole and firm, but not dogmatic. People must be able to leave room for leaders of freewheeling genius to have fun innovating in their disciplined approach of achieving the objectives they are accountable. These individuals will become the extraordinary thought-leaders in the Future Picture for some of the most successful organizations in the world beyond the 21st century and creative economy.

Exitus or Exigo also means to never surrender control back to the incumbents with their outdated norms, because control is the prerequisite of speaking this aspect of the vernacular in the language. Among the other characteristics it embodies, it speaks of "good-growth." The real benefit from Exitus or Exigo being spoken is the knowing of absolute defeat that follows a leader who is able to finish with finesse by defending the event horizon. It is the drum march for people to move with a different rhythm to get inside of the competitor's mindset to mentally and systemically breakdown his will. Similar to a boxing match when the two fighters after a brutal slugfest return to their corners between a match. One sits down and his opponent stands to send a message saying *"you're already defeated; you just haven't come to understand it yet!"* This action allows a decision to be made in that very instance and time is of the essence because the clock to return to the center of the ring is ticking away.

For the smart fighter sitting, he quickly becomes aware that the situation is beyond his control, which is in turn a by-product of throwing in the towel. This maneuver was successful in the February 25, 1964 Muhammad Ali vs. Sonny Liston fight. As the bell sounded for the seventh round, Muhammad Ali (known as Cassius Clay during that fight before changing his name later to Muhammad Ali) was the first to notice that Liston had spat out his mouth guard while sitting on the stool in his corner after noticing Clay standing across the ring. After seeing Liston had spat his mouthpiece on the floor of the ring, Clay moved to the middle of the ring with his arms raised, dancing the jig that would become known later as the "Ali Shuffle" while Howard

Cosell, broadcasting at ringside, shouted *"wait a minute! Wait a minute! Sonny Liston is not coming out!"* Liston failed to answer the bell for the seventh round and Clay was declared the winner by technical knockout. It was the first time since 1919 that a World Heavyweight Champion had quit sitting on his stool.

The Language of Performance-Driven Execution using this last aspect of the vernacular, Exitus or Exigo to finish with finesse with maneuver warfare, is within itself, a powerful dynamic that forms an incredible reason for all leaders to learn how to speak this language today. It is a game changer.

With the requirements for learning the Language of Performance-Driven Execution that's outlined to inform you what it takes to increase impact and productivity, now it's your time to make some choices about the decisions used to guide your way forward. Are you prepared to start speaking the language that changes everything about your 'way to play' that also achieves greater impact, purpose and productivity—for you and in the lives of others? Learning to speak the Language of Performance-Driven Execution will help you, as a leader, to develop one of the more appropriate and disruptive forms of behavior known in the world of business for some time. Never before has anything of the likes of the Language of Performance-Driven Execution been seen as a new innovation spoken to elicit action. This is planning to execution at its best because the filler is the language that requires succinct and direct actions to follow. It will meet any form of growth objective efficiently and effectively today and into the future. The focus remains on two very important things:

1.  Imparting to leaders the importance of employing strategy execution skills they'll need to increase impact and productivity, while practicing a new language that successfully wins organizational and business strategy.

2.  Helping leaders build great strategies that they can understand, believe in and will execute strategically and flawlessly, allowing all stakeholders to think strategically, focus sharply and move quickly to finish with finesse.

If you are committed to making your organization more strategic in thought-leadership and action, learning to speak the Language of Performance-Driven Execution will meet your needs, while helping you and your teams to:

*   Build an overall strategy that is both understood and supported throughout the organization, that will create a focused strategy to result a new 'way to play' using a common language that wins both the event horizon and Future Picture.

The true value in the language is the clear, concise and easy format in which it is developed. It has valuable lessons for people in leadership.

Languages aren't supposed to do these things, but the Language of Performance-Driven Execution does because it represents something special... and different. Anyone would find their time well spent in learning to speak this language. The entire approach is what learning a new language of strategy should be: quick, fun and easy. You'll absorb your new language without any complexities or added tension because all you have to learn is six words. The Language of Performance-Driven Execution has a 100% guarantee that leaders will change how they and their organizations will play in the leadership sandbox: Amaze yourself by learning the language to change how to attain *Breakthrough Achievable Results* and more!

A question comes to mind that you should consider for yourself before using the language: *"what allows us to convert the success of greatness into the mastery of extraordinary in leadership?"* I can tell you that it is the near-wins and absolute failures that truly motivate us to master our destinies. Are you aware of what doggedness looks like with a high level of exactitude? What it means to align discipline with objectivity to hit a target after pursuing a kind of excellence and obscurity? To be in a position to witness what's so rare to glimpse that difference between success and mastery—success is hitting the objective, but mastery is nothing without knowing that it can be done again and again. Success is an event, a moment in time, whereas mastery is a commitment to achieving an objective and the constant pursuit of a constant accomplished task with a win at the end.

In other words, the pursuit of mastery is a forever, an onward and an almost; it is the reaching and not the arriving. It is that constant for wanting to close the gap between where you are and where you want to be—the sacrificing for your craft and not the sacrifice of yourself or others. It is the lineage of near wins and a fresh perspective that can compel us on an ongoing quest to learn something new.

The Language of Performance-Driven Execution is set on a trajectory of mastery. It has a compulsion that changes our view of the landscape and puts our objectives, *which we on occasion place out in the distant future,* into a more proximate to our current conditions and where we stand now. The language has resemblance to a more practical clarity. It inspires us to make decisions in the present to achieve that far off in the distance objective. And, the language moves us to experience not what we are, but what we can become at sometime in the future.

The language allows us to thrive at our own leading edge and it's why, in its deliberate and completeness, it is tuned to innovation. Mastery of the language is not so because it allows a leader to take it from its inception to a desired point in the future.

Mastery happens because you, the leader, know that there can be and will be more once a higher level of greatness is achieved—only to continue onward looking for something else. Like mastery, the

Language of Performance-Driven Execution is a veracious unfinished path that requires more. Leaders must build from an unfinished idea even when the idea is a foreign vernacular, a language that must be understood to realize what can become a new reality. It's all about developing new landscapes and environments that ultimately require new maps. Finally, academics and consultants alike can come together to revisit the popular idea that new languages form to increase productivity and efficiencies. Even those that have profoundly shaped existing best practices that are already in use such as Clay Christensen's views on disruptive innovation and his identified nomenclature on the subject. Models like these are widely used and accepted because they're user-friendly, make things simpler and reassure executives that they've acted on well-substantiated knowledge. And the Language of Performance-Driven Execution is no different.

When we think about established firms attempting to become disruptors, the Language of Performance-Driven Execution would be a good starting point to change their way of thinking. Although disruptive innovation is not a model for universally applicability, the Language of Performance-Driven Execution is, and can start a disruptive way of thinking that will go on to show up in the way people, cultures and an entire organization behaves. There are many "ifs" and "buts" that popular frameworks lack however the Language of Performance-Driven Execution is *not* one of them. Sadly, though, mainstream leadership folks aren't interested in testing, applying or updating strategy frameworks, let alone new strategy languages, for they are simply interested in practical implications. But when you think about the applications of this newly proposed language and the simplicity that inherits its construct, the added value will be realized after objectivity about the conditions under which established views do and don't work well.

In all of these areas, what really excites me is the prospect of a stronger link between getting things done using best practices and achieving execution excellence leveraged by a new language that promotes more productive creativity. Together, we can simplify reality without distorting it and uncover the social laws that we don't yet understand, but shape our world using Novo (to make anew, change), Distinctio (to distinguish, differentiation), Cretum or Cresco (to increase, expand), Socius (to share, association) OrgSx (to get it done, execution), and Exitus or Exigo (to finish, exit) to explore a better meaning and purpose.

Those of us who are in positions of leadership responsible to drive change and be accountable to the actions that follow most likely do so because we're strong-minded individuals who know what we want. That's our strength and we tend to play to it. The problem is, knowing what *we* want isn't the same thing as knowing what our *customers* (internal and external) want. And that's where the very thing that drives us into situations that may not be healthy. This level of single-mindedness *will always* be the Achilles heel showing our weakness that *will always threaten* our success. To succeed for the long term, leaders must learn to embrace change by connecting their ways of thinking to their communications and actions. In Go Slow to Go Fast strategy, this is known as *The Art of Strategy Connectedness that shows reasons for a much needed pivot to embrace change.*

I urge you to begin learning the Language of Performance-Driven Execution and using it in your new strategy language to realize what the future can become. It defines *The Art of Strategy Connectedness and* I promise that you'll wish you had learned it sooner.

# 6

# The Rule of Three:
# Leadership Triplicity™

*"Making three things happen in parallel with consistency to cause an effective change to follow is mastery. It requires the understanding of the power that lies in simplicity; the ability to go away so that you may be able to come back to see the fruits of your labor. And on your journey, people will be able to see you differently, offering something of value. Going away from your starting place is not the same as leaving."*
— **Damian D. "Skipper" Pitts**

T he second Next-Level Practice in the Go Slow to Go Fast strategic approach is known as Leadership Triplicity™. This concept states three things must happen in parallel for people to understand, learn and do *something* to impact the Future Picture.

The word *something* is the operable word to focus on here. There is an underlying structure and logic to leadership today and it has been lost within the fragmented and confusing state of misinformation over the years. Every year without fail, more authors release yet another series of books (or eBooks) on the topic of leadership attempting to either dispel a theory or to build upon the noise while introducing their own strategy. Added to the mounds of literature, we can't even fathom the untold number of leadership seminars, motivational speakers, executive coaches, and leadership ideas taught in business schools and corporate training centers across the globe with little to no continuity between the projects or cases.

No wonder leadership has lost its way today (it really has); not that we don't need the abundance of knowledge and birthing of thought-leadership to help guide our way forward. But, the fragmentation of misguided information and the confusion that follows it continues to cause challenges while navigating through the noise to decipher what has value and what does not. Figuring out which strategy to follow and which will simply just become another fad has become unavoidable and somewhat disheartening.

The main problem that is very apparent today is that there's too much noise and far too many divergent approaches to leadership with little to no guidance on how to select the right theory for any specific situation. I do know that we cannot have a one-size-fits-all, but there should be a guide that exists to explain which approach to use for dealing with specific situations. When we go into any restaurant in the world, there are choices on the menu that explain the ingredients for the hungry person to decide if an item will be enough to fulfill the hunger. In some cases, the menu even goes as far as to explain the calorie count and whether or not the item will be harmful should the recipient suffer from allergic reactions. Nonetheless, in the leadership scheme of things, there's little or no acknowledgement that any one leadership approach will or will not work in any situation, or even in a significant number of situations. There's little guidance on how to size up a situation or to align an approach using a specific strategy to get the expected outcomes for the given situation a leader is dealing with.

And just as every theory can be right, they can all be wrong, depending on the situation and influences from the people in the scheme of things. We all know that a theory that works well under some conditions fails miserably under others.

None of them can be relied upon to guide every leader in every situation; nor can the aspiring leader predict which theories will work under which conditions because each condition presents a rapidly challenging and unpredictably changing dynamic that never remains the same from one minute to the next. As more people enter into the situation, it changes due to varying perspectives and situational behavioral dialects. It is unequivocally a myth that a good leader can lead successfully in any situation. Not for any minute can we expect that Dr. Martin Luther King would react today as he did in the sixties to overcome the oppressions against mankind. Responding to violence with non-violence today is simply different because the world has become a more dangerous place causing for a different set of decisions to bring resolve to conflict.

Different situations call for different leadership capabilities, decision-making and unique approaches to achieve the results from the demands of the situation. Leaders today are forged in the furnace of conflict and stress, and it's fair to say that the demands from the conflict and stress fail more people than it turns out actual effective leaders who are proficient in their duties when leading others to be better at leadership and followership.

So, a question that should be running through your head at this point is *"does this publication offer more noise to fall in line with the statements up to this point?"* Or, *"what makes this text any different?"* These two questions should also be the considerations we use to examine all bodies of work in the marketplace before exploring their validity to an existing situation, but I want to answer them for the Go Slow to Go Fast approach to leadership and strategy.

I've learned by watching and listening that most leaders don't have a strategy today. And although I can't prove that statement and back it up statistically, I can say that over the years I've been invited into my share of discussions, trainings and seminars when leadership strategy was introduced—and I can tell you that an alarming number of people don't have a clue about what is required to actually lead. This is true regarding leading people as well as process and strategy. This is scary when you think about the state of leadership across the world today.

In answering the first question, *does this publication offer more noise to fall in line with the statements up to this point,* I have to stand on the evidence from the previous chapter with the outlining of a new language. So my answer would be NO; "we don't need any more noise! The context of this publication is designed to offer a different perspective to leadership. Go Slow to Go Fast requires a pause to step back and look at existing conditions to evaluate the best way to precede using "disruption" as the North Star objective for achieving a task—and NOTHING else.

The second question, *what makes this text any different,* goes to the heart of the entire Go Slow to Go Fast strategy and takes a very pointed approach to the leadership that states: *"to become extraordinary coaches of extraordinary men and women, a culture must shape how a society behaves."* So, the two perspectives combine to establish one very specific mandate in a Go Slow to Go Fast strategy: *"**Achieve disruption to the incumbent strategy, allowing the actions predicated from the Go Slow to Go Fast strategic approach, to deliver globally responsible results through the people that make up the organization with great impact!***" Herein lies the difference; to move forward using a Go Slow to Go Fast approach and strategy, leaders MUST ensure they're aligned with causing a significant disruption with a radical change to follow from their actions. If this is not the case, the strategy cannot and does not qualify for use. As such, a Go Slow to Go Fast strategy causes the traditional approach to leadership to no longer have relevance because Go Slow to Go Fast sets-out to explore what is beyond great; hence, the word *extraordinary* having a place in this segment. Should a strategy not be aligned to meet such an outcome, including the people chosen for the journey, it does not fit the Go Slow to Go Fast mandate that allows a culture to shape how a society behaves. These are the rules and nothing else matters!

Setting out to shape *how a society behaves* and causing *a significant disruption* to experience extraordinary outcomes and results from your actions is a matter of importance that not all leaders or leadership approaches are tuned into and this is a great differentiator to impact the Future Picture. If you haven't figured out for yourself how to become the disruption that is represented in this text, there are a few things that you must do in order to begin the process for yourself. First, you must understand the importance of the *Rule of Three* as a Go Slow to Go Fast strategy. Next, you must understand *divergent-convergent-emergent methodology* in a Go Slow to Go Fast strategy. And finally, you need to fully understand what it means to appropriately *change what you can, manage what you can't and lead everything else*—an outcome known as *Singular Accountability*. Let's look at the *Rule of Three* to ensue you are able to grasp a full understanding of this perspective before considering to make a Go Slow to Go Fast strategy the course of action to realize real change that WILL matter and stick as you decide to go forward.

## The Rule of Three

The Rule of Three in a Go Slow to Go Fast strategy relates to a term and philosophy known as Leadership Triplicity; otherwise known as a Next-Level Practice.

It's defined meaning offers a very general rule that states how simple concepts or ideas presented in threes are more interesting, more enjoyable and most of all, more memorable. It's no accident that the number three is universal in well-known stories: The three musketeers, the three stooges, or the three wise men. It's no accident that you are likely familiar with these three part quotes: *"Life, liberty, and the pursuit of happiness; "sex, drugs, & rock n' roll"; "truth, justice, and the American way"* (of course, these are the causes for which Superman fights), and it's no accident that good stories have a beginning, middle and an end.

I've come to understand the power of the *Rule of Three* and how it can be used to create real change in life (I mean change that actually matters). And, when you think about it at work in a Go Slow to Go Fast strategy, you cannot move forward without also thinking about putting Leadership Triplicity to work to Better *your* Best (come on, you really didn't expect any thing but three words here did you?). This little idea explains why the majority of people and organizations continue to experience the norms, why a few get the results they'll be happy with, and why others experience extraordinary greatness and then go on to inspire others to do the same. The *Rule of Three* is at work here; it comes down to three words that relates to *divergent-convergent-emergent methodology* and they each explain how people behave when seeking to complete a process with success, improve upon a process to move closer to greater levels of success, or CREATE new habits to change their situational circumstances by identifying factors that others have yet to consider for themselves. The three words are Many-Most-Some:

- **Many** people know what they do and how they do it, and they get mediocre results.
- **Most** people know what they do and how they do it, and get the results they expect.

- **Some** people actually figure out WHY they do what they do, and get extraordinary results… then, they go on to teach others to do the same, and they live their lives improving upon their individual purpose day-after-day to keep achieving the extraordinary results they seek—they understand the concept of purpose!

Leadership Triplicity sets it sights on these three words and place them in categories to better understand which people should be teamed together to make three things happen, in parallel, in order to do *something* that achieves extraordinary outcomes while impacting the Future Picture.

There is clearly a difference between the types of people in each category and the values or motivators they carry with them. Mediocre results are only experienced when people become complacent and comfortable in their every day happenings. They're not seeking to make a big impact, but they're quite happy with the normal structure each day offers them in a given situation.

These people are not those individuals who will light a spark to ignite the flame of change; hence, they fall into the "Many" category. Clearly by the definition, these individuals will not do well in a situation where Leadership Triplicity is at work. Next, when people are doing only enough to get the results they expect, no one will be pulling the others along to rise-up above their individual potential. There's little to no pursuit in the everyday challenge to exceed expectations. When these things occur, the people here will demonstrate reasons why they should fall into the "Most" category. But then, there's another category that focuses on the very reason WHY Leadership Triplicity was developed.

This category, "Some," is where the greater of your efforts should be focused because it fits the perfect storm to become an extraordinary and salient event. This category explains the purpose for having people aligned with the strategy who want more than the expected results. They push instead of pull while working to respond more effectively each day than the prior, and they understand the very meaning of the words from the 35th U.S. President, John Fitzgerald Kennedy, spoken at Rice University on September 12, 1962: *"We choose to go to the moon in this decade and do the other things, not because they are easy, but because they are hard."* In other words, the people who reside within the "Some" category do the things that are hard because they want more and choose to help others along the way achieve more for themselves and others. They understand partnership, collaboration and the importance of the perfect storm blowing in to disrupt everything while pushing things out of balance. And more importantly, they understand the reasons why strategy must become extraordinary to create a new mandate that will not only eliminate existing incumbent playbooks, but will change how the game is played all together.

Leadership Triplicity and the *Rule of Three* is a powerful movement. It is powerful because it defines three different but very valuable perspectives that every situation must have. One that goes along to get along; one that accepts traditions as they are; and one that sees the world as it is and knows what to do for others to see how it can become. The final perspective is the *something* that is talked about in the definition of Leadership Triplicity that achieves extraordinary outcomes while impacting the Future Picture.

Leadership Triplicity is a mash-up of concerts between divergent-convergent-emergent methodologies within the Go Fast to Go Slow strategic approach. It starts with the comforts of our well being and slowly converts the comforts into something we never thought we could achieve. It then progresses onward to realize what the world can become if we only apply a different perspective to the way we think about accomplishing things in life. In divergent perspective, people only conform to what is comfortable, a routine of sort, to guide their paths forward.

As they move down the path, they are introduced to new perspectives that take form from wider perspectives and putting on different lenses. They converge on potential new possibilities and opportunities from a wider field of view. As they converge on the possibilities and opportunities, they're able to focus at different distances, giving multiple frames of reference to more people at the same time. The two perspectives offer a different way to see what the world can become. The path from divergence to convergence opens the lens for a wider viewpoint to consider *something* new to ultimately focus on a three-dimensional window of newly formed perspectives known as 30-60-90 Promethic Forethoughts.

30-60-90 Promethic Forethoughts glean insight from the Greek God Prometheus who is known for giving mankind foresight and fire (desire). 30-60-90 represents the corporate stop-watch, 30-60-90 days used to achieve specific objectives. So, in essence, 30-60-90 Promethic Forethoughts are a combination and a result of divergent and convergent perspectives used to make better decisions from a three-dimensional window of new perspectives. Divergent and convergent perspectives do two things. First, they expand (divergence) the innovation sandbox to offer a new 'way to play.' Next, they narrow (convergence) the innovation sandbox to offer a disciplined and focused perspective to achieve a better way or approach to win. Divergent perspectives offer things like "creativity, brainstorming, strategy mapping, etc." Convergent perspectives foster things like "prototyping, flowcharting and mind mapping." Together, they create small wins or fans to want more because they represent more options to realize a better way, meaning or purpose. Where the excitement lies is in the *Moment of Truth* where people understand that the two perspectives actually represent a transitioning point. Divergence offers as many options as possible while convergence allows for choices to be made in order to decide which one to select for implementation. The *Moment of Truth* identifies the birthing process whereas emergence is realized as a significant breakthrough. All of these three things are conducted within the 30-60-90 Promethic Forethoughts or the stopwatch to ensure momentum remains fluid.

The emergence perspectives, that place where *"some"* people reside and hang their hats, are where the explosion happens. Exploration into new opportunities and new possibilities with a focus on *Singular Accountability* is achieved. Characteristics of the likes of *Shared Consciousness and Purpose* (discussed in the follow-on *Crisis Leadership* book), collaboration, team maneuvers, disruptive innovation, and more reside in this category. This is where the magic happens and why Leadership Triplicity exists.

The first two qualities, divergence and convergence are where things are teased out and shaken up to stir Right-time Decision-making in the pot of explored possibility. Emergence is also where edgy unconventional wisdom is applied to overcome incumbent behavior and strategy using a hell-fire approach (large amounts of force happening in parallel, at the same time, as in the Language of Performance-Driven Execution) to force the hand of your rivals to conform to your new 'way to play.' Leadership Triplicity is all about bringing the rule of three to life through *divergent-convergent-emergent methodologies* to make sure the right people are in the right categories and focused on doing the right things to get the right things done. It is a Next-Level Practice worth getting familiar with and one that will add significant more value to your step-wise path into an impactful future.

In the end, *Singular Accountability* pervades as the 'Moment of Truth' through Leadership Triplicity. This means that everyone, not just the bosses and leaders, are being held accountable for the outcomes. Everyone lives and dies with the sword so to speak. No one person is larger than the organization, its objectives and the impact it will be making on the Future Picture. And more importantly, everyone involved in a Go Slow to Go Fast strategy will be most creative because they feel motivated primarily by the interest, satisfaction and challenge of the work itself, and not by external pressures or individual perspectives (wants and gains).

For your review, the diagram on the next page outlines the Leadership Triplicity™ framework and includes the underpinnings known as KWAPS (Key Words And Phrases). The outlined KWAPS are those direct actions used to ensure Right-time Decision-making is accomplished within each of the objectives and people within the Many-Most-Some categories are able to journey through each category successfully when applying the *divergent-convergent-emergent methodologies*. To learn its full use, you'll have to glean insight into the full Leadership Triplicity framework in the *Crisis Leadership: How to*

Diagram 3. Leadership Triplicity™

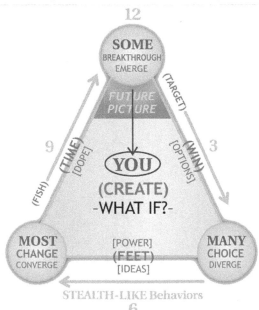

*Avoid Risk, Lead out from Crises before they Happen and Go beyond Best Practices* publication. Or, you can simply send me an email to discuss how to integrate this Next-Level Practice as a new 'way to play' into your organization to explore new opportunities and new possibilities with your processes and teams to impact your Future Picture and Better *your* Best. Email me at dpitts@damianpitts.com.

# 7

# Leadership Code Switching and the Four Action Behaviors

*"Each day, our fate is created from our actions and yet we wonder still today why so much remains out of our own control. At the end of the day, your ability to behave responsibly is all that stands between accountability and irresponsibly? "*
— **Damian D. "Skipper" Pitts**

There are Four Strategic Imperatives that come to play in any form of structured organizational setting or environment: People, Teams, the Organization and the Environment. Understanding how they each add value in the decision-making process allows for the opportunity to sit and analyze how significantly they each play in the whole leadership scheme of things. What I mean by this statement is several things, mainly: leaders make decisions quickly based on the patterns in their situations; leaders make decisions from the emotional associations they have in the situations they are members; leaders make decisions based on the process they've become reliant upon to get the results they are seeking; and leaders make decisions based on the relationships they have with others in the same situations they've found themselves dealing with; good, bad or indifferent, at any given time.

What I've come to learn while developing Go Slow to Go Fast strategy is that nothing will test a leader like noticing the signs of crises on the horizon. They will do whatever is required to avoid the turbulence at all cost. However, getting them to understand the behaviors that make up the natural habitat in which a crisis resides is important for survival in today's world. And more than that, it is even more critical to possess the Next-Level Practices (NLPs) and the skills to recognize and respond to the effects of the highly charged and dramatic events that surround the circumstances that lead up to a crisis in leadership. Although many programs exist to reference how to manage or flourish under pressure in the face of chaos, few acknowledge, or explain, the behavioral influences leading up to the defining moment before disorder is experienced—until now.

Go Slow to Go Fast strategy as Next-Level Practices (NLPs) identifies and facilitates how to change the outcomes from within the leadership sandbox and what behaviors must be called upon for people, teams, organizations and environments to do so with impact. One of these behaviors is known as Leadership Code Switching. It helps to make a significant difference with a simple set of ideas resulting in small changes that deliver big results.

This is a phenomenal behavior used by Crisis Leaders to make sure they are doing what is necessary to avoid operating in a world of VUCA: Volatility, Uncertainty, Complexity and Ambiguity. Code switching in leadership is the ability to modify behavior in response to rapidly changing environments using past experiences to manage psychological challenges when moving toward the Future Picture. Having the experience to successfully code switch in the heat of a battle offers a different '*way to play*' and changes the lens of leadership in an active leadership sandbox; one that allow other leaders to change their lens of leadership while achieving greater results and improved outcomes.

Leadership Code Switching carries with it an ethos that goes unmatched, providing the significant ability to slow things down in order to go faster with greater effectiveness.

Learning to modify behavior, in response to rapidly changing environments, using past experiences to manage psychological challenges (limiting) when moving toward the Future Picture is a great skill that all leaders must learn to not only do, but adapt their own skills by learning and mastering the skills for themselves. In essence, Leadership Code Switching represents the direct action and strategic operational approach that also helps to identify *Recon for Risk* perspectives to seek out potential for risk that may harm any one aspect of the four strategic imperatives. And for this reason, Go Slow to Go Fast strategy is important (risk assessing) to win the future and ultimately the Future Picture.

What Leadership Code Switching shows us is that there's three different forms that all leaders must consider to remain relevant when setting out to stimulate disruptive change to their respective environment. They are outlined as borrowing (context), maneuvering (management), and adapting (acclimation).

The first form refers to borrowing or context. The book, *In Their Time: The Greatest Business Leaders of the Twentieth Century*, the authors talk about context-based leadership. They describe it to mean that an opportunity emerges when environmental factors and individual action come together—and "come together" is the most important part. They explained how the environmental factors created a specific and sometimes unique context for business. Within this contextual framework, some individuals envisioned new enterprises or new products and services. Some saw opportunities for maximizing or optimizing existing businesses. Others found opportunities through reinvention or recreation of companies or technologies that were considered stagnant or declining.

Context stimulates a leader's approach to change and the direction the change will happen with respect to the specific opportunities that lay ahead. It is a determining factor that when applied wrongly, has created a long list of past CEOs and leaders to fail in their approach to changing the strategic context within a system. This is due to their records of success in one context and thinking that the success can be moved over into a different context to experience the same successful outcomes. Context is specific, so it requires specific thinking and more so, specific behavior and borrowing context is a tricky business. It goes to say that just because a person is an excellent worker within the context of their role in a large organization; it does not mean that they will be as successful in a growing start-up.

Well established organizations have significant systems and large supportive teams in place to pull resources and knowledge from, whereas a strong start-up may require the individual to actually take trash out, wear many hats outside of their intended role and more. Context is critically important and must be held as a critical component in Leadership Code Switching when borrowing plays a part in the success or failure of a strategic initiative.

The second form of Leadership Code Switching refers to maneuvering or simply stage management. Managing process or achieving process transformation is the intended practice that flows from maneuvering management process to win business transformation. Google went public 10 years ago *(August 19, 2004)*, and since then has dramatically changed the way the world accesses information. It has also helped shape the practice of management. Staying true to its roots as an engineering-centric organization, Google has stood out both for its early skepticism of the value of managers as well as for its novel, often quantitative approaches to management decisions. The 20% Time rule at Google is now a well documented management practice. Since its start, the organization encourages its employees to spend 20% of their time on interesting side projects, with the idea that some of these projects would become new products. Both Gmail and AdSense, the company's ad software for publishers, started out as 20% time projects. But back in 2010, Chris Trimble, *a well-known innovation speaker, consultant faculty member at Tuck School of Business, Dartmouth College, and the coauthor of Reverse Innovation: Create Far From Home, Win Everywhere* criticized the 20% time rule both for being expensive and for emphasizing ideas over execution.

Writing last year, amid reports that the company was ending the policy, Michael Schrage, *a research fellow at MIT Sloan School's Center for Digital Business, is the author of Serious Play, Who Do You Want Your Customers to Become?, and The Innovator's Hypothesis (forthcoming)*, took a slightly different view, arguing that 20% time is great for some employees but not for others. As for deciding who gets it? He suggested letting the data decide, an approach Google could no doubt get on board with. The point here is management offers a significant ability to code switch or maneuver between new ideation or to remain in a traditional box using managed outdated processes to get left behind.

Using the concept of maneuvering in Leadership Code Switching, like Google, leaders are able to allow their leadership experiences to yield unique and powerful insights while their business acumen, at the same time, facilitates the articulation of ideation for practical application.

Maneuvering in Leadership Code Switching remains a rapidly evolving practice used to instill the seven guiding principles used to manage process well: the targeting of critical vulnerabilities, boldness, surprise, focus, decentralized decision-making, tempo and combined arms.

The third and final form of Leadership Code Switching refers to adapting or acclimation. This type offers the ability to succeed in multiple contexts, based on what authors Warren Bennis and Robert Thomas in *Geeks & Geezers: How Eras, Values and Defining Moments Shape Leaders* refer to as adaptive capacity: the ability to change one's style and approach to fit the culture, context or condition of an organization. Success in the twenty-first century will require leaders to pay attention to the evolving context and to adapt or acclimate themselves to the specificity within those contexts to be successful.

This type of Leadership Code Switching will definitely shape the context of business leadership, and at the very essence, it will become the mainstay in leadership to change how we view not just leadership, but the very way we learn and ultimately live our lives. It presents a compelling new perspective that predicts who is likely to become, and remain, a leader, and why. At the heart of this type in Leadership Code Switching is what Bennis and Thomas referred to as "crucibles;" utterly transforming periods of testing from which one can emerge either hopelessly broken, or powerfully emboldened to learn and to lead. Crucibles are the turning points, the defining and salient events that force us to decide who we are and what we are capable of becoming. This Leadership Code Switching type reveals the critical traits people must learn to master, including adaptability, vision, integrity, unquenchable optimism and "neoteny;" the youthful curiosity and zest for knowledge, highlighting the forces that enable any of us to learn and lead not for a time, but for a lifetime.

We've seen several early examples of this code switching ability across our worldly communities. One that stands out is Tracy Martin, the mother of Trayvon Martin, the 17 year old African American male who was shot and killed in Sanford Florida in 2012. The incident that took the young man's life ignited a national examination about race, gun rights, our laws, the U.S. Constitution and politics. But, even with all of the debates and national outcry about right and wrong, Tracy Martin stood tall above the noise to not only become a grieving mother, but to also keep her composure to adapt to a higher purpose. The higher purpose that was more important in the eyes of the nation was to establish a voice for the "unalienable rights" of all men and women, regardless of race.

And, consequently, she believed that her son's *right* to continue on with his life was not to be an issue of conversation or to be taken in death by anyone and for any reason. Ironically, unalienable rights became an underpinning throughout the entire situation, but still today, some two years later and after the fact, Tracy Martin's voice still represents leadership on the issue and although there are other mothers across the world whose voices are also heard loud and clear on the issue, it is Martin's voice that has been thrust into the spotlight of late.

All three forms of Leadership Code Switching refer to switching back and forth throughout a series of organizational behaviors to both communicate reason and to offer a compelling purpose for people, all people, to look at life to consider what they can become versus what they have become up to a specific point in time. And, in the end, the three different forms of Leadership Code Switching can not only improve situations, but will define them as the salient events that they are to become and represent in the field of leadership, Crisis Leadership, in the eyes of everyone around the world.

None of this is possible without first allowing leaders to accept new challenges using *focus* and *differentiation* in the discovery of concrete solutions for managing events long before they have a chance of turning into turbulent situations. Learning to Go Slow to Go Fast using Next-Level Practices (NLPs) provides the creative juices to respond more effectively to the distinctly challenging new world. Changing the lens of leadership requires people to first examine their perspective about how they see the world. Is the glass half full or half empty? Or, do you simply need a new glass? Regardless of how you answer these questions, how you see the world presents a significant impact on the level of success you'll achieve.

I'm referring to the essence of classic strategy that argues reasons why people must look beyond potential rivals in order to consider threats from the hidden influences in life. There are four competitive forces or *action behaviors* that form the best means of dealing with these hidden influences that will allow you to become more viable as an individual, team, organization and environment. Known as the Four Action Behaviors in Crisis Leadership & Performance-Driven Execution, they're outlined for Go Slow to Go Fast strategy to close the gaps between high performance and irresponsibility. They are listed as: *Design the Future, Target for Success, Campaign to Win, and Finish with Finesse.* They each show how strategy is all about guiding the outcome of individual effort to produce sustained success. In strategic terms, success is producing a sustainable outcome that is valuable and satisfying over time.

Strategy then, is not winning fierce battles; rather it is winning the overall war that continues to show up to cause volatility, uncertainty, complexity and ambiguity—and more particularly, strategy is set on winning the peace that follows. Not being able to initiate a good strategy limits your ability to change your lens on something new and this is a dangerous and expensive state that subsequently never leads to long-term success.

Many people think that strategic thought and execution are very difficult. To the contrary, almost everyone can learn to do both in parallel. The operative word, however, is "learn." We all grow up in a tactical world where looking both ways before we cross the street is a necessity for survival. Likewise, in our education we spend the overwhelming majority of our time learning details while we spend little time trying to integrate what we have learned. This relates to the essential things learned on various principles and disciplines of strategy that will ultimately deliver the greatest impact.

So, unfortunately, strategy is foreign to most of us; we have had little exposure to it and we are normally rewarded for tactical (doing) and not strategic (planning) prowess. If however, we really want our efforts to actually change how we see things in the world to produce sustained success, then we must learn *situational strategy* used to navigate the *Four Strategic Imperatives* in Go Slow to Go Fast strategy: People, Teams, Organizations and Environments. Situational strategy means that with every situation, things are different and no one strategy is poised to deal with the elements in individual situations successfully. Fortunately, despite the mysteries surrounding strategy, learning to think and act strategically is not too difficult, but it does require you to view the world through a lens that offers a wider perspective and on a much different set of terms.

## Design the Future

The first step in strategic thinking that changes the lens of how you see the world is to identify the future that you want to create. In Go Slow to Go Fast strategy, the desired future takes on a three dimensional perspective known as the "future," the "event horizon" and the "Future Picture" (talked about earlier). Designing the future is a very hard, very objective, very measurable picture of the future you want to create. This action behavior requires that you break the Future Picture into six (6) separate, but critical echelons to ensure a balanced future is embraced by all involved:

1. Leadership GPS System
2. The *Other* Cardinal Rules
3. Guiding Precepts
4. The Five D's of Execution

5. Persuasive Negotiations

6. Strategic Measures of Merit

Changing the lens of leadership in Go Slow to Go Fast strategy assumes that the people in an organization generally know more about their business than anyone else in the world. It also assumes that people in an organization or on a team responsible to improve the results across an environment will make and execute smart plans if they have access to the disciplined process for doing so.

Creating such a process should only be done in an open planning environment where more than just one or a few strong individuals have a say in the matter. Everyone's voice needs to be heard and contributions from everyone are required to ensure the plan is effective in its approach to lead into successful outcomes. The more people who are involved in the planning process, the better the opportunity to integrate effective and qualitative information into the mix. Things will seem to pick up in momentum causing the development process to go faster and the plan will more likely be well executed.

In general, it is good to have all six echelons involved in the planning process. Otherwise, the results can be harmful by skipping a sequence in the strategy planning process. Allowing everyone to take part in each area of discussion regarding the six echelons ensures that there will be various perspectives to add to the knowledge and experiences in the room. It also means that as the planning permeates down-range, people will have the disciplined focus they need to be held accountable for their individual contributions.

## Leadership GPS System

First discussed in chapter 3.1, the Leadership GPS System is the key concept that allows you to scope the environment to understand existing conditions and where you would like to end up (the final destination).

The first of the four action behaviors, Designing the Future, means that you are able to think about an operating environment and what will be required to build and measure, in high resolution, the pictures of the desired future includes how to craft the rules of engagement (behavior) that will become an integral part of realizing the actions within the event horizon and the Future Picture.

The three-dimensional window that allows for multiple perspectives becomes very apparent here. We talked about them earlier, but it cannot hurt to discuss them again because of their critical importance in the strategy planning process. Known as the "future" (compass heading) the "event horizon" (the place right before the Future Picture) and the "Future Picture" (how you expect the distant future to look prior to arriving) the Leadership GPS System helps to capitalize on the intelligence and energy of the organization's own people to create and execute winning strategies, *business and products,* in collaborative environments.

The Leadership GPS System, also known as the Five W's Agenda, provides the answers to these five focus-centric questions known to align people at all levels of the organization against the following strategic essentials:

1. **WHY** are we doing this? ...WHY will it be disruptive as a behavior and action? These questions are the descriptors about your purpose.
2. **WHO** will be impacted? ...WHO will benefit? ...WHO will be eliminated? And, WHO will be limited?
3. **WHAT** are we applying our resources and energy (inertia) against? ...WHAT is our compass heading and target (Zulu) time (end point)?
4. **WHERE** are we going? ...WHERE are the gaps in our knowledge and experience for the journey?

5. **WHEN** do we plan to arrive? …WHEN should we expect the future, the event horizon and the Future Picture? This includes 'descriptive memos' regarding the decisions to achieve the organization's objectives.

This system and highly useful strategic planning tool and instrument, helps decision-makers identify and overcome problems and challenges before they occur. Consider this when thinking about using the Leadership GPS System. You can take another look at the Leadership GPS System at the end of this chapter.

### The *Other* Cardinal Rules

The second critical echelon is known as The *Other* Cardinal Rules. This is a set of guidelines that are invaluable for people and organizations to follow while planning and executing at the strategic or tactical level. These rules, once established by the individual(s) or teams, are the rules that govern forward movement and must not change. Consider these Cardinal Rues when designing the future:

#### *Be the King that Builds the Rock of a Nation*

As an influencer of self and people, stay away from weak-kneed questions such as *"Can I do this?"* and assertively ask *"How are we going to get this done?"* Personally take action and refuse to make excuses for inaction. Be a Leader-Reader to seek understanding before seeking to be understood. Create, initiate, and shape change to influence an improved way to play that taps new opportunities to seize new possibilities. Never stop driving vision, but arrest signs of uncertainty—defend purpose and be reminded that relentless movement calms wrath with a mild answer to the meek, but a harsh word stirs up anguish to the strong.

### Exit the Lands of the Terracotta

Do not continue to live in your past greatness that allowed you to be where you are today. Regardless of your past triumphs, power offers a double-edged sword with a tyrannical reign that will quickly end in a peasant's uprising. Exit your past, empower your future and allow your greatness to assist you in the conquering of new states through humility.

### Remember the Alamo

Leadership must remain on one accord through a high level of trust, accountability and commitment in order to win the front and back gates of their desired outcomes (perspective). Man has all he needs to effect change and thus his own success. By reforming his world-view, he can affect his own success. All he needs he has and transforming his thinking will bring forth progression, success and a much respected competitive edge.

### Remove the Jars' Lid

Allow for profound growth by employing performance-driven thinking to navigate the maze of organizational politics—*and the schedule to do so*—to accept real change that actually matters and will stick. Accept a new lens to expand your growth beyond your mind's limits. A new world awaits you on the other side. Explore!

### Understand the Bus

Explain clearly what is expected from everyone you are responsible to and the implications should they fail in their own responsibilities. This is to ensure that each person is on the right bus, in the right seat, and on the move together as one to achieve the same objective.

The bus cannot move until everyone is properly seated and buckled in safely, having cleared their minds and their hearts to focus on the journey ahead.

*Open the Gateway*

Provide a deep understanding of your strategic intent, tactical approach, and business acumen (process) to form an unrelenting system that wins political, economic and social systems in the favor of your realized state.

*Remember Baghdad*

Never start what cannot be completed with poise, tact, discipline and the prowess to achieve excellence through unrelenting peak performance. Identify areas to apply warfare principles: identify and target competitive forces, set and maintain favorable terms of battle and, find and exploit the "gaps" within the strengths of your competitor's energy to impede behavioral movements. The greater the success at utilizing these principles, the easier it is to find gaps—chinks in their amour—to compromise their integrity and willingness to advance.

## On to Iwo Jima

I can't, says who? Communicate and facilitate a measurable, well-timed and executable strategy-forward—this is the way to build, manage and sustain extraordinary greatness in teams to allow them to flawlessly execute their assigned missions—regardless of challenges, lack of resources and the spillage of blood, sweat and tears. Get to the top of your mountain without fail and finish with finesse for all to see. This will fuel others to also want to win in their task to also achieve the experience of climbing their own mountain regardless of the challenging real-estate that lies ahead. Never give-in. Never give-up. Never again say never. Now that the Cardinal Rules are outlined, it is important to understand that they act as an unbinding set of rules that when in use, must not be misinterpreted the wrong way. In their current context, they work to specify the powers and functions that an individual can use to protect the integrity within his/her own good-growth behaviors when deciding on an approach to win in life.

## Guiding Precepts

The third critical echelon is Guiding Precepts; describing the essence of the organization and the boundaries you intend to accept regardless of the circumstances. They are designed to inform people what they should and should not be doing in accordance with executing a well designed strategy to win.

They also inform of the reasons "why" an action must occur and the repercussions should the individual/organization fail at meeting the tasks. More importantly, Guiding Precepts carry with them a set of General Orders; the broad, community-wide "need statements," designed to encompass a variety of related issues in a person's life or within the life cycle of an organization. These related issues are referred to as "Guiding Objectives," which are specific items that need to be addressed. Additionally, Guiding Strategies (developed to fit current and future circumstance) are the methods identified for addressing the Guiding Objectives, and the Guiding Policies are the specific action steps that are recommended to implement the Guiding Strategies.

Establishing real-world Guiding Precepts is critical to designing the future because they provide the ability to explore implications in an open and reflective manner, and reinforces the Cardinal Rules when providing coherency and wholeness that often lacks in life cycles.

## The Five D's of Execution

The fourth critical echelon is the Five D's of Execution; a substantive transformation in "thought" about how people achieve a certain perspective on things in life. They refer to an orchestration of systemic and evolutionary new world-views resulting in a "change" of societies, cultures and marketplaces due to behavioral influences and perspectives. This is today often called "systems theory," which sees a web of relationships coalescing to become something greater than the sum of its parts. Individuals must be able to look at things from a perspective that they are always changing and evolving into new forms; able to *Think Above the* Bar to attain *Breakthrough Achievable Results.*

We are doomed to a slow death unless radical change occurs in the way we think; change your way of thinking using the Five D's of Execution to cause *Disruption, Discipline, Determination, Development, and a Desire* to avoid dying a slow death. Consider this in establishing your Guiding Precepts that will ultimately pervade your organization or environment:

- Leadership must be *Disruptive* when times are good.
- Leadership must be *Disciplined* when momentum needs building.
- Leadership must be *Determined* when faced with possible setbacks.
- Leadership must understand *Differentiation* and innovation to *Think Above the Bar* to accomplish *Breakthrough Achievable Results* when continuous improvement requires ongoing learning to change, and…
- Leadership must have the *Desire* and focus to do what is right when high levels of commitment are needed to *establishing targets* over *setting goals* to become the change others will look to follow. Absence of *Desire* forces us to spend more time doing things right due to poor results from always go-go-go.

## Persuasive Negotiations

PERSUADING involves being able to convince others to take appropriate action. NEGOTIATING involves being able to discuss and reach a mutually satisfactory agreement. INFLUENCING encompasses both of these. The fifth critical echelon is Persuasive Negotiations and examines how to move people in the direction that best suits the overall organization and environment. This echelon forms the *Three Cs Process* and leads to greater reciprocity and effective collaboration of like-minded people:

1. Collaboration: who you are "is" who you'll attract.
2. Collective Intelligence: the collective efforts of many people to achieve a consensus in decision-making.
3. Connectedness: requires you to touch a heart before asking for a hand.

With this echelon, you can influence more conversations in your direction by becoming interested in other people than you can by trying to get people interested in you. Likewise, Persuasive Negotiations also utilizes Professor Robert Cialdini's *Six Laws of Influence* that govern how people influence and are influenced by others:

- **The Law of Scarcity. Intellectual property is more valuable to us when its availability is limited.** Scarcity determines the value of an item.
- **The Law of Reciprocity.** If you give something of value to people without expecting anything in return, they feel compelled to return the favor. People feel obliged to return a favor when somebody does something for them first. They feel bad if they don't reciprocate. "You scratch my back and I'll scratch yours."
- **The Law of Authority.** We are more likely to comply with someone who is (or resembles) an authority. In other words, people prefer to take advice from "subject matter experts" (SMEs). There is a deep seated duty to authority within us that has been learned from parents, school, authorities, etc. Become a SME!
- **The Law of Liking.** We are more inclined to follow the lead of someone who is similar to us rather than someone who is

dissimilar. We learn better from people who are similar to us. We are more likely to help people who are already moving in the direction that we already believe to be right.

- **The Law of Social Proof**. We view a behavior as more likely to be correct, the more we see others performing it. We assume that if a lot of people are doing the same thing, they must know something that we don't. Especially when we are uncertain, we are more likely to trust in the collective knowledge of the crowd (known as the influence of the herd). This, by NO means suggests becoming the norm. It does however suggest becoming different to change the norm for others to follow you as the herd!

- **The Law of Commitment and Consistency**. Consistency is seen as desirable as it is associated with strength, honesty, stability and logic. Inconsistent people may be seen as indecisive: never committing themselves for long enough to complete tasks. People will do more to stay consistent with their commitments and beliefs if they have already taken small initial steps that delivered the results they are looking to achieve.

## Strategic Measures of Merit

Strategic Measures of Merit (MoM); those measures that tell you when you have achieved your Future Picture or when you are on the right course for achieving it, must be in place to keep responsible people accountable for their actions. MoM must be in place because they offer the system checks for continuity and consistency within the strategy-forward to ensure plans remain on course with respect to predetermined criteria.

The six (6) separate, but critical echelons combine to add significant value to the first of the four action behaviors, Design the Future, to ensure balanced futures are embraced by everyone with a stake in the expected outcomes. They work to help leaders find and overcome problems and obstacles before they occur; the main purpose of the Go Slow to Go Fast initiative.

Next, we move into the second action behavior with Target for Success that explains how to understand your organization and markets in system terms in order to find the key Centers of Gravity (the leverage points) that will provide the most return on talent energy investments.

## Target for Success

There are a very large number of things against which an organization can put its resources. You know intuitively that some of those things will have much higher impact than others. The organization which targets the right things, the Centers of Gravity, will be far more effective at a much lower cost than the organization that has no disciplined way to choose and affect its targets. The Go Slow to Go Fast Process recognizes that everything takes place in the context of a system and that systems have such annoying characteristics as inertia and resistance to change. But, they also have Centers of Gravity; the components of a system that's related to achieving your Future Picture. This action behavior focuses on the leverage points that, when affected, have a disproportionate impact on their parent system and on the Future Picture. The best way to change a system (your organization or your market) is to affect its Centers of Gravity.

Again, Centers of Gravity are the essential points within a system that if you want to win your plan with effectiveness, even when or if your resources are limited, you apply your behaviors against them to achieve the greatest leverage or energy towards the vulnerabilities or areas that threaten your desired outcomes.

Centers of Gravity are relational synergies that total five: Leadership (decision makers), Processes (strategies and tactics), Infrastructure (the organization and emerging markets), Populations (people) and Action Units (customers and vendors). No matter the system, organization or marketplace, these five Centers of Gravity exist and are the starting point to cause change to occur.

If you want to put your organization or market on a new track, it is necessary to create rapid and hard-to-reverse system change using the action behavior Target for Success. To create hard-to-reverse change, you must affect the Centers of Gravity in the system in a compressed period of time. Doing so significantly reduces the ability of the system to resist what you want it to do and the change tends to stick.

## Campaign to Win

The third action behavior, Campaign to Win, explains why champions are needed along the way and along the path to success. With the Future Picture standing before everyone as a clear beacon to guide actions, this action behavior allows you to begin your attack against the Centers of Gravity previously identified. Why use the word "attack" here?

Simply because when you're moving your energy towards or against the leverage points within a system, you're essentially launching a preemptive strike against the gaps in performance to cause momentum to move in the direction you would like to go. You do this with campaign teams drawn from across the organization consistent with the talents required to exert the greatest leverage possible.

Campaign to Win is essential to the Future Picture and people responsible for driving success from within the system to the maximum extent possible of those who participated in the creation of the Future Picture and the identification of the Centers of Gravity. The campaign teams' objective is to ensure the continuation of the change work being done. This means that the system is relying on people to think strategically, focus sharply and move quickly with the decisions and action in an open planning environment to affect the Centers of Gravity in parallel.

For decision-makers and leaders to affect them in a very compressed time frame using parallel operations, the Centers of Gravity have far higher probabilities of success than do stretched-out serial operations and paradoxically cost are lowered within the compressed time frame.

It is almost always the case that the current organization structure will not be optimum for a new strategy, especially if it involves an aggressive Future Picture. That being said, part of Campaigning to Win is to modify the structure as required to allow the organization to move fast and accurately against the Centers of Gravity. The campaign teams themselves, of course, are designed for rapid action and will normally provide the bridge to a new-normal and new formal structure. In the interim; however, the organization is acting and winning in the real world and is not waiting for the development of a new structure—all the reason why this action behavior, Campaign to Win, is so critically important in the change process.

### Finish with Finesse (Complete the Succession Process)

At its most basic level, effective strategy has four static components: knowing where you would like to end up; knowing where you would like to place your energy against; understanding the methodology for applying your energy resources; and knowing the parameters of the inevitable end game. When systems fail at dealing with these four strategy components, they're deficient in their abilities to win their overall objectives in the long run. The fourth and last action behavior, Finish with Finesse, also extends itself into completing the succession process; meaning, once the objective is met or the system has changed from leveraging the Centers of Gravity in the direction that improves effort or increases outcomes, decisions must be made about next steps.

In the real world, every business cycle and product has a beginning and an end, also known as the target [Zulu] time. Even though we know this to be the case, very few organizations plan for the back side of the inevitable cycle. The failure to plan in advance to achieve positive organizational behaviors during the target [Zulu] time means that too much energy is devoted to the wrong things. Using the four action behaviors in the Go Slow to Go Fast Process and initiative allows you to plan so as to exit cycles and products with maximum gains.

Changing the lens of leadership within the context of the four action behaviors allows leaders and decision-makers to have a clear starting point and end time within a mapping sequence designed to win. It offers a different perspective to experiencing mastery (differentiation) over success (the norm) causing real change not only to happen, but to stick in the end. Go Slow to Go Fast understands strategy as being the single-most important component of any success for an organization.

The Four Action Behaviors are the starting point for changing the lens of leadership within a system that is primed for change. The Go Slow to Go Fast strategy can be called on to learn how to effectively use it for leadership and management teams who are committed to developing and executing winning business or product strategies to win by thinking strategically, focusing sharply and moving quickly to achieve the objectives. However, more simply, anyone can just follow the outline that makes up the process and initiative to complete an effective change process that is designed to win in the end.

Changing the lens of leadership is the process that creates objective, actionable descriptions of the organization's desired future with accompanying strategic measures of merit and guiding precepts. The process employs a real-world systems approach to find critical Centers of Gravity within an organization and in its markets. The process also helps to create and support open, flexible organizations, efficient at operating in parallel operations and orchestration of the greatest resources at every level—the people. And, the process of the Four Action Behaviors combined with Leadership Code Switching provides for the ability to be highly successful, specifically when planning the end game for every facet of the organization or business.

These Next-Level Practices (NLPs) are significant to Go Slow to Go Fast strategy and is essential to changing the lens of leadership for effective organizational change—or changing the constructs within the other strategic imperatives in teams and the environments they operate—ultimately the overall culture.

*"Business is a continual dealing with the future... a continual calculation, an instinctive exercise in foresight."*
— **Henry R. Luce** (1898 - 1967) U.S. Editor and Publisher

# PART II

# EXPLORE THE OPPORTUNITIES OF GOING FAST

# 8

# Understanding and Using
# TABLE Methodology

*"When sharing your table with others, it requires a 'them first' before 'me first' perspective to and help them with finding their place—at the table—to add value from a different perspective than your own. This gives you the chance to observe other's etiquette to see what you can offer that does not yet exist."*
**— Damian D. "Skipper" Pitts**

We've been talking about Next-Level Practices (NLPs) in Go Slow to Go Fast strategy and how they combine to add more value to your approach when setting out to create a new 'way to play' in the leadership sandbox. Before wrapping up these practices, we need to also address the ethos in Leadership Code Switching as well as the importance of placing your decisions on the TABLE to allow others to have a chance to examine your thoughts on the issues that will or can ultimately affect them. There are principles that define the ethos in Leadership Code Switching. Understanding Leadership Code Switching is one thing, but getting familiar with the principles that defines the Ethos in Leadership Code Switching is an even greater opportunity for experiential growth.

Our current crisis in leadership shows us why edgy and unconventional methods of growth can quickly become a lost art that will continue to be elusive over time. This is mainly due to folks thinking that far too much work is required to make the much needed pivot to continue the growth over the long-term. Using the Go Slow to Go Fast strategy, we define this lost art as *"the spirit of showing moral character that guides our beliefs, and in turn, becomes the foundation for influencing self and others."* For the well educated folks in the field of leadership, this is closely related to the ethos in leadership. But, I'm referring to something bigger. The *Ethos in Leadership Code Switching* is the ability to make the best moral decisions and judgments possible, *in rapidly changing environments,* and using those decisions to not only overcome limitations, but to also create ethical momentum while transitioning toward the Future Picture with greater impact. There are a few simple principles to be aware of while executing such a task. These principles must be used to define and make up the meaning for having an Ethos in Leadership Code Switching; they're outlined as:

1. Right-time Decision-making
2. Fast Strategy
3. Ethical Momentum
4. Transitional Prowess
5. Impact

## Right-time Decision-making

Leaders and their teams can make hundreds if not more decisions throughout any given day and, in most cases, their decisions don't require a standard automatic response due to familiar circumstances. It does seem that from time to time, they have to make decisions based on where the course of the future leads and the actual choices that follows the decisions to be made.

In essence, these decisions will either move people using direct actions to respond more favorably to something of importance, or simply be a wrong decision in the end. The question then is *"what must be done to ensure they are making the best decisions in the moment and, before doing so, are also making sure the decisions are right?"* One way to do so is to place your decisions on the table long before they'll be required for use. This is what I refer to as owning your own TABLE in Right-time Decision-making. Owning your own TABLE or using your TABLE Methodology refers to:

**Time-them:** there are two traps which people fall into when making decisions; making them too soon and making them too late. Some people make decisions too swiftly and without due thought. This may be because they are uncomfortable with the tension and turbulence that gets created when a decision has to be made, but they don't have all the information needed. Instead of living with tension, they make the decision ahead of time. Most leaders delay making decisions because they fear making a mistake or fear the changes that will result. The best decisions are hot-iron decisions: those that are well-timed, which you make when the iron is hot and the time is right.

**Align-them:** the more decisions you make consciously, the more you can align them with your objectives and purpose. Studies show that the average person makes 612 decisions a day. Each one takes us closer or further from our ultimate objectives in life. In a week, that would mean a single individual makes up to 4,284 decisions and in a year, the same individual makes 222,768 decisions; wow! As you can see, the results, *good or bad*, are cumulative over time. Strategic thinking means looking at how your decisions today affect your tomorrows. When your decisions are in alignment with what's important to you and the people directly impacted by your decisions, then life becomes meaningful, productive and satisfying.

**Become-them:** there is a balancing act that comes with making good decisions. First, you must become your decision making ability. This means that your decision making must be as critical to you as the air you breathe. Now, some would say that life is too short to be so serious about making decisions. And in using conventional thinking, this would be absolutely correct. However, there's nothing conventional in a Go Slow to Go Fast strategic approach when you as a leader are slowing things down to avoid risk by leading out from crises before they happen. The Go Slow to Go Fast approach is NOT for traditional folks who continue to do traditional things.

Instead, it is for those individuals who see themselves as unconventional and unusual who are willing to cause disruption to existing conditions, existing thinking and definitely to the way things are currently being done. There are three balancing acts to be aware of when getting into **the practice of becoming your decisions.** They are:

1. **Do or don't do; there is NO try!** Commit yourself through effort and intention to doing or get the hell out of the way to let someone else make the decision to get it done.

2. **Think and act.** Too much thinking puts off the action causing a paralysis of analysis; too much action may be at the expense of thought. Seek the right balance.

3. **Look before you leap and leap long and far when you do!** See and understand fully the possible risks when making your

decisions but, once decided, take the plunge with courage and live with the decisions made with no regrets. There's no more time for second thoughts. Once the action is completed, it is a past-tense situation that will always be in your rear-view mirror. Keep your eyes on the front windshield moving forward.

**Lead-them:** act when you must, but lead your decisions with excellence through performance. You should only make decisions when you have to. Margaret Thatcher is known to have made a focused comment on decision making where she stated, *"If there's one thing I've learned in politics, it is: never make a decision until you have to."* Here's a look at five "don'ts" to guide you.

1. DON'T make a decision unless you have two or more equally valid options.
2. DON'T make a decision if the responsibility belongs to someone else—unless you must.
3. DON'T make a decision unless there is disagreement, conflict or turbulence.
4. DON'T make a decision about irrelevant matters; time matters more.
5. DON'T make a decision if it can't be turned into action; strategically and flawlessly.

**Execute-them:** understand the importance of your gut instinct and follow it ONLY if it works well in your favor. Evidence will express the chances your gut instinct will keep you out of trouble. No matter what method we use to make a decision, there comes a moment when we know instinctively whether the decision is right or not. Many of the biggest business deals ever taken were taken on instinct. But, they were rarely taken on a whim.

Intuition works best when we have done the groundwork, accumulated plenty of expertise and researched the field using empirically-based outcomes over time. Take time to cultivate your intuition for it is never wrong and has your best interests at heart.

## Fast Strategy

One of the most important and critical principles that defines the Ethos in Leadership Code Switching is known as Fast Strategy. Successful leaders and organizations often become victims of their own success: when their business matures, they find it impossible to renew themselves and keep their decisions under review. To regain and maintain growth they need to learn to thrive on change and disruption while ensuring their decisions, under all conditions, undergo a Recon for Risk assessment before making them a reality. To achieve this and more, there are three essential capabilities they need to have in place as the catalyst for growth:

1.  Strategic Sensitivity: both the sharpness of perception and the intensity of awareness and attention in the face of making moral decisions.
2.  Resource Fluidity: the internal capability used for process transformation while employing the use of *right-time* resources rapidly for the situation.
3.  Collective Commitment: the ability of the top decision-makers to make bold decisions—fast, without being bogged down in "win-lose" politics within the system.

## Ethical Momentum

A natural progression with the Ethos in Leadership Code Switching, this principle breathes life into the other four because it involves systematizing, defending and recommending right and wrong behavioral conduct that keeps momentum moving in the right direction and at the right time—all of the time. Momentum cannot exist without first making sure that the people involved have the ability to make moral decisions to protect the integrity of the mission and objectives for the overall team.

Ethical Momentum is closely related to normative ethics, as they both represent the study of what makes actions and behaviors right and wrong. And since it is the one critical essential that must be present to allow the other principles to collaborate, it must become the spirit that motivates ideas and customs while moving into the future—*the disposition, character or fundamental values particular to a specific person, people, corporation or culture.*

There are five (5) fundamental considerations that people must uphold to be responsible professionals using the Ethical Momentum principle:

1. Integrity: does the person exhibit this quality all of the time?
2. Authenticity: how does the person help the team achieve differentiation?
3. Objectivity: will the person be able to make decisions without following the pack?
4. Professional Competence: is the person competent about their responsibilities?
5. Professional Behavior: how will the person behave under pressure?

To ensure your people fully understand this principle, leaders must make sure they use the guiding precepts when considering current and future performance prior to deciding to move down range with a group of individuals who will ultimately become the team that will be held responsible for driving momentum ethically.

## Transitional Prowess

The notion that great ideas come completely out of left field, as an extraordinary ability to cause an incredible moment to finally be witnessed by the masses, is not, unfortunately, how the world works. But, having the extraordinary ability to form a coalition of people or organizations to create mutual trust between them in order to achieve mutually beneficial progress or profit, is known as creating "transitional prowess" in Go Slow to Go Fast strategy. Creating *transitional prowess* is important because it relates to a simple word that smart decision-makers use on a daily basis; "coalition." When used in the context and the Ethos in Leadership Code Switching, it creates a purposeful treaty for individuals and teams working towards a mutually beneficial objective in the long-term, during which they cooperate in joint fashion, each in their own self-interest, joining forces together for a common cause. The alliance may be temporary or a matter of convenience, but in the end, the formation understands the importance of using preparedness and its extraordinary ability to defeat any threat to the overall system the joining forces represent.

## Impact

Impact is the ultimate objective with the Ethos in Leadership Code Switching. Its basic meaning states: to "make a difference in times of rising uncertainty" using each of the five (5) principles together when moving toward the Future Picture. At the core of this principle is a manifesto for process transformation and disruptive thought-leadership that is the underpinning of Leadership Code Switching. Decisions made by leaders will have extraordinary and enduring impact on their own futures and on their organizations, the global economy and society at large, consequently shaping how whole societies behave.

With impact, the Ethos in Leadership Code Switching prepares leaders by developing the required capabilities needed to fluidly pivot one way or the others depending on the circumstances they face. The key objective is to make sure they put themselves in the best conditions possible at all times and to do what is required to change the way to play in their favor to command the future. The impact principle when combined with right-time decision-making, fast strategy, ethical momentum and transitional prowess provide the extraordinary attributes to help leaders own their futures and Future Picture. These attributes are essential with the Ethos in Leadership Code Switching, allowing leaders to do the work that earn them their position, not only as an individual of significance, but as the game changer when they show up to any situation they are a part. The impact attributes are outlined as:

- Adaptive Acclimation: becoming comfortable with matching their strategic prowess to their competitive environments and rapidly adapting in response to turbulence.
- Disruptive Change: seeking evolutionary transformation, not just in the environmental sense, but also through innovative business process and gamification models that drives profit and strategic advantages by addressing unmet customer needs that Eliminate-Raise-Reduce-Create chokepoints at point of entry—this is your Strategy Canvas at work. Eliminate process and factors others take for granted. Raise process and factors beyond industry standards.

Reduce process and factors below industry standards. And, create process and factors the industry has yet to consider.

- Connectivity: embracing new opportunities and new possibilities to navigate the disruption inherent in the explosion of growth connectivity—and seeking tighter connections within each Center of Gravity: Leadership, Processes, Infrastructure, Populations and Action Units.

- Customer Centricity: creating a positive consumer experience that stands out from industry norms and stands on a deep understanding of how to meet and satisfy customer needs while overcoming customer frustration by disrupting how they are connected to and delivered upon that will exceed their expectations.
- Boldness: having the disruptive vision, controlled confidence and focused courage to take disciplined calculated risks, investing in alternative futures and making the kinds of transformative moves to ultimately shape how societies behave to upend rivals.
- Values-Driven: reconciling the imperative for long-term value creation with the need for short- to medium-term results, ensuring expectations go far beyond ideation, but develops superiority on all functional and operational dimensions that is critical to achieving strategic advantage.

Providing impact; making a difference in times of rising uncertainty provides the disruptive spark, the story, and the vision that empower others to adapt to turbulent times that follow in the footsteps of disruption. It also inspires others to follow into new economies of scale, building trust through strategic and flawless execution to win in any situation.

## Strategic Implications

Leadership Code Switching carries with it an ethos that goes unmatched, providing the significant ability to slow things down in order to go faster with greater effectiveness. It means that you are able to set out on a journey that will allow you to learn how to modify behavior, in response to rapidly changing environments, using past experiences to manage psychological challenges (limiting) when moving toward the Future Picture is a great skill that all leaders must learn to adapt. In essence, Leadership Code Switching represents the direct actions and operational approach to Go Slow to Go Fast (assessing risk) to win the future and ultimately the Future Picture. We've seen that there are three types of Leadership Code Switching that all leaders must consider to remain relevant in their own unique ecosystem. This will enable them to stimulate disruptive change that refers to how they can switch back and forth fluidly throughout a series of community or organizational behaviors—helping them understand what they can become versus what they have become up to a specific point in time.

Basically, Leadership Code Switching offers the needed fluidity (key word) to move throughout situations without stumbling, but if they do stumble, and they will, their level of competence will bring them through. This chapter is all about owning the future with impact on the Future Picture; leaders must understand how to code switch in leadership. And, in doing so, two things must happen; first, leaders must fundamentally understand their markets and fix their sights on what is required to win. This is the strategic imperative that ultimately wins competitive landscapes. Second, and most importantly, they need to be accountable for their actions using the guiding and foundational principles designed to ensure their success across all aspects of life. These guiding principles; Right-time Decision-making, Fast Strategy, Ethical Momentum, Transitional Prowess and Impact are the social imperatives to support Next-Level Practices (NLPs) in Go Slow to Go Fast strategy. Anyone can use them in any situation to become victorious, and not only in the business context.

In fact, Leadership Code Switching represents an ethos that is unconquerable when used the right way because it focuses on achieving and supporting one very specific objective: avoiding risk by leading out from crises before they happen using disruption, change and behavioral fluidity to shape how societies behave. And if leaders are to change their perspective to seek out a different 'way to play' and win in the competitive landscape, and if they are to put their stamp on tomorrow with greater impact, they must decide to do so today.

To provide you with additional information that will be of great assistance in helping you to do that, this section provides you with some great questions to use when making decisions. These are questions to ask the people you influence to align with your Next-Level Practices (NLPs) when making Next-Level Practice Decisions (NLPDs).

With help from *Leigh Buchanan's article, *editor-at-large for Inc. magazine,* who originally published the 100 great questions every entrepreneur should ask, we adapted them for use within the Go Slow to Go Fast strategy. With a few tweaks, the 100 questions have been transformed for use to help leaders feel comfortable with placing their decisions on the TABLE in the open to allow others a chance to examine their thoughts about the issues that will or can ultimately affect them. By doing so, their approach and the use of the Next-Level Practices (NLPs) of Leadership Code Switching can be used more effectively to lead their organizations into the future with impact. And with the help from Leigh Buchanan's article on the 100 questions every leader should ask, this shared information will also improve the step-wise path to achieving extraordinary success and outcomes.

Additional assistance and inspiration from the shared wisdom of some of the great leadership minds of our times, *namely Paul Graham, Jim Collins, Tony Hsieh, and other business leaders,* we learned from Buchanan's article that there's no Superman versus Batman face-off between asking questions and finding answers to identify ways of creating innovation throughout your environment. However, because people have their own opinions (as they should) and are willing to express their views on the subjects that are important to them, namely those subjects that will influence their own growth, asking the right questions will be a wise thing to do to add to the value needed to form your own Next-Level Practices (NLPs).

We all know that questions ignite imagination, avert catastrophe, and sometimes reveal unexpected paths to brighter destinations. Jim Collins, Marshall Goldsmith, and other thinkers have compiled their own stock of questions, which they urge leaders to pose to themselves and their teams. The right questions don't allow people to remain passive. They require reflection, followed by action… direct action to overcome the obstacles that stand in your way.

Warren Berger, author of *A More Beautiful Question*, praises inquiry's ability to trigger divergent thinking, in which the mind seeks multiple, sometimes non-obvious paths to a solution. Asking good questions and doing so often *"opens people to new ideas and possibilities,"* says Berger.

To compile this list of provocative questions, Buchanan and her Inc. magazine team reached out to entrepreneurs and management thinkers, put in the exhaustive time and arduous work to scan the millions of blogs, and revisited their favorite business books (though they tried to identify the origin of each question, some had competing claims of authorship. In those cases, they made their best call) to bring to us, their readers, more valuable information to use. Rigid mindsets and shared insights are dangerous things when allowed to gallop without have the abilities to ethically pull the reigns back at the right times. In doing so, information compiled to form opinions that are both ethical in nature and responsible in use provides the tools that can no longer be locked away out of reach.

I am so happy and grateful to have found this article after following the Inc. magazine folks like Leigh Buchanan. Thankfully this shared information has allow me to now share it with you here as we wrap-up the Next-Level Practices (NLPs) in Go Slow to Go Fast strategy. I hope that you'll continue to help me share this information, and I also strongly suggest that you also follow the team at Inc. magazine (I don't get any royalties and I am a paid subscriber) to keep your mind (in a word from Buchanan) supple.

I welcome your insights and willingness to add your own questions to this list when sharing with your work colleagues, family and friends.

1.  How can we become the company that would put us out of business? —*Danny Meyer, CEO of Union Square Hospitality Group*

2.  Are we relevant? Will we be relevant five years from now? Ten? —*Debra Kaye, innovation consultant and author*

3.  If energy were free, what would we do differently? —*Tony Hsieh, CEO of Zappos*

    Hsieh explains, "This is a thought experiment to see how you would reconfigure the business if you had different resources available or knew that different resources would one day become available. Another question might be; what if storage was free? Or what if labor costs half as much as or twice as much?"

4.  What is it like to work for me? —*Robert Sutton, author and management professor at Stanford*

5.  If we weren't already in this business, would we enter it today? And if not, what are we going to do about it? —*Peter Drucker, management expert and author*

    The late Drucker posed a variation on this question to Jack Welch in the 1980s. It inspired General Electric's "fix, sell, or close" strategy for exiting or restructuring unprofitable businesses.

6.  What trophy do we want on our mantle? —*Marcy Massura, a digital marketer and brand strategist at MSL Group*

    Massura explains, "Not every business determines success the same way. Is growth most important to you? Profitability? Stability?"

7. Do we have bad profits? —*Jonathan L. Byrnes, author and senior lecturer at MIT*

    Byrnes explains, "Some investments look attractive, but they also take the company's capital and focus away from its main line of business."

8. What counts that we are not counting? —*Chip Conley, founder of Joie de Vivre Hospitality and head of global hospitality for Airbnb*

    Conley explains, "In any business, we measure cash flow, profitability, and a few other key metrics. But what are the tangible and intangible assets that we have no means of measuring, but that truly differentiate our business? These may be things like the company's reputation, employee engagement, and the brand's emotional resonance with people inside and outside the business."

9. In the past few months, what is the smallest change we have made that has had the biggest positive result? What was it about that small change that produced the large return? —*Robert Cialdini, author and professor emeritus of marketing and psychology at Arizona State University*

10. Are we paying enough attention to the partners our company depends on to succeed? —*Ron Adner, author and professor at Tuck School of Business*

    Adner explains, "Even companies that execute well themselves are vulnerable to the missteps of suppliers, distributors, and others."

11. What prevents me from making the changes I know will make me a more effective leader? —*Marshall Goldsmith, leadership coach and author*

12. What are the implications of this decision 10 minutes, 10 months, and 10 years from now? —*Suzy Welch, author*

13. Do I make eye contact 100 percent of the time? —*Tom Peters, author and management expert*

14. What is the smallest subset of the problem we can usefully solve? —*Paul Graham, co-founder of Y Combinator*

15. Are we changing as fast as the world around us? —*Gary Hamel, author and management consultant*

16. If no one would ever find out about my accomplishments, how would I lead differently? —*Adam Grant, author and professor at Wharton*

17. Which customers can't participate in our market because they lack skills, wealth, or convenient access to existing solutions? —*Clayton Christensen, author, Harvard Business School professor, and co-founder of Innosight*

18. Who uses our product in ways we never expected? —*Kevin P. Coyne and Shawn T. Coyne, authors and strategy consultants*

19. How likely is it that a customer would recommend our company to a friend or colleague? —*Andrew Taylor, executive chairman of Enterprise Holdings*

    "Taylor's use of this question at Enterprise Rent-A-Car inspired Fred Reichheld to create the Net Promoter Score, a widely used metric for customer loyalty."

20. Is this an issue for analysis or intuition? —*Tom Davenport, author and professor at Babson College*

    Davenport explains, "If it's a decision that's important, recurring, and amenable to improvement, you should invest in gathering data, doing analysis, and examining failure factors.

    If it's a decision you will only make once, or if for some reason you can't get data or improve the decision-making process, you might as well go with your experience and intuition."

21. Who, on the executive team or the board, has spoken to a customer recently? —*James Champy, author and management expert*

22. Did my employees make progress today? —*Teresa Amabile, author and Harvard Business School professor*

    Amabile explains, "Forward momentum in employees' work has the greatest positive impact on their motivation."

23. What one word do we want to own in the minds of our customers, employees, and partners? —*Matthew May, author and innovation expert*

    May explains, "This deceptively simple question creates utter clarity inside and outside a company. It is incredibly difficult for most people to answer and difficult to get consensus on—even at the highest levels. Apple = different. Toyota = quality. Google = search. It's taken me three years to get one of my clients, Edmunds.com, to find and agree on their word: trust."

24. What should we stop doing? —*Peter Drucker, management expert and author*

25. What are the gaps in my knowledge and experience? —*Charles Handy, author and management expert*

26. What am I trying to prove to myself, and how might it be hijacking my life and business success? —*Bob Rosen, executive coach and author*

27. If we got kicked out and the board brought in a new CEO, what would he do? —*Andy Grove, former CEO of Intel*

    In 1985, with the company's memory-chip business under siege, CEO Grove famously posed this hypothetical to Intel co-founder Gordon Moore, leading them to ditch memory for microprocessors.

28. If I had to leave my organization for a year and the only communication I could have with employees was a single paragraph, what would I write? —*Pat Lencioni, author and founder of The Table Group*

Lencioni explains, "Determining the substance of this paragraph forces you to identify the company's core values and strategies, and the roles and responsibilities of those hypothetically left behind."

29. Who have we, as a company, historically been when we've been at our best? —*Keith Yamashita, author and founder of SYPartners*

30. What do we stand for—and what are we against? —*Scott Goodson, co-founder of StrawberryFrog*

31. Is there any reason to believe the opposite of my current belief? —*Chip and Dan Heath, authors who teach at Stanford's and Duke's business schools, respectively*

32. Do we underestimate the customer's journey? —*Matt Dixon, author and executive director of research at CEB*

Dixon explains, "Often, companies don't understand the entirety of the customer's experience and how many channels may have already failed them. They don't understand that the customer goes to the website first, pokes around but can't find the answer to their question, and then tries to start up a chat with an agent, only to get frustrated by the delayed response. Only then do they go to the Contact Us tab and call. From the company's perspective, the call is square one. The customer sees it as, you've already wasted 15 minutes of my time."

33. Among our stronger employees, how many see themselves at the company in three years? How many would leave for a 10 percent raise from another company? —*Jonathan Rosenberg, adviser to Google management*

34. What did we miss in the interview for the worst hire we ever made? —*Alberto Perlman, CEO of Zumba Fitness*

35. Do we have the right people on the bus? —*Jim Collins, author and management consultant*

36. What would have to be true for the option on the table to be the best possible choice? —*Roger Martin, professor, Rotman Business School*

    Martin uses this question when members of a group bring diverse opinions to a decision. It allows people to step back from their strongly held beliefs and contemplate a range of circumstances that might—or might not—support each option.

37. Am I failing differently each time? —*David Kelley, founder, IDEO*

38. When information truly is ubiquitous, when reach and connectivity are completely global, when computing resources are infinite, and when a whole new set of impossibilities are not only possible, but happening, what will that do to our business? —*Jonathan Rosenberg*

39. Do we aggressively reward and promote the people who have the biggest impact on creating excellent products? —*Jonathan Rosenberg*

40. What is our Big Hairy Audacious Goal? —*Jim Collins*

41. Is our strategy driving our strategy? Or is the way in which we allocate resources driving our strategy? —*Mark Johnson, co-founder, Innosight*

    Johnson explains, "You might think you have a strategic plan, but your people may be doing things on a day-to-day basis that are undermining it. It's essential that people believe in the strategy so they can make the daily decisions that support it."

42. How is the way you as the leader think and process information affecting your organizational culture? —*Ari Weinzweig, co-founder Zingerman's Community of Businesses*

    Weinzweig explains, "Describe the culture you'd love to have in your organization. Then check the desired characteristics of the culture against the way you think and process information. Are they congruent? Do you want collaboration but think in isolation? Do you want a flat organization but think hierarchically?

43. Why don't our customers like us? —*James Champy*

44. How can we become more high-tech but still be high touch? —*James Champy*

45. What do we need to start doing? —*Jack Bergstrand, CEO, Brand Velocity*

46. Whom among your colleagues do you trust, and for what? —*Charles Handy*

    Handy tells this story: "One CEO had a problem with his best subordinate, who was very good at his job. But he was also personally ambitious, so the CEO could not trust him to be totally loyal. The dilemma was whether to keep him because of his abilities or lose him because he couldn't be sure of him. The answer was for the CEO to either assign the subordinate jobs where his loyalty wasn't relevant or to confront him with his feelings. After some pushing from me, the CEO did the latter, and it cleared the air."

47. Are you satisfied with your current role? If not, what is missing from it? —*Charles Handy*

48. Do you keep 50% of your time unscheduled? —*Dov Frohman, engineer and executive, author*

    The 50% stat may be somewhat arbitrary. But Frohman's point, laid out in his book "Leadership the Hard Way," is that leaders should make sure they maintain sufficient "slop" in their schedules to allow space for reflection and the assimilation of lessons learned from experience.

49. What would I recommend my friend do if he were facing this dilemma? —*Chip and Dan Heath*

50. What kind of crime could a potential new hire have committed that would not only not disqualify him/her from being hired by our organization, but would actually indicate that he/she might be a particularly good fit? —*Pat Lencioni*

    Lencioni explains, "In this case 'crime' is a metaphor. This question speaks to values. A particularly idealistic organization may be okay with hiring someone that was previously reprimanded for standing up for his beliefs or blowing the whistle on something. A particularly competitive organization may be okay hiring someone who in prior positions was reprimanded for being overly arrogant or difficult to work with."

51. If our customer were my grandmother, would I tell her to buy what we're selling? —*Dan Pink, author*

52. If our company went out of business tomorrow, would anyone who doesn't get a paycheck here care? —*Dan Pink*

53. What is something you believe that nearly no one agrees with you on? —*Peter Thiel, partner, Founders Fund*

54. Do you have an implicit bias for capital investments over people investments? —*Tom Peters*

    Peters explains: "Capital enhancements are important. They're also cool. You can get your picture taken next to a new robot. People investments are invisible and hard to measure. The tendency is to favor the hard stuff over the soft stuff. But the soft stuff is invariably more related to long-term strategic success than the hard stuff."

55. Do we have enough freaky customers in our portfolio pushing us to the limit day in and day out? —*Tom Peters*

56. Who are you going to put out of business, and why? —*Brad Feld, managing director, Foundry Group*

57. What happens at this company when people fail? —*Bob Sutton and Jeff Pfeffer, Stanford professors*

58. How will you motivate the dishwashers? —*Bill Keena, independent casino consultant*

    Job interview questions comprise a genre unto themselves, so we chose not to include them in this article. With one exception. Keena says the only correct answer to this question, posed to manager candidates in a hotel chain, is "If they are overloaded I would roll up my sleeves and start washing right alongside them." That speaks to the candidate's ability to create employee engagement. Turned inward, however, the question reveals even more about culture. Ask yourself this: Are we the kind of company that cares whether our dishwashers are motivated?

59. Do your employees have the opportunity to do what they do best everyday? —*Marcus Buckingham, author*

60. Where is our petri dish? —*Tim Ogilvie, CEO. Peer Insight*

61. What Microsoft is this the Altair Basic of? —*Paul Graham*

62. Do we say "no" to customers for no reason? —*Matt Dixon*

    You may have created your customer policies at a time when you lacked resources, technology wasn't up-to-snuff, or low service levels were the industry norm. Have those circumstances changed? If so, your customer policies should change too.

63. Instead of going to current contacts for new ideas, what if you reconnected with dormant contacts—the people you used to know? If you were going reactivate a dormant tie, who would it be? —*Adam Grant*

64. Do you see more potential in people than they do in themselves? —*Adam Grant*

65. Are you taking your company in the direction of better and revenue or cheaper and cost? —*Michael Raynor, director, Deloitte Services LP*

66. Would you rather sell to knowledgeable and informed customers or to uninformed customers? —*Don Peppers, founding partner, Peppers and Rogers Group*

    Partly it's a matter of values: uninformed customers can be easy targets who swallow your pitch without pushing back. Selling to knowledgeable customers, by contrast, "is a mark of a trustable firm—one that is working to advance its customers' best interests," says Peppers.

    And there's another benefit: "Your most valuable customer references are not the ones who spend the most, but the ones who have the most expertise and authority. That gives them credibility with their peers."

67. What are we challenging, in the sense that Mac challenged the PC or Dove tackled the Beauty Myth? —*Mark Barden and Adam Morgan, founders, eatbigfish*

    Barden and Morgan explain that for companies challenging market leaders with greater resources, competing on the status quo is death. Instead they must assault the dynamics of a category (the dominance of PC) or a cultural meme (what society defines as "beautiful" in women).

68. In what way can we redefine the criteria of choice in our category in our favor, as Method introduced style and design to cleaning and Virgin America returned glamour to flying? —*Mark Barden and Adam Morgan*

69. In the past year, what have you done (or could you have done) to increase the accurate perception of this company/brand as ethical and honest? —*Robert Cialdini*

    Cialdini explains: "Of course, the preferred way to increase the perception of a company as ethical is to foster ethical practice within the organization. However, sometimes a company can be ethical without a corresponding perception in the marketplace that this is indeed the case. Therefore, companies should strive not only to enhance and reinforce an ethical culture but also to arrange for a warranted perception of that ethicality to be part of their brand."

70. To whom do you add value? —*Dave Ulrich and Norm Smallwood, co-founders, The RBL Group*

71. Why should people listen to you? —*Dave Ulrich and Norm Smallwood*

72. How would our PR, marketing, and social media change if we did not use outside agencies? —*Guy Kawasaki, founder, Garage Technology Ventures and Alltop*

    Kawasaki explains, "Let's see what happens when a company can't abdicate these functions to hired guns. I'd bet that employees, because they know and love their product more than any agency, can do a much better job at less expense to boot."

73. What was the last experiment we ran? —*Scott Berkun, author*

74. Are your clients Pepsi or Coke drinkers?" —*Marcy Massura*

    Massura explains: "This is a symbolic question that gets at how deeply you have researched your target clients. Business leaders can find out more about their customers than ever before thanks to the ability to collect data on a grand scale. Such detailed information allows the company to interact with targets in new ways and to assess current product development and marketing roadmaps."

75. What is your BATNA (best alternative to a negotiated agreement)? —*Roger Fisher and William Ury, negotiation experts*

76. What's the best design framework for an organization in a post Industrial-Age if the top-down, command and control model is no longer relevant? —*Traci Fenton, CEO, Worldblu*

77. Who are four people whose careers I've enhanced? —*Alex Gorsky, CEO, Johnson & Johnson*

78. Where can we break convention? —*Shane Snow, co-founder, Contently*

79. Whose voice (department, ethnic group, women, older workers, etc) might you have missed hearing from in your company, and how might you amplify this voice to create positive momentum for your business? —*Jane Hyun and Audrey Lee, partners, Hyun & Associates*

80. In retrospect, of the projects that we pulled the plug on, what percent do we wish had been allowed to keep going, and what percent do we wish had ended earlier? —*Ron Adner*

81. Do you, as a leader, bounce back quickly from setbacks? —*Bob Rosen*

82. Who do we think the world wants us to be? —*Geoffrey Moore, organizational theorist and management consultant*

83. How will we build a 100-year startup? —*Phil Libin, CEO, Evernote*

84. What successful thing are we doing today that may be blinding us to new growth opportunities? —*Scott D. Anthony, managing partner, Innosight*

85. If you could go back in time five years, what decision would you make differently? What is your best guess as to what decision you're making today you might regret five years from now? —*Patrick Lencioni*

86. What stupid rule would we most like to kill? —*Lisa Bodell, CEO, FutureThink*

87. What potential megatrends could make our business model obsolete? —*Michael A. Cusumano, professor, MIT*

88. What information is critical to our organization that our executives are ignoring? —*Max Bazerman, professor, Harvard Business School*

89. What have we done to protect our business from competitive encroachment? —*Tom Stemberg, managing general partner, Highland Venture Capital*

90. If you had to rebuild your organization without any traditional competitive advantages (i.e., no killer a technology, promising research, innovative product/service delivery model, etc.), how would your people have to approach their work and collaborate together in order to create the necessary conditions for success?" —*Jesse Sostrin, founder, Sostrin Consulting*

91. What are the rules and assumptions my industry operates under? What if the opposite were true? —*Phil McKinney, innovation expert*

92. Do the decisions we make today help people and the planet tomorrow? —*Kevin Cleary, president, Clif Bar*

93. What is your theory of human motivation, and how does your compensation plan fit with that view? —*Dan Ariely, professor, Duke University*

94. How do you encourage people to take control and responsibility? —*Dan Ariely*

95. Who do we want out customers to become? —*Michael Schrage, professor, MIT*

96. How do I stay inspired? —*Paul Bennett, chief creative officer, IDEO*

97. Do I know what I'm doing? And who do I call if I don't? —*Erin Pooley, business journalist*

98. Do they use it? —*Howard Tullman, CEO, 1871*

99. What is our question? —*Dev Patnaik, CEO, Jump Associates*

100. How is business? Why? —*Thomas A. Stewart, executive director, National Center for the Middle Market*

*Leigh Buchanan's original article, *editor-at-large for Inc. magazine:*
http://www.inc.com/magazine/201404/leigh-buchanan/100-questions-business-leaders-should-ask.html

# 9

# NLP Innovation: Next-Level Practices (NLPs)

---

*"There's always a way to Better your Best! Start looking in different places to find it and get it done!"*
— **Damian D. "Skipper" Pitts**

N LP Innovation: Next-Level Practices (NLPs) are simple. It's about aligning today's talent and tomorrow's skill requirement to meet the needs in current realities. While doing research to unpack the Five Ps in Crisis Leadership: Purpose, Perspective, Progression, Perseverance and Persuasion, I set-out to tee the readers up to easily generate ideas for their next BIG thing. I go on to ask the reader; *"what if you could solve problems before they happen or even identify those you missed… as efficiently as the greatest innovators do around the world?"* *"Would you like to out-problem-solve, out-THINK, or even out-*

*innovate your competitive landscape?"* Next-Level Practices (NLPs) are designed to clearly move you out of the competitive landscape and into the innovation countryside.

In NLP Innovation, you'll be walked into a simulated place to glean insight from the power of design think, gamification and neurolinguistics. They are used to help flip the innovation switch on in your mind… quickly, while also inspiring the same action in the minds of the people on your team. The world is moving in hyper-speed. With so many things going on, how are we able to keep track of it all in our daily and professional lives? Time seems to be a significant luxury that we need more, but don't have enough. Father-time is one of the few things that still remains out of our control and with that said… **What if** you could innovate faster than your competitors? You can! **What if** you could avoid risk by leading out from crises *before* the turbulence hits? You can! **What if** you could transform incumbent behaviors and thinking within your existing conditions to change how you achieve objectives and allow your organization to differentiate itself from the competitive landscape away from the chaos? Guess what? You can! **"What if?"** … seems to be the common thread that runs through the *actions* of achieving *extraordinary* outcomes. And coming up with an answer, the answers, is no easy task, but at the same time, you'll learn in this chapter how it CAN be done.

Understanding how to unpack today's talent and tomorrow's skill requirement will change the way you work, but not before answering a key question: *"What does the perspectives of turbulence, chaos and extraordinary have in common?"* They're all preemptive behavioral events that result in a form of change when they've completed their cycles as an individual salient event that normally shows up at its individual choosing.

To operate using high performance-driven execution equates with your ability to become different from the others in your industry.

Turbulence, chaos and extraordinary are the three things that will allow your company or organization to become the substance that others will need and be compelled to follow. They are the things that will allow you, your people and the organization to really matter!

But, with two of the three, they can cause a good day to turn upside-down if you don't understand how to use them to your advantage. In order to avoid that from happening, a few things must be put into action as the underpinning behaviors within the context of where you are now and where you are seeking to travel later.

To start, you'll need all of the Next-Level Practices (NLPs) and techniques introduced up to this point, but you'll also be introduced to a final one known as TIME methodology: Target-Identify-Minimize-Execute. This methodology is a proven, powerful process that works across most of the challenging industries and organizational boundaries you'll face. No matter what the issue, this methodology offers a course of action that aligns directly with the Five Ps of Crisis Leadership to generate billion dollar ideas that will go on to comprehensively solve future challenges and problems while also predicting even better solutions.

Next, you'll need to understand how to use the **"Ideation to Disruptive Innovation"** methodology that outlines the process of achieving **disruptive-incremental-distributed innovative** behavior to start a new, rapid and parallel-centric evolution and process for organizations to become the trendsetters in their marketplaces. Once that is completed, the process is then facilitated throughout the divergent-convergent process to result breakthrough initiatives that lead to emergent outcomes (the discovery of new possibility and new opportunities)—while recognizing today's talent to align it with tomorrow's requirements. None of this is possible without having the right people (relationships in place). **Disruptive Innovation objectives** often seem mutually exclusive. **Incremental innovation objectives** normally requires more time. And **distributed innovation objectives** remain fluid, *always in motion,* to allow the three to come together as one quickly. Making better decisions with Go Slow to Go Fast strategy allows the dichotomy between the three to happen in parallel using the best approach combined with the best attributes of the Target-Identify-Minimize-Execute Next-Level Practices (NLPs) and techniques.

This will ultimately ensure that the organization using the process and practices is able to launch preemptive and disruptive new products and services in record time. This is how today's talent and tomorrow's requirements come together to form dynamic synergies to help people to stop underestimating the importance of effective collaboration to achieve organizational objectives. While some people sometimes undertake solo journeys, my time as a United States Marine has taught me the importance of engaging with like-minded people to win the often tough objectives that stand before us.

And, the model that forms the entire framework when using Next-Level Practices (NLPs) and techniques being offered in this chapter, also requires people to come together to experience high performance-driven execution and the preemptive behaviors that produce breakthrough achievable results—*Think Above the Bar.* This outcome is known as **"NLP Innovation;"** the result of Next-Level Practices (NLPs) and techniques combined with **disruptive innovation objectives, incremental innovation objectives and distributed innovation objectives.**

## The Evolution of NLP Innovation

In today's economic environment, organizations are required to create differentiable value, but they don't always achieve this objective. However, to do so requires a certain synergy between strategy and innovation. The evolution of NLP Innovation methodology does just that by moving from a defined opportunity or problem to disruptive behaviors that transform into a plausible prototype of new products or services developed in compressed timelines, normally 90-days or less. The resulting direct action is referred to as a "90 day Short-range Target," or simply, 90-SRT. The choosing of a compressed 90 day timeline was carefully selected because 90 days is a standard corporate stopwatch; one working quarter, and often the limit of a team's ability to focus on new functions and features. The 90-SRT discipline integrates another KWAP into the framework with direct ties to the TIME methodologies: Target-Identify-Minimize-Execute Next-Level Practices (NLPs) and techniques.

90-SRT offers the ability to have clarity of mind and purpose when surrounded by turbulence and/or chaos. When the time requires operating under risk situations, 90-SRT will help you to performance at your peak without fail. It increases your ability to see clearly when others are blinded by fear, and act when others are paralyzed. It offers a way to devise and craft objective plans even with incomplete information, then execute those plans decisively while still being nimble and adaptable enough to iterate as the terrain changes (and we all know that it will). When used in collaboration with TIME methodology: Target-Identify-Minimize-Execute Next-Level Practices (NLPs) and techniques, users will be able to build teams with high impact perspectives on the brain 24/7. They'll be able to inspire others to follow them into the fire on their way to extraordinary with little to no resistance to change.

Essentially, the linkage between today's talent and tomorrow's requirements relies on the combining of NLP Innovation and 90-SRT strategy that must align with the leader's strategic intent to meet the objectives within the Future Picture with great impact. In the thick of things, they combine to form the context of applied ideation and disruptive innovation.

And while most business situations have limited knowledge and practice in leading this form of applied ideation and disruptive innovation across their organizations, the results in recent years from the fast-paced hyper-competitive world of business and organizational development requires them. Not having the knowledge and practice will be like being thrust onto the front lines in a time of war; business is a battlefield and those individuals who cannot equate their environments to this way of thinking—having the ability to think and behave using high performance-driven execution—will quickly find out why and how they will be needed in the daily functions of their operations and decision-making.

The synergies between the two are the keys to value creation and lead the idea-driven organization down a path of step-wise methods to unlock the power that lies within its underlying capabilities.

They refocus the organization's drivers on achieving the results that must be extraordinary (nothing else matters), specifically when the stakes are high. And, the innovation perspective provides an unencumbered clean sheet view of the future and is only concerned with what opportunities lay ahead. They prompt the decision-makers to consider the question *"what future state do we want to achieve?"*... as opposed to the orchestrated approaches of strategic planning that promote incrementalism. The synergies and the actions of the decision-makers will ultimately determine whether the organization is in the business of becoming a strategic innovator or competitive imitator. The following diagram on the next page illustrates what NLP Innovation looks like before being put it into action—your how.

Diagram 4. NLP Innovation: Next-Level Practices (NLPs) —TIME

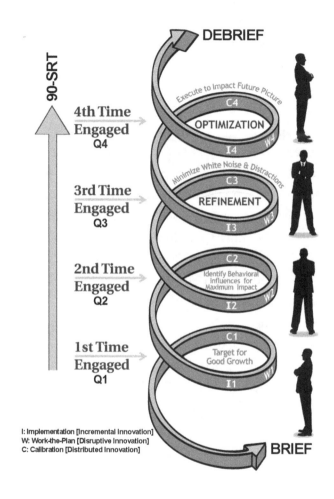

In a Harvard Business Review article (May 2010), Jocelyn Davis and Tom Atkinson refer to a study they conducted with the Economist Intelligence Unit of 343 businesses, which found *"companies that embraced initiatives and chose to go, go, go… ended up with lower sales and operating profits than those that paused at key moments to make sure they were on the right track."* How can you not only make sure you are on the right track, but also stay on the tracks and avoid derailment? The NLP Innovation model is one way to make this objective a reality. In my research, results showed that within one to six months, most sales and service organizations achieve a significant improvement in sales growth and customer retention through effective execution after embracing initiatives to make better decisions by slowing things down.

Effective execution simply means prioritizing action plans to overcome the most common barriers to strategy execution, while calibrating the process along the way to achieve a successful completion. This breakout strategy is codified into Four NLP Stages known as TIME: Target-Identify-Minimize-Execute.

**The first is the "Target" Stage (Engineering).** This includes your leadership system such as the vision, strategies and core values. Most organizations use an outside-in approach in developing their leadership system by scanning their environment for the strategies to be aligned with incumbent actions and behaviors to provide the direction and abilities to capitalize on opportunities. With incumbent strategies, this is used to inspire teams to behave a certain way. However in NLP Innovation, "targeting" focuses on good growth behavior using a 90-SRT perspective. This means that decision-makers align with the Four Action Behaviors, specifically here being the first of the four in *Design the Future*:

## The "Target" Stage (Engineering) involves the first Action Behavior, Design the Future]

- **Target for Good Growth**: Instill accountability by your actions; create a high resolution and compelling set of measurable objectives to achieve and impact the Future Picture.
- Build alliances immediately with all direct reports and the key players most important to your team's success.

- Make sure your destination (where you are headed) is crystal clear to lift your team's performance to build congruence between strategy and execution.
- Share success stories that are directly linked to your leadership system that is built on a disruptive innovation foundation (if it is not, STOP).

Before you begin the cycle in this stage, ALL stakeholders must ask and answer the Five "W" questions within the Leadership GPS System, and these questions MUST be repeated in each of the Four NLP Stages:

**The second is the "Identify" Stage (Navigate).** This stage translates the leadership system into action by management's sensitivity to various team member attitudes, skills and capabilities. It is here that performance- driven thinking transforms into high performance-driven execution. Translating the leadership system and the organization's incumbent behavior and direction (strategy) into new perspectives will never be an easy task. Communicate one message to several direct reports and it is not uncommon for respondents to use selective filtering on what they want to hear. Overcoming those things that cause and lead up to *dysfunctional behaviors in a crisis* within your messaging and communications is critical on all matters important (e.g. promotions, recognition, and feedback) and must be aligned with the strategies and core values in your disruptive innovation activities. This stage ensures the objective is achieved. The Identify Stage in NLP Innovation also focuses on the Four Action Behaviors, specifically *Target for Success*, using the 90-SRT perspective.

### The "Identify" Stage (Navigate) involves the second Action Behavior, Target for Success]

- **Identify Behavioral Influences for Maximum Impact**: Assess your team's abilities and attitude. Adapt your leadership

# LEADERSHIP GPS SYSTEM

## GPS COORDINATES

### COMPETENCE AND CONFIDENCE

Can the leaders take the organization to its objective? Do they truly believe the *purpose* is worth the effort?

## DIRECTIONS

### TRUST AND PURPOSE

Has trust been earned due to past behaviors and achievements? Do people believe they are part of something of worth and value?

 **WHY**
... Are we doing this (purpose)?
... Will it be disruptive as a behavior and action?

 **WHO**
... Will be impacted?
... Will it benefit?
... Will be eliminated?
... Will be limited?

 **WHAT**
... Are we applying our resources and energy (inertia) against?
... Is our compass heading and target (zulu) time?

 **WHERE**
... Are we going?
... Are the gaps in our knowledge and experience for the journey?

 **WHEN**
... Do we plan to arrive?
... Should we expect the future, the event horizon and the Future Picture?

style and process to each member of your team with laser-focused feedback.

- Target the areas for the greatest potential (Centers of Gravity). Identify and leverage Centers of Gravity; those things that, when impacted, have the greatest effect for the least amount of time, energy and resources.
- Move from strategic perspectives to tactical outcomes. Armed with the big-picture perspective within a Future Picture window and a campaign plan, your team must identify potential risk factors when planning and executing tactics.

**The third is the "Minimize" Stage (Agitate).** This stage removes distraction or noise from the system to ensure behavioral influences remain on track to achieve the desired effects within the system. It ensures refinement to the system, specifically when plans disintegrate because of poor alignment or when people allow their personal agendas to get in the way (it will happen). Especially during times of rapid change, people tend to get self-protective (they'll revert back to their incumbent behaviors). They turn inward and stop communicating or behaving in alignment with the Future Picture. They become information misers instead of information sharers.

The result; tactically-focused organizations full of friction, frustration and poor strategic performance. However, in NLP Innovation, behaviors are refined and perfectly synchronized to the execution processes that are governed properly across the diverse teams involved in executing the new behaviors.

This stage in the model, Minimize, also focuses on the Four Action Behaviors, specifically *Campaign to WiN* in the using the 90-SRT perspective. The letter "N" is title capped on purpose to bring attention to the activities within the stage. The emphasis on the letter basically means that everyone involved in the process must "now" focus their efforts towards the unified behavioral stream of high performance-driven execution to make sure their efforts are still aligned with the Five W's Agenda.

### The "Minimize" Stage (Agitate) involves the third Action Behavior, Campaign to WiN]

- Minimize White Noise and Distraction: Refinement.
- Navigate the Five W's Agenda: **WHY, WHO, WHAT, WHERE and WHEN.**
- Campaign to WiN means that ALL stakeholders understand that they must think strategically, focus sharply and move quickly to shake things up. This means that they must move with force while considering all sides of the plan's equation (the three dimensions of the future) to cause what incumbent behavior will see as irregular action to resolve any issues still lingering around up to this point in the entire process.

And finally, **the fourth is the "Execute" Stage (Framing).** This stage develops and reinforces the desired behaviors that will move the organization to its Future Picture vision with significant impact. In this stage, leaders are reminded clearly that execution is a discipline, one that is aligned and integral to optimizing strategy. Optimizing the stages leading up to the Framing is the greatest strategic challenge confronting an organization today where disruptive innovation is concerned. In most cases, leaders believe that a problem of strategy formulation or some competitive threat facing the organization takes higher priority.

Likewise, strategy formulation, while extremely challenging and difficult, is not what should concern them the most. It must not be the planning that should cause the greatest worry. It is something even bigger and more problematic; the execution of strategy above all else.

Making any plan work will be an even greater challenge than creating the plan.

Execution (both strategic and flawless) is the key to removing yourself from the competitive landscape where everyone is fighting for successful outcomes. NLP Innovation takes discipline, rigor and unrelenting effort to achieve it. In NLP Innovation, execution becomes *maneuverability* and *warfare*; the core elements in the strategy execution Framing process to optimize the efforts that *will* impact the Future Picture.

Framing is also where the challenging journey is realized and encourages leaders and their organizations to do what is required to embrace their greatest potential to exceed their own performance-driven expectations. This stage offers the most valuable resource in the entire system when it comes to developing a hunger and a drive for precise decision-making to realize ultimate high performance-driven execution with extraordinary success. This stage is also the powerful tool that provides leaders with *everything* they need to know to be successful to achieve their objectives with a sense of urgency. The Execute stage using Framing helps people to put an end to their lackluster behavior, allowing them to begin to go fast from this point forward.

### The "Execute" Stage (Framing) involves the fourth Action Behavior, Finish with Finesse]

- **Execute to Impact the Future Picture: Optimization**.
- Progressively improve performance-driven execution tactics thru Right-time Decision-making and training.
- Walk your team through the powerful process of planning how you are going to exit your strategy after disrupting the competitive landscape to Eliminate-Raise-Reduce-Create industry factors within your predefined actions within a disciplined and compressed timeline.

Whether you are a field operations manager or a leader within the senior ranks as one of the vice presidents or chiefs, these four stages in NLP innovation will help your discover the secrets behind effective business strategy execution. Keep in mind that the effectiveness from the process is greatly benefited when each of the four stages are used in the proper sequence and in parallel to completion. NLP innovation remains rooted in the foundational aspects that make-up each stage and is ONLY revealed during the training and development process when outlining how to use the Engineering, Navigate, Agitate and the Framing perspectives.

Staying aligned and on the tracks means making the most important choices and actions every day. So you can prioritize action plans, using *the Cardinal Rules* and *Guiding Precepts* in *Go Slow to Go Fast strategy*.

They will guide you through each of the four stages and cannot be forgotten. Engineering, the Target Stage, relates to the principles that tie to accountability—one of the most important key success factors (Design the Future). Navigate, the Identify Stage, relates to the principles used to tenderize your movements for effective feedback, so that your team can chew on and digest the intended strategic direction (Target for Success). Agitate, the Minimize Stage, relates to the principles to refine and remove unnecessary behaviors and influences, enabling you to overcome the most common obstacles to execution excellence—*maneuverability* and *warfare*, to measure what matters most when achieving the objectives (Campaign to WiN: think strategically, focus sharply and move quickly).

And finally, Framing, the Execution Stage, relates to the principles to optimize the process to create a high resolution and compelling set of measurable outcomes within the Future Picture (Finish with Finesse). And unlike a "vision statement," your Future Picture will help you achieve the kind of clarity you need to drive NLP Innovation throughout your entire organization while becoming a learning organization.

## NLP Innovation Rules, Consideration and Key Ingredients

NLP Innovation has its own set of critical rules where disruptive innovation (the strategy) is the foundation from which it is used. Strategy is all about guiding the outcome of individual effort and events to produce success. In strategic terms, performance-driven execution produces a sustainable outcome that is valuable and satisfying over time. Strategy, then, is not winning battles; rather it is winning wars and more particularly the peace that follows them. Focusing only on battles (objectives) at the expense of wars (overall mission) and the subsequent peace (competition) is dangerous and no longer enough in business and organizational behavior today. We now know that it almost never leads to long-term success.

Many people think that strategic-thought and execution are very difficult. To the contrary, almost everyone can learn to do both using NLP Innovation. The operative word, however, is "learn." We grow up in leadership and operations in the tactical world, where looking both ways before we cross the street is a necessity for survival (metaphor). Likewise, in our education, we spend the overwhelming majority of our time learning details, while we spend little time trying to integrate what we have learned. So, unfortunately, strategy is foreign to most of us let alone NLP Innovation. We've had little exposure to it, and we are normally rewarded for tactical, not strategic, prowess. *If, however, we really want our efforts to produce sustained success, then we must learn strategy at both an organization and a personal level within the context of NLP Innovation.*

Fortunately, despite the mysteries surrounding this form of strategy, learning to think and act strategically is not too difficult, but it does require you to view the world through a different set of lenses to change how you think, speak, behave and execute on the most basic things before moving to the more trivial. And, this is where the rules add value.

## New Circumstances Require New Approaches—the Rules!

Any strategic system that does not deal with all four of these elements will become deficient and will not likely achieve 90-SRT and/or lead to high performance-driven execution abilities. With TIME methodology: Target-Identify-Minimize-Execute Next-Level Practices (NLPs) and techniques, each of these necessary elements (the rules) must be addressed by an "Action Behavior" (AB), or key step known as the Four NLP Stages in NLP Innovation:

Table 2. The Four NLP Stages in NLP Innovation

| THE STAGES: STRATEGY EXECUTION | THE FOUR ACTION BEHAVIORS | BEHAVIOR/ACTION (OUTCOMES) |
|---|---|---|
| 1. Target Stage (Engineering) | AB#1: Design the Future | Target for Good Growth |
| 2. Identify Stage (Navigate) | AB#2: Target for Success | Identify Behavioral Influences for Maximum Impact |
| 3. Minimize Stage (Agitate) | AB#3: Campaign to WiN | Minimize White Noise and Distractions: Refinement |
| 4. Execute Stage (Framing) | AB#4: Finish with Finesse | Execute to Impact the Future Picture: Optimization |

You won't win by following the incumbent rules of yesterday. NLP innovation allows you to set your own rules with disruptive innovation leading the way to change the usual suspects (incumbents) in you space. A winning grand strategy with an integrated plan that will take you from concept-to-execution-to-completion is a MUST.

NLP innovation and process *is built on a series of natural laws of strategy*:

- *Every action* **affects the Future Picture.**
- *Specific* **actions create a** *specific* **future** and **event horizon.**
- **Everything and every action** *happens within a system.*
- *All systems have inertia* **and resistance to change.**
- **All systems have** *Centers of Gravity.*
- *Systems change* **when their** *Centers of Gravity change.*
- **The** *extent and probability of system change is proportional to the number of Centers of Gravity affected and,* **the** *speed and impact at which they are affected.*
- *All* **known systems** and things have **a beginning** *(the Future),* **a middle** *(the event horizon) and* **an end** *(the Future Picture) without fail!*
Specific actions produce specific ends.

When the competitive landscape was simple, leaders and organizations could mostly afford to have complex strategies. But, now that the competitive landscape is so complex, changing in hyper-speed, they need to be simplified. Smart organizations and decision-makers have done just that using disciplined and simple approaches: a few straightforward, hard-and-fast rules that define direction without confining them as in NLP innovation. It only has four step-wise approaches to get to the end objective with significant measures of merit along the way to avoid risk by leading out from crises before they happen. In essence, the simple rules are... rather simple in TIME methodology: Target-Identify-Minimize-Execute Next-Level Practices (NLPs) and techniques:

- Target Stage (Engineering), Design the Future; Simple Rule: target for good growth and pursue a better meaning.

- Identify Stage (Navigate), Target for Success; Simple Rule: identify behavioral influences for maximum impact and rapidly change ambiguous markets.

- Minimize Stage (Agitate), Campaign to WiN; Simple Rule: minimize white noise, distraction (refinement) and eliminate unnecessary STUFF out of the way: Situations That are Unclear and Fertilized by Fallacies to focus your energy to move away from the critically important things.

- Execute Stage (Framing), Finish with Finesse; Simple Rule: execute to impact the Future Picture (optimization) and jump into the confusion while remaining in motion (keep moving) to seize opportunities to finish strong.

## New Circumstances Require New Approaches—Considerations

The future of incumbents in any way, shape or form does not look promising in any measure of the word. In fact, the word incumbent has become a significant impediment to progress.

Efforts have been made to (re)define the behavior that follows the word in ways that would make it more relevant to 21st century organizations and endeavors. Efforts to date, however, have not been able to overcome the deeply ingrained belief that the word incumbent is synonymous with a specific approach, namely a new 'way to play' over the traditional means of getting things done using better or improved approaches.

The word has become unalterably frozen in time because it represents nothing new for tomorrow; it is stuck in yesterday's significance that is no longer relevant. New circumstances in business, leadership, organizational behavior, decision-making, strategy and execution require new approaches or considerations that will also require people to begin thinking differently. And, the new considerations due to circumstances present key terms that form the core of a new conceptual foundation; one that is filled with edgy unconventional wisdom to provide a point of departure for the systematic exploration of future "incumbent" behavior.

Three concepts combine to form this core: divergence (agility), convergence (focus) and emergence (discipline). In brief, agility is the critical capability that organizations need to meet the challenges of complexity and uncertainty. Focus provides the context and defines the purposes for the endeavor. Convergence is the target objective and the process that guides actions and after effects. Learn the three words and consider using them in place of the one word *incumbents*. They'll add a different perspective to any (most) situations you'll face, specifically a situation where NLP Innovation can be used to change your existing (incumbent) conditions (circumstances).

## New Circumstances Require
## New Approaches—Key Ingredients

Incumbents offer an approach that, while it was once very effective in achieving its ends, is no longer the only possible or even the best approach that is available to meet the requirements in the future. Incumbents used to be a solution to a problem that has changed. The situations for which incumbents are best adapted have been transformed by the realities of the Information Age. Thus, the assumptions upon which incumbents were basing their responses (actions and behaviors) to past problems are no longer valid.

Incumbents are not well suited for coalition operations, particularly the kind of complex endeavors called for in the 21st century. Furthermore, while it may come as a surprise to some, incumbents are not necessarily the best choice for most operations today and into the future.

Before any changes to incumbents can be made successfully, leaders must first, before anything else, address their talent pools to unearth potential issues that lay beneath the surface. In NLP Innovation, there's one key ingredient that is more important than any incumbent strategy, leadership trait, behavior and action, or impending outcome to achieve this and more. It is known as relationships (people)—one of your Centers of Gravity (CoGs).

It is also known as Leadership Snake Eyes; however, this topic is covered in great detail in the upcoming Crisis Leadership book. You have the opportunity to unpack this strategy more in that publication as the follow-on to Go Slow to Go Fast strategy.

But, let's explore a minimum version of Leadership Snake Eyes here. It's a very simple concept to understand. Continuing to do more of the same versus changing the lens of leadership to begin doing something different, NLP Innovation, is essential to everyone's success. Leaders must be able to see the complexities of the relationships and stories in their minds before they are able to make a moral decision to respond by doing what is right for the people they are responsible to—doing the right things to get the right things done. Changing norms and having the strength to stand alone as the unwavering flag that blows in the wind for all to see and to make a statement simply by using differentiation as the strategic advantage, is how to remain disruptive in your approach to lead trends and stop following the trends others create.

Extraordinary greatness knows the importance of keeping greatness around at every turn for everyone to grow from the unified efforts of everyone involved. Leaders who want more for their organizations while doing what matters most to achieve Next-Level Practices (NLPs), must possess the ability to see the good in all people. People are *today's talent* and *tomorrow's skill requirements* if they are given the right tools to grow from within. Change is an inside-out process, but in most cases, it requires the guidance to tap what has not been tapped to reach its full potential.

In the words of Kare Anderson, "mutuality matters" and can be achieved in as little as 90-days (90-SRT) when it comes to NLP Innovation with the *rules, considerations and key ingredients* leading the charge with the full application and strategy. They culminate to define a specific meaning to leaders today: humanity's egotistical varicosity cannot laugh at itself and if that is the case, it will crumble from the rigidity and the compression of its own uncelebrated faults. With this, leaders must do what is best to build healthy relations for the greater good of their organization when responding to the greater cause that leads to further disruptive innovation efforts to win without being opposed by any potential threat that might show up (and something will show up). Understanding today's talent and tomorrow's skill requirement will help you understand why people, good people, make bad decisions and how NOT to allow it to happen to you.

# 10

# Navigating the Labyrinth of Disruptive Innovation

*"You can't navigate the rough waves of the sea simply by standing on the water's edge contemplating how you're planning on doing it. At some point, you'll need to decide to cast off to get to your destination... regardless of the rough waves."*
**— Damian D. "Skipper" Pitts**

D o you even know what it means to navigate the labyrinth of disruptive innovation? Or, what it means to do so using the Go Slow to Go Fast strategy? First, you need to understand the meaning of a labyrinth: it represent a journey towards your objectives, where there might be unexpected turns. Passage through a labyrinth is not easy, simple or direct. It will require purpose, perspective, the will to progress in the face of chaos, the ability to persevere, and the ability to persuade others to follow you on the same journey to achieve more meaning at the end.

As we think about the current crisis in leadership where it doesn't seem like our national leaders understand the concept of leadership, we can see how so many of the wrong decisions as being made and followed to continue us on a path filled with unhealthy behaviors. Unfortunately, as far back as the start of the 21st century, those of us in leadership have been making some basic and poor decisions that have led others to where we are today. And, although the Go Slow to Go Fast approach offers a clearly defined strategy to slow things down to reconsider the decisions within the approach decided on, tomorrow still holds a labyrinth of obstacles to navigate. The unique attributes in Go Slow to Go Fast strategy, coupled with the supportive context of LEAN Leadership, will enable anyone seeking a better road map to navigate these obstacles to a point of personal and professional fulfillment. Some of the main obstacles to overcome will be to:

- Understand the importance of slowing down to go fast.
- Realize when you're stuck with a bad hand dealt by the dealer: the Poker's Bluff—and how to rely on your 'Cardinal Rules' and 'Guiding Precepts.'
- Balance the need for 'trust and purpose' with 'competence and confidence.'
- Know the differences between 'best-practices' and 'Next-Level Practices (NLPs).'
- Learn the importance of being bilingual in change speak to transform existing conditions: The Language of Performance-Driven Execution.
- Understand fully your role when the time requires you to bridge the gaps between planning and execution with more meaning for improved outcomes.

Remembering the saying, *"Chi va Piano va Lontano... Chi va Forte va alla Morte!"* Again, it is translated to mean *"Who goes slow goes far... Who goes fast dies."* No labyrinth, regardless of the reason, can or should be navigated quickly. This book represents its own labyrinth and should be taken slowly because it is specific to exacting a needed change to incumbent thinking, and behaving to improve outcomes. It offers the many strategies to overcome the many unforeseen issues and obstacles that will hurt you in the long run when you don't know the best ways to navigate them successfully. To ensure your organization does not fall into the deep abyss that the team and I refer to as the *Tyranny of Success*, the Go Slow to Go Fast strategy argues the case of applying a uniquely developed utilization process to avoid risk and lead out from crises *before* they happen using a "preemptive" approach to getting things done. The Tyranny of Success, is by any measure, a very tough measure to deal with as an organization. It is the residence of traditional thinking folks, from the disenchanted to the revolutionists against change who's efforts conspire to keep things like the way they are in the traditional sense. Leaders definitely need to be aware of these folks and the situations that lead up to them becoming a reality in order to be alerted in their defense against them due to the challenges they cause.

## The Perils of the Tyranny of Success

John Kotter as far back to 1996 in his book Leading Change basically laid this road map out to recognize the perils of the tyranny of success. Let's begin with the lack of alignment for positive organizational behavior. As opportunities to change behavior become increasingly important to the organization's culture, the Tyranny of Success works to foil any progress on those efforts. Next, we can look at not establishing a great enough sense of urgency to realize the needed change. The Tyranny of Success will steer the attention away from the change efforts, causing the decision-makers to be distracted to not look hard at the organization's competitive environment, market position, technological trends and financial performance over a specific period of time. Next, we can even explore things such as not anchoring needed change to the organization's culture and having the wrong teams in places where certain capabilities are required to compete or remain relevant as an actor in the marketplace. Essentially, change sticks only when it has a chance to move away from such sayings and attitudes that promote "... the way we do things around here..." When this attitude and negative behavior seeps into the bloodstream of the organization's culture, new thinking and new behaviors have uphill battles to get rooted in shared values and meaningful purpose. Having the wrong people on the team opens opportunities for decisions to be subjected to degradation as soon as the pressure for change is realized.

These and many other perils are hard to overcome when the leadership culture is not strong enough to make the needed decisions to enact improvements in the needed areas. There are several factors that are particularly important for leaders and decision-makers to choose when change is needed in a specific area or culture. The first is a conscious attempt to show people how the new approaches, behaviors and attitudes will help improve performance within the culture. The key to getting people to see the value with adding new approaches relies heavily on effective communications. Time must be spent explaining why performance is the essential part in moving something to the next level.

Next, decision-makers must make sure that they have the right people on the team and those people *must* represent the new approaches through their work, the way they think, and through their efforts towards making sure the new approaches are being institutionalized by others. It's all about leadership succession and those key individuals who are willing to step up to become the champions of change. Without these folks and the leaders that are responsible for driving the new approaches, behaviors and attitudes throughout the culture, more perils in the Tyranny of Success are likely to become apparent obstacles for the organization.

These are two of the more critical perils in the Tyranny of Success that must be pointed out. Communications and people; two of the most important aspects leaders and decision-makers must align to overcome the Tyranny of Success. They must think and behave differently to change the level of strategic intent, critical tasks, competencies and frameworks to build healthier cultures and leadership roles when introducing new approaches to the organization. This chapter explores how to repurpose, and then how to exploit to reposition value, differentiation and growth when dealing with the Tyranny of Success. It focuses on *exploring* innovative ways to stimulate increased utilization and growth. It births new formulations for personal and professional development to move existing conditions *(repurposing)* to a higher level of quality to impact the value stream along with the buyer's utility to improve the user experience. And, it offers an adaptive structure with the control mechanisms to impose incremental growth from the change behaviors that ultimately goes forth to become the force multiplier within the changing environments.

Although this chapter is one of the shortest in the book, it details why the Go Slow to Go Fast strategy is not for everyone, nor for the faint at heart. Creating a change platform that others may follow takes time. And for the leaders looking to cause a disruption to their existing conditions that will ultimately look radical when done, navigating the labyrinth of disruptive innovation to overcome the Tyranny of Success, will take time. Essentially, leaders will need to take time to make time to take the time to learn how to lead differently. This requires some heavy lifting to pivot from where you are in order to get to where you are hoping to be in the near future. Simply, this journey is different because it is not easy. Change is never easy and learning a new paradigm as in the Go Slow to Go Fast strategy using LEAN Leadership is no different. It requires you to have to actually *think*, and lead others to *think* about making the future a better place with meaning and purpose. Differentiation is exactly with you think that it is… different, and why should it be easy? Navigating the labyrinth, this very labyrinth called Go Slow to Go Fast to make better decisions, is both disruptive and filled with innovation. It requires a leader and h/her organization to operate in parallel, moving multiple disciplines of behavior down-range, all at the same time and for the same outcome. And, it utilizes the disciplines of maneuver warfare as its directives to navigate the labyrinths in leadership successfully by: targeting critical vulnerabilities, using boldness, surprise, focus, decentralized decision-making, tempo and combined arms. Commanding when applied individually, but devastating when applied in subsets or as an integrated whole, these directives ensures any one person or organization will be able to:

1. Analyze and probe competitors with the aim of rapidly exploiting their weaknesses to affect their competitive position.
2. Take calculated risks that have the potential to achieve major, market-shifting results.
3. Use volatility, uncertainty, complexity and ambiguity (VUCA) as a deceptive strategy to degrade the quality of information available to competitors and impair their ability to deploy competitive resources efficiently.
4. Concentrate resources at critical places known as Centers of Gravity in compressed timelines to capitalize on key market opportunities to meet and exceed customer demands.
5. Give authority to those who are closest to the point of Right-time Decision-making to effect mission critical targets.
6. Identify opportunities, make better decision (go slow), and implement plans more quickly than competing forces

to seize the initiative and force them into a constant state of reaction. This is all done by combining resources so that the returns generated by the whole are greater than those generated by the individual parts.

A distinction in Go Slow to Go Fast strategy is its "prescriptive" and "preemptive" approaches to getting things done, which brings me to the first approach, "prescriptive." This approach is identified by its short name "REx." This is all about focusing the attention on the purpose for taking a much needed "gemba walk" *to reposition the organization, exploit new thinking and achieve execution excellence* to begin a simultaneous pursuit of differentiation and growth using low risk experiments. The gemba walk (discussed in the introduction) focuses on *exploiting* preemptive measures to lower cost and risk, while increasing value to the user experience using high performance-driven execution.

The gemba walk has a formal structure with a series of behavioral controls for incremental improvements to be made along the way. It promotes high efficacy, quality and breakthrough achievable results—the *repositioning*. Through research, my team and I found that the idea of attacking challenges, problems or crises using a preemptive strategic approach regularly fails when the leadership body is successful at meeting turbulence and tension head-on. Simply put, navigating the labyrinth of disruptive innovation by first using Go Slow to Go Fast strategy to slow things down is important when setting out to take a three-pronged approach to improving the root of the problems and challenges. This three-pronged approach focuses on putting the gemba walk to use and completing its application by unpacking the vertical axis in performance-driven execution. A gemba walk is only valuable when the entire process is completed fully to achieve execution excellence at the end.

Let's take a look at the gemba walk again now:

### Diagram: The Gemba Walk

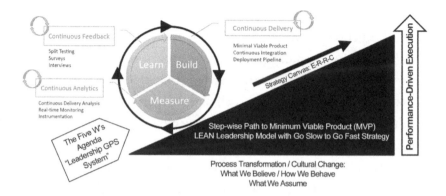

The design in a gemba walk eliminates risk so that leaders, decision-makers and the organization will be equipped to complete the journey across the bridge to execution excellence from the point of planning. It repurposes directional effort and focuses a leader's strategic intent on identifying reasons why the organization must take a different path that, in most cases, is less likely than its traditional approach. And sometimes taking a different path may be just what the organization requires. In doing so, there needs to be alignment in the internal capabilities using five leadership considerations (C1-C5) to neutralize the Tyranny of Success:

1. **C1:** How do you change the leadership DNA to support a new, embryonic risky approach in order to avoid near-death business experiences? —**Leadership DNA**
2. **C2:** How can you align leadership across an organization when their DNA is committed to driving profits in today's franchise? —**Leadership Alignment**

3. **C3:** How can you adapt management systems on process that are used to manage short-term performance to become capable of supporting a "test and learn" leadership approach to innovation? —**Experiential Leadership**

4. **C4:** How do you stop from becoming another hero only to lose your edge when competition strikes? Why not move early? Why seem flat-footed? —**Preemptive Leadership**

5. **C5:** How can you scale new business within existing organizations that are disciplined to support only one mature, core business? —**Lean Leadership**

The five leadership considerations allow for thought-leadership and performance-driven thinking around Leadership DNA, Leadership Alignment, and Experiential Leadership to be aligned *to reposition the organization, exploit new thinking* for the organization (REx). They enhance the leader's strategic intent in the planning process to ensure a real-time response to opportunity is achieved, whereby a leader or leadership team is able to identify potential new opportunities and new possibilities within the five leadership considerations.

Thought-leadership and performance-driven thinking are used to orient the greater organization toward the planned objective using behavioral methodologies to explore or exploit successful outcomes. For these reasons, the "prescriptive" (REx) approach is very important and this is where the *Six Essential Insights* from the introduction add value and impact. You cannot exploit successful outcomes without doing the following:

1. Declare a Process Transformation is Required
2. Establish the Strategy Forward
3. Train While Working—GODOs (Tacit Knowledge)
4. Develop Master Discipline Trainers (MDTs)—Mentoring

5. Achieve a State of Crisis Leadership & Performance-Driven Execution™
6. Focus Implementation on Flawless Execution

Doing the *six essential insights* using the "prescriptive" (REx) approach starts the *repositioning* process for the organization to get on the right path. Leaders and decision-makers would be wise to use the approach to ensure their organization is capable to realize maximum impact with minimal expenditure of resources. Where it get interesting is when the last two *leadership considerations* come into play to support performance-driven execution using the Leadership Triplicity approach to achieve *execution excellence* and begin the simultaneous pursuit of differentiation and growth using low risk experiments—the "preemptive" approach. This approach focuses back on the three required things, or organizational behaviors, (also from the introduction) to successfully *reposition* and then *repurpose* the organization to realize a more meaningful existence (the "pivot"). The three organizational behaviors to use here are:

✓ Managing the Probable
✓ Habits of the Mind
✓ Leading the Possible

The table that was offered in the introduction is essential here to explain each of the three organizational behaviors. They must be used to complement the *12 Considerations When Driving Performance-Driven Execution*. And as stated earlier, they provide reference points in the *repurposing* process to help improve project performance, increase project satisfaction, promote innovation and encourage leadership to move beyond best practices to begin using Next-Level Practices (NLPs) in its new state with impact on the Future Picture.

In order to achieve to achieve *execution excellence* and complete the simultaneous pursuit of differentiation and growth using low risk experiments successfully, leaders and decision-makers must ensure the organization achieves its Minimum Viable Product (MVP) internally or externally before reintroducing itself to its emerging markets and existing marketplace. "Managing the Probable," leads to "Leading the Possible," but not before passing through "Habits of the Mind." These three behaviors represent the "preemptive" approach and their uses to achieve differentiation and growth using low risk experiments.

Table: Three Organizational Behaviors to
Drive Performance-Driven Execution (PDE)

| Managing the Probable: the "Future" | Habits of the Mind: the "Event Horizon" | Leading the Possible: the "Future Picture" |
|---|---|---|
| When facing challenges, most people typically fall back on their familiar standard operating procedures: provides assurance of predictability. | Ask different questions; refer to your "Strategy Canvas:" Eliminate- Raise- Reduce-Create. Take multiple perspectives. See Systems: develop 'safe-to-fail' experiments to nudge existing systems in a better direction. | Broaden your range of interventions by breaking away from your familiar behaviors, habits and patterns using a whole new approach to expand your options. Experiment in low risk ways, and realize potentially out-sized payoffs: "move beyond the check-box" mentality. |

In order to change incumbent thinking, behaving and performing at the organizational level, the two distinctions to successfully *reposition* and *repurpose* the organization on a better path are required. This is what I refer to as Better *your* Best in Go Slow to Go Fast strategy. Essentially, it comes down to a simple formula:

A **"Prescriptive"** approach (*repositioning*) + **"Preemptive"** techniques (*repurposing*) = the ability to **Better *your* Best** in doing the right things to get the right things done.

They epitomize the three dimensional window on the future when navigating the labyrinth of disruptive innovation and this is critically important. The combination of the five (5) leadership considerations and the three (3) organizational behaviors illustrates the path to a more meaningful purpose when change is needed in an organizational environment. Think of the transformation as a 3x5 transition to a better future: "Managing the Probable" (the "Future," your compass heading) *must* pass through the "Habits of the Mind" (the "Event Horizon," your bridge between planning and execution) to achieve "Leading the Possible" (the "Future Picture," your expected future state prior to arriving to it) when executing a "prescriptive" (repositioning) and "preemptive" (repurposing) approach to impact the organization's Future Picture. And all that it takes, essentially, is *changing how you think*— there will always be leadership implications along the way, specifically in *Habits of the Mind* residency and you must be prepared to deal with them.

The most critical of the implications is Organizational Efficacy (OE). At its core, OE simulates the aggregate confidence levels across an organization's culture, starting with the people, their sense of mission, purpose, effectiveness and resilience that relates to an overall "can do" attitude and approach to doing the right things to get the right things done. The transformation using a 3x5 transition to a better future will not only achieve this objective and more, but it will definitely provide a pathway to overcome the Tyranny of Success while navigating the labyrinth of disruptive innovation.

Excited and optimistic, my wish for you is that you'll accept the ideas put before you to change how you see the world, your world, with the ability to see what it can become from your actions. This is not another fad, but a credible source of influence to be used for inspiring extraordinary greatness and outcomes through process transformation. Incidentally, my role as an instructor at Temple University in Philadelphia, PA allows me to test these theories in an academic setting using real-world applications from my executive education students who bring their business challenges to class with them for low-risk experiments. We have the opportunity to watch the strategies being applied in real-world situations to bring resolve before being integrated back into the organization's system.

Why is this important? Simply because adopting this same format allows you to also test your own theories using low-risk experiments to form new doctrines, rules and guiding precepts to be tested long before you have a chance to use them. And if the idea of navigating the labyrinth of disruptive innovation catches hold as a Next-Level Practice (NLP), then perhaps more leadership professionals that you'll go on to influence will also be inspired after seeing the need more often to break from the status quo. You'll see how navigating the labyrinth of disruptive innovation offers a more real-time and real-world empirically-based option to use when attempting to overcome the Tyranny of Success.

Finally, there are ten keys in Go Slow to Go Fast strategy that everyone should learn in order to navigate their own labyrinths in leadership:

1. Be committed to extraordinary success and even better outcomes.
2. Be disruptive when times are good—set priorities.
3. Be disciplined when momentum needs building—set and demand performance-driven thinking that leads to high performance-driven execution.
4. Be determined when faced with possible setbacks—ensure you are tough, but fair when dealing with the relationships you most count on.
5. Be sure your leaders understand *differentiation* and innovation to *Think Above the Bar* to accomplish *Breakthrough Achievable Results* when continuous improvement requires ongoing learning to change.
6. Be focused on doing what is right to get the right things done in compressed timelines—develop and maintain a strong sense of urgency.
7. Be compelling in your approach to lead or navigate others through the labyrinth in leadership—pay close attention to detail.
8. Be prepared to do what is right when high levels of commitment are needed to *establishing TARGETs* over *setting goals* when deciding to become the change others will look to follow.
9. Be ready to fail because no matter what, you will—get up and shut up…work still needs to get done!
10. Be hands-on while having fun in your learning. Lead your people, teams, organizations and environments in a way that others have yet to consider themselves—become the trends others will seek to follow.

Be aware that navigating the labyrinth of disruptive innovation successfully will not only allow you to overcome the Tyranny of Success, it will also force you to use the "gemba walk" as well as the 3x5 transition to a better future. Yes, this will take some time to complete, but not as much time as it will take to close your doors if you don't pivot when required as a culture and organization. The key is to remain relevant in your marketplace. This process takes as many excuses away as possible for you to get stuck in another labyrinth, specifically in leadership. CONSIDER THIS as you start to bring Go Slow to Go Fast to a close allowing you to make better decisions before going fast. You can no longer continue to live your life using traditional and outdated thoughts, behaviors and processes to change your circumstances—nor can you lead your organization using best practices that are outdated. A new 'way to play' lays waiting directly on your path. The world has changed and continues to change at a very rapid and unforgiving pace. You must focus on becoming a performance-driven thinker who *Thinks Above the Bar* in order to deliver *Breakthrough Achievable Results* that are guided by your ability to slow down to go fast.

There are still more mistakes that people make, but failing to make the decision to navigate the labyrinth of disruptive innovation to overcome the Tyranny of Success are the critical ones. I realize that in a short chapter everything is made to sound a bit too simplistic, but in reality, even successful change efforts are messy and full of surprises. However, just as a relatively simple vision is needed to guide people through a major change platform using the Leadership GPS System and the Five W's Agenda while taking a simple walk—gemba walk—so a vision of the change process can reduce the opportunity for a poor performance. Achieving execution excellence simply by navigating your labyrinth can be the difference between planning and execution and, success and failure.

# 11

# Understanding your Role: Planning to Execution

*"Learning to plan is easy. Following through on what you learn is the hard part."*

— **Damian D. "Skipper" Pitts**

U p to this point, we covered a wide range of topics that are used to construct the Go Slow to Go Fast strategy concepts and approach. Examining them through a lens of leadership and strategy focuses the topic on the critical tasks that a leader must undertake to develop and execute the initiatives of doing the right things to get the right things done. In choosing this focal point, decision-makers may find that some of the activities such as the Poker's Bluff, Leadership Code Switching, or the tasks of transforming 'best-practices' into *Next-Level Practice Decisions (NLPDs)* that ultimately transition into *Next-*

*Level Practices (NLPs)* are secondary priorities because they are not the important things to do that requires their immediate attention.

Likewise, they may think that these activities (and others like them) are more important to delegate the authority to someone else. Remember the lessons from Jack Welch mentioned in the introduction. This would be a grave mistake because the leader as the decision-maker must own all activities that make up the Go Slow to Go Fast strategy concepts and approach. Mainly because they require a sense of urgency with discipline and precision to arrive at the outcomes that support disruptive innovation inside and out of the organization. A sense of urgency within three (3) specific objectives (stages) are important:

1. Develop the Design (don't copy, create)
2. Execute the Process (high velocity delivery is advantage)
3. Achieve Agility in Performance-Driven Execution (momentum matters)

Understanding your role in this step-wise process means you'll need to explore new internal ports of fortitude: plotting your sails to discover new untapped character traits using edgy unconventional wisdom. This serves up the meat and potatoes to put some girth on the bones of Go Slow to Go Fast strategy. Introducing this very interesting and dynamic concept into the annals of leadership at a time when we're experiencing a crisis in leadership plays a critical role and part in overcoming the Tyranny of Success. You cannot Go Slow to Go Fast without having a need for addressing a sense of urgency to deal with change using disruption as the essential element for achieving disruptive change with impact. The three stages are incredibly important, but without having a sense of urgency and ability to *Think Above the Bar*, disruptive change cannot be achieved.

Could you imagine operating a business in an industry where disruption and change became the constant catalyst for significant growth almost on a daily basis? I'm not talking about iterative growth whereby systems gradually progress from one change paradigm to the next by improving upon themselves. No, what I am referring to is disruptive innovation through process transformation introduced to challenge your existing processes within your existing conditions because they no longer deliver or exceed your expected results to impact the organization's future.

Understanding your role in this scenario means tough choices must be made, and the leader (you) must be the one to force the issue. Forcing the issue with a sense of urgency builds the fabric for a Go Slow to Go Fast strategic approach to drive real change that will matter and will stick consistently and without fail.

What if you could predict the winning strategies each year to keep your organization ahead of the curve before the curve is actually experienced? Or, what if in a race for innovative growth, your decision makers can integrate disruptive change that is so radical that it sets your organization apart from the competitive landscape year after year? What if you could choose your competitive battles knowing you would win nearly every time regardless of the other competitors entering into the market? And finally, what if you knew in advance which growth strategies would succeed and which would fail before launching a disruptive strategy that will change how your emerging leaders behave to explore the factors your markets have yet to consider?

These are the questions that explain the importance of knowing your role in the planning and execution process using a Go Slow to Go Fast strategy and approach. Not so long ago, strategy was golden. Leaders at every corner of business and industry immersed themselves in the planning process to determine how best to achieve their organization's objectives. They assumed that the strategizing would pay off. And yet, for too many organizations, the strategy results and outcomes from these well-crafted viewpoints (or, so they thought) were very few and far between. Quite simply, leaders weren't able to fully achieve their objectives because they couldn't execute. They were unable to strategically and flawlessly achieve a sense of urgency to complete three important and specific stages:

- Develop the Design (don't copy, create)
- Execute the Process (high velocity delivery is advantage)
- Achieve Agility in Performance-Driven Execution (momentum matters)

So, to ensure that you are well informed about what your *authentic* role is in bridging the gaps between planning and execution using the three important stages, I'll unpack each of them to show how they'll require your existing leadership acumen to change you and the conditions where you will be applying them.

## Develop the Design (don't copy, create)

We all know that change is inevitable and despite their best efforts, most organizations and decision-makers can't seem to translate that knowledge into positive direct action with forward motion. Today, that's a serious and dangerous deficiency. One way of embracing the spirit of innovation and change is to adapt to the whole concept of Go Slow to Go Fast to reach new levels of success. This disciplined approach overcomes the challenges that stem from an inability to change; a serious issue that leads to irreparable harm in the long-run.

Make no mistake: If you want to run a successful business or organization that responds favorably in the face of change today, the option that will most likely win your efforts is to *"Develop the Design"* that fits the requirements that are forthcoming and *not* in the moment. This means that you need to stop copying past actions and behaviors and replace them with direct actions created to meet future requirements. My consulting colleague, Mark Hefner, President & Chief Operating Officer at N2Growth put it this way; *"Culture is a strategic imperative that must be created/transformed by design, not by default."* You must be willing to create and implement innovative strategies while adjusting to the changes in the markets. That's true of start-ups, small businesses and international corporations alike. If you're not flexible enough to flow with the waves of change, your ship snap in half when the first storm comes along—and, it's coming. Let's face a real fact here before moving on; effective execution starts with a plan. The ability to execute effectively is undermined early in the implementation process for several reasons that go on to cause challenges later. Few people use action plans to manage the many initiatives required to achieve a vision.

Too many leaders fail to hold people accountable for developing and using well designed action plans and when a series of direct actions are developed, they are not always aligned with the immediate project needs that are critical for delivering real-world results with impact.

Make no mistake; action plans are the cornerstone of strategic execution that wins in the long-term. Rather than being seen as a burden and a waste of time, action plans that are directly aligned to expected outcomes need to be recognized for what they can do: clarify expectations and accountability, align individuals and teams around a common objective, coordinate the effort of individuals and groups, ensure adequate resources are allocated to the project initiatives, and help identify and take action against the problems before they derail the initiative. Action plans by themselves don't have the ability to get things done, but in conjunction with the other Go Slow to Go Fast strategic approaches, they increase the likelihood that you'll execute well and get or exceed the results you're expecting.

Having a sense of urgency provides the means of connecting tomorrow's capability requirements to today's talent by analyzing how the existing capabilities will either create the expectation or slow the momentum for achieving it. Develop the Design utilizes a critical direct action from the Four Action Behaviors, *Target for Success*. With this direct action, there are a very large number of things against which an organization can put its resources. You know intuitively that some of those things will have much higher impact than others. The organization which targets the right things, the Centers of Gravity (CoGs), will be far more effective at a much lower cost than the organization that has no disciplined way to choose and affect its targets.

The Go Slow to Go Fast process recognizes that everything takes place in the context of a system and that systems have such annoying characteristics as inertia and resistance to change. But, they also have Centers of Gravity (CoGs); the components of a system that are related to achieving your Future Picture. Target for Success as the direct action used to Develop the Design focuses on the leverage points that when affected, have a disproportionate impact on their parent system and on the Future Picture. The best way to change a system (your organization or your market) is to affect its Centers of Gravity (CoGs) that were discussed earlier. These are also the essential points within the system that if you want to win your plan with effectiveness, even when or if your resources are limited, you apply your behaviors against them to achieve the greatest leverage or energy towards the vulnerabilities or areas that could threaten the success within your desired outcomes.

To provide a brief recap, Centers of Gravity (CoGs) are the relational synergies that total five known as the *Five Rings*: Leadership *(decision-makers)*, Processes *(strategies and tactics)*, Infrastructure *(the organization and emerging markets)*, Populations *(people)* and Action Units *(customers and vendors)*.

No matter the system, organization or marketplace, these five rings exist and are the starting point to cause change to occur—the reasons that you Target for Success. It would not be wise to *Develop the Design* without the *Target for Success* direct action applied. If you want to put your organization or market on a new path, it is necessary that you set-out to create rapid and hard-to-reverse system change using *Target for Success* as your direct action behaviors to affect your system's Centers of Gravity (CoGs) to meet the requirements of the future. To create hard-to-reverse change, you must affect the Centers of Gravity (CoGs) in the action plans first to affect the system in a compressed period of time. Doing so significantly reduces the ability of the system to resist what you want it to do, improving your chances and the probability for the change to deliver an innovative solution that will ultimately stick.

So, STOP duplicating and start creating. Think about it this way, *Develop the Design* by applying another *Next-Level Practice (NLP)* and you'll be able to see in real time how your outcomes will set the organization apart using the best performance results and those that are more effective at execution.

## Execute the Process (high velocity delivery is advantage)

Next, we move on to the most overlooked strategic initiatives. Leaders forget that although planning is important, doing the right things to get the right things done—execution that is both strategic and flawless—is the grease that keeps the wheels and gears moving in a system. However, none of this is possible without first making sure you involve the right people in the right decisions.

Involving emerging leaders in decision-making, those people who show promise to meet tomorrow's requirements today, is the best thing a leader can do to help their cause. This may mean that friendships are harmed because the friend is NOT the best resource to fulfill the need for the organization. Far too many people believe in their minds that they are the best fit for a given situation and this is NOT always the case.

For example, I continue to run into people who are very talented in their own right as coaches using off-the-shelf products to improve their recipient's perspective on growth. But, when it comes to developing a uniquely designed process to meet tomorrow's needs today, the off-the-shelf perspective is not always the best answer. At some point, authenticity has to show up and the skills to perform at a higher level must pervade existing norms and behaviors. Off-the-shelf does NOT deliver in a Go Slow to Go Fast strategic approach. Execute the Process (high velocity delivery is advantage) will and does day-in and day-out.

I've come to understand that some people view not having authenticity as a sign of weakness while others fear it as giving up control. In reality, though, the world is too complex for any person or leader (not all people are leaders) to go it alone. To offer Right-time Decision-making, you must seek out the perspectives of a wide range of people. Involving the right people in the right decisions gets them focused on generating solutions to problems rather than complaining or waiting to be told what to do. Your employees shouldn't feel like they exist only to help your company make a profit. They need to feel respected as key players with valid viewpoints while having a seat and voice at the table. They should be involved in decisions that affect them and should be encouraged to share their thoughts and concerns. When people feel they don't have a sense of ownership, nothing truly can get done or be accomplished, and this brings me to yet another issue.

People today MUST be held accountable, more accountable, to the outcomes and performance when executing. People with a high level of accountability will take initiative to ensure the success of a project. They'll provide early warning detection of potential problems and try to resolve the problems even when they are not within their areas of responsibility.

In Go Slow to Go Fast strategy, we identify this approach to another KWAP (Key Word And Phrase) known as **FISH: F**ind **I**solated **S**ystem that will cause **H**arm. One reason we hesitate to tackle the accountability problem in a timely manner is from a lack of clarity on what people should be held accountable for in the first place. Discussions about accountability can be straightforward and potential conflicts less intense when everyone knows ahead of time (during the Develop the Design stage) what is expected and how success will be measured.

Establishing this clarity ultimately reduces the likelihood of having to partake in this form of discussion in the first place. Being accountable comes naturally for some people and these are the individuals you want at your side. For many of us; however, the more natural tendency is to justify and explain why we are not responsible when things go wrong. This goes against the entire Go Slow to Go Fast approach! Although it is very tough to change human nature and behavior, the people in leadership roles today (some are called into leadership, while others are told they are leaders; I believe some people see the word as a title versus a series of actions and behaviors that need not be explained) can help create an environment that enables others to operate at a higher level of responsibility. As stated earlier, Kouzes' and Posner's *Exemplary Leadership Practices* are important here to *Model the Way, Inspire a Shared Vision, Challenge the Process, Enable Others to Act and Encourage the Heart.* The key is to set people up for success by clarifying expectations up front and building a step-wise procedural approach that wins in competitive environments and on time at all cost—all of the time and without fail.

This helps avoid the need to make excuses, and by-the-way, GOALS don't exist in Go Slow to Go Fast strategy. Goals are opportunities to make excuses (i.e., "we tried, but…" "if Jack had completed his task, we would have been able to…;" or "if the manufacturer didn't provide us with a faulty part, our product would be better"…and so on). Go Slow to Go Fast approach demands that goals be exchanged with TARGETs because targets have one reason for existing; to get hit dead center or destroyed. This means that excuses are eliminated and have no place in the matter of things.

TARGETs are looked at as critical objectives to be measured, sighted-in and eliminated using one shot because time is of the essence to keep momentum moving. TARGETs in a Go Slow to Go Fast approach require people and NOT a person to have a voice to decide on the outcomes in a given situation. **TARGETS** offer a critical KWAP in a Go Slow to Go Fast approach. It is defined as **T**ake **A**ction **R**ight-now **G**iving **E**veryone **T**imely-value…**S**trategically. This basically means that actions are strategic in nature to affect the outcomes in a situation, whereas everyone is held accountable for the outcomes— Singular Accountability (talked about in the Rule of Three, Leadership Triplicity™). There are three questions to consider in the Develop the Design stage to ensure targets are hit to solve challenges and problems:

1. What can we do better to do the right things to get the right things done now?
2. How did our actions contribute to this situation?
3. What MUST be done going forward to ensure we're able to eliminate risk by leading out from crises before they happen— avoiding the turbulence and chaos within the systems we are being held accountable?

This approach is NOT allowed to pinpoint blame and helps to minimize the threat to anyone's self-image. The three questions also minimize the need to make excuses because they target specific actions to collaborate on finding a solution. This creates a structure that supports execution. In developing the Go Slow to Go Fast approach, research found that striking the right balance between centralization and decentralization differentiates top-performing organizations from all others in their marketplaces.

While many organizations emphasize developing a realistic strategy that engages the right people for the right decisions, problems develop when leaders assume that the current organizational structure will support the new strategy. In most cases, this is simply not true. You cannot continue to be successful using strategies from the past. Don't assume that organizational structure is just about efficiency. The right structure can also enhance accountability, coordination and communication, and ensure that decisions are being made as close to the action, in real-time, as possible and needed. These are key components of doing the right things to get the right things done—providing high velocity that delivers a strategic advantage that wins.

## Achieve Agility in Performance-Driven Execution (momentum matters)

Think for a moment what the definition of the word agile represents: being or remaining flexible in the approach to achieve objectives regardless of challenges within a given set of circumstances. Agility is like water; fluid always in motion to venture wherever and whenever it chooses a path to proceed.

Now, let's look at the definition for Performance-Driven Execution: the GODOs and the ability to become contagious beyond the contact sport of leadership by learning how to do the right things at all times, over and over again—to achieve mastery. Combine the two and this is what you have: Agile Performance-Driven Execution is the ability to remain fluid when deciding to move with impact (GODOs) to do the right things at all times, over and over again to achieve mastery. This definition sets up the conversation about the importance of bringing alignment between a leader's direct actions and the organization's values, priorities and impacts within its Future Picture; where you want to be and how you want the future to look prior to arriving to it in the distant future.

No organization should ever have two sets of values and expectations, one within the leadership ranks and another within the staff ranks. This is NOT leadership and when leaders say one thing and do another, business suffers. It might surprise you to learn exactly how much execution depends on the consistency of a leader's ability to ensure positive organizational behavior aligns with organizational values/ priorities. People observe their leaders to pick up on the signals that are the most important and appropriate. They pattern their behavior after what has been confirmed as doing the right things to get the right things done in a timely manner. If your behavior signifies that "we are all in this together" as in a Go Slow to Go Fast approach, people are more likely to be motivated to do what is necessary or required to win. When you expect people to behave a certain way, help them see the importance of using the Exemplary Leadership Practices offered from Kouzes and Posner. There's no other way that matters; showing a 'do-as-I-say, not-as-I-do' approach or attitude sends mixed messages and does NOT conform to the meaning of Go Slow to Go Fast. If you're operating a business or running an organization where people think things such as *"why is it necessary for us to... but not for them to...?"* don't be surprised when momentum is stalled and a resistance to change shows itself causing performance to fall short of expectations.

And with that, this offers another perspective to the Agile Performance-Driven Execution approach: organization-wide collective intelligence, collaborative effort and connectedness (defined roles) through positive organizational behavior. Most people in the world today have good intentions (my belief). They want to cooperate with like-minded people to achieve specific tasks. Yet, ensuring that decisions and actions are coordinated using collective intelligence across organizational boundaries requires more than wishing and elaborate speeches.

It takes collaborative effort and connectedness (clearly defined roles) to achieve what must be done to accomplish tasks. These provide the foundation upon which significant cooperation can be built. In addition, people must be held accountable to fulfill commitments and take responsibility for doing their jobs properly. This requires a combination of direct leader behavior and systems that encourage and reinforce the appropriate behavior.

Effective execution from the three facilitates change readiness, especially when large-scale strategic initiatives are the objective targets to meet the needs of the organization. Frequent change in behavior on the part of those who you depend on to deliver the expected results that do not focus on these three change readiness behaviors and direct action will become a problem later. However, following these perspectives delivers three disciplined outcomes:

1. Leader behavior will have a direct impact on the level of resistance demonstrated by other people—collective intelligence.
2. People are more likely to make a behavioral change successfully if they are inspired to move into action when they are ready—collaborative effort.
3. People are more willing to align to specific strategies to help move systems and organizations through the levels of change, though they must be used at the right time to achieve specific outcomes—connectedness.

Agile Performance-Driven Execution ensures that momentum matters because it *campaigns to win* in order to allow people to *Finish with Finesse*. It enhances opportunities to cooperate on the things that are important. We all know that organizations are complex structures containing many moving parts and interdependencies. And because we already know this, it is important that we rely on others to help get things done to meet our objectives. This means that cooperation and collaboration are critical to our success. The challenges faced in the workplace cannot be overcome if the conditions that create and sustain cooperation and collaboration are not in place.

For this reason, the Agile Performance-Driven Execution utilizes its own critical direct actions known as *Campaign to Win* and *Finish with Finesse*. The *Campaign to Win* direct action facilitates a clear and concise communications style in the leadership traits that elicit share d informed perspectives to clearly define the roles of each stakeholder on the team. These conditions help encourage and motivate people to focus on the team's best interest without feeling that they are trading off their own interests. Once in place; however, sustaining cooperation is a delicate task.

People will still have different points of view about how and when things should happen. A leader's ability to influence others constructively to gain their support is critical to maintaining cooperation. In every instance, losing cooperation is mainly caused by mistakes being made and miscommunications, and when unhealthy occurrences cause disagreements to go unaddressed or not well managed.

The *Campaign to Win* direct action explains why champions are needed along the way and along the path to success. With the Future Picture standing before everyone as a clear beacon to guide their actions, this direct action and behavior allows you to begin your attack against the Centers of Gravity previously identified. Why use the word "attack" here? Simply because when you're moving your energy towards or against the leverage points within a system, you're essentially launching a preemptive strike against the gaps in performance to cause momentum to move in the direction you would like to go. You do this with campaign teams drawn from across the organization consistent with the talents required to exert the greatest leverage possible. *Campaign to Win* is essential to the organization's Future Picture and the people responsible for driving success from within the system to the maximum extent possible of those who participated in the creation of the Future Picture and the identification of the Centers of Gravity.

The campaign teams' main objective is to ensure the continuation of the change work is being done, which means that the system is relying on people to think strategically, focus sharply and move quickly with the decisions and action in an open planning environment to affect the Centers of Gravity in parallel. This means that for decision-makers and leaders to affect them in a very compressed time frame using parallel operations, the Centers of Gravity have far higher probabilities of success than do stretched-out serial operations and paradoxically cost are lowered within the compressed time frame. It is almost always the case that the current organization structure will not be optimum for a new strategy, especially if it involves an aggressive Future Picture.

That being said, part of campaigning to win is to modify the structure as required to allow the organization to move quickly and accurately against the Centers of Gravity. The campaign teams themselves, of course, must remain poised on developing rapid parallel actions to provide the bridge to a new-normal and a new formal structure. In the interim; however, the organization must still be able to conduct its business activities competitively and for this reason, the *Campaign to Win* direct action is so critically important in the change process allowing the organization to Finish with Finesse at the end.

Using the three important stages in Go Slow to Go Fast to understand fully your role in planning and execution [develop the design (don't copy, create)... execute the process (high velocity delivery is advantage)... and achieve agile performance-driven execution (momentum matters)], builds incredibly important organizational strategic execution methodologies to help leaders understand that a well-conceived vision along with realistic strategies are critical to meeting the demands of the future successfully. Leaders appreciate the need for having highly engaged like-minded people around them when striving to achieve high performance-driven execution. But, to do so, everyone must fully understand their roles to achieve such an initiative. Yet, even when these core factors are in place, many organizations are still not able to deliver consistent results. The reason is that although essential, these factors are clearly only prerequisites. Organizations and the decision-makers who are being held responsible for leading successful outcomes must be the best at execution to create the needed operating plans that are coordinated across all boundaries of the enterprise. When everyone understand their individual roles within the context of achieving higher levels of excellence in performance, expectations can be met without fail and step-wise procedures can be formed to ensure the pathway to success is established. When this becomes the daily behavioral occurrences, the three stages will become the salient events that everyone will look to follow. People won't mind being held accountable for the behaviors they will be required to contribute on behalf of the overall organization or environment.

Individual change readiness becomes a collaborative effort. Execution becomes less challenging and organizations are more disciplined to develop, create and maintain the necessary strategies used to close the execution gaps. Of course, organizations cannot bridge the execution gap overnight, nor can people fully grasp the concept of what they will be held accountable to when asked to be self-sustaining within a system.

Still, getting this 'construction project,' because that's actually what it is underway, will require more than one perspective and more than one person to build a real-world architectural framework that works in the end. This is an important step in the right direction.

As I start to wrap things up, most notably the evidence shows that leaders today can no longer enter into the conversations of tomorrow until they have a complete understanding about where they are (existing conditions), where they want to end up (the Future Picture), and how they intend to respond to the current demands on their systems and enterprises. This will require them to keep the Centers of Gravity in the forefront: Leadership, Processes, Infrastructure, Populations and Action Units. The response is determined by their ability to effectively code switch in leadership to respond more favorably to each of the five Centers of Gravity.

What continues to be disturbing today is how leaders are able to read about similar methodologies to understand the reasons why they make sense, yet we continue to experience a crisis in leadership around the world. A crisis in leadership requires a complete breakdown of leadership purpose to fully understand its perspective before progressing into the future. This would be the case if leaders would be doing more of the right things to get the right things done. But, actually getting them to want to learn a better way to use improved processes that will ultimately lead to disrupting and changing outdated process, is the real challenge in all things becoming possible. Inspiring people to do the right things to get the right things done presents a whole different set of circumstances all together.

We understand that change is tough, uncomfortable and hard for some people, but continuing to proceed each day using outdated thinking and outdated norms is just foolish. Launching an evolutionary process that leads to change using the combination of the Go Slow to Go Fast stages will, in most cases, provide the capacity to understand the reasons why disruptive behavior is required today. And, although no change paradigm can be seen as the silver bullet that kills the big bad wolf of failure and failing systems, this step-wise process is one for the ages to allow you to command the change in any organizational situation.

To help you to further understand how the three events combine to change your perspective within your existing conditions, I developed a fun philosophical, but healthy debate between *rationalism* and *empiricism* that I believe offers much to consider when deciding on changing your approach on the future. I refer to this debate as the *"65 Leadership Reasons for Change"* that offer a considerable perspective to learn how reason and experience should be the basis of your actions *(rationalism)* or another perspective that states all knowledge originates in experience *(empiricism)*.

Whichever perspective you believe, rationalism or empiricism, the *65 Leadership Reasons for Change* will challenge your beliefs about why change is so critically important today. This upcoming journey will challenge your thought-leadership and existing thought processes to add more value to the Go Slow to Go Fast approach by sharing additional insights to improve your acumen when deciding to make a greater impact. It means that people today must really learn how to *Think Above the Bar* to accomplish *Breakthrough Achievable Results* using a transformative change perspective. What I'm suggesting is that people, not only people in leadership, must be able to change their beliefs, change their attitudes, change their behaviors and ultimately, change their outcomes while being more receptive to the power of *differentiation* because it (differentiation) has quickly become a bar of expectation that contributes greater impact to the overall success of change when it is needed to respond more favorably in the world today.

## The Strength of Intuitiveness

I know that you want to see the *65 Leadership Reasons for Change,* but there's one last thing to understand before we go into them. They are like a mind's Bootcamp of learning how to use disruptive-thought to change existing norms and conditions to differentiate yourself from the rest of the pack. It is tough to remain positive when deep down in your heart you know that change in a certain set of circumstances is needed to move *something* (people, teams, an organization or an environment) into a better state.

Have you ever been in a situation where you knew that the people involved were the wrong people (values, personalities and behaviors) for the state of affairs? Or, have you been on a workplace team that wasn't really a team causing momentum to stall or move at a snail's pace? An overarching lesson to learn when it comes to facing needed change is one that comes hard to some people, but it is still a lesson that anyone can learn to use to make greater impact on the future. The lesson here refers to what is known as the Strength of Intuitiveness: your ability to understand or know something without any direct evidence or reasoning process due to past experiences. Developing exceptional change and leadership monikers as positive initiatives require us to live above the daily metaphors and common speak to bring into focus our strengths-based approach to making things better.

Improving existing conditions to ensure they are influential enough to differentiate your strengths from their norms to awaken your creative potential means that you must be prepared to expose the needed areas of change when necessary. This is another form of Leadership Code Switching.

Preparing to expose those areas awakens your creative potential to modify your behavior in response to rapidly changing environments using past experiences (knowledge) to manage the personal and psychological challenges (limitations) when moving toward a new objective. At that point, it is your obligation to facilitate the faculties of the mind and push your personal change paradigms to their limits regardless of the opportunities you'll seek to resist, kick-back or stall your own needed growth.

The Strength of Intuitiveness offers you an optimistic viewpoint and the forward-thinking you'll need to open the vast opportunities and possibilities within the systems and processes you are responsible (or will be responsible) to influence. As an agent for change, you have to be willing to take full advantage of how the change will not only affect your own growth, but the growth of the people, teams, organizations, processes, systems and environments you are responsible for leading. In the end, you'll be surprised to learn just how many people will be intrigued to follow your lead to find their own voice and inspire change in themselves and in others.

And now that the Strength of Intuitiveness is out of the way, the *65 Leadership Reasons for Change* are ready for its introduction to the stage. Remember, they represent a healthy dispute between rationalism and empiricism when it comes to tapping your untapped potential. They are your guide to influence or stop small challenges from becoming BIG problems. And, inspired by the Strength of Intuitiveness, you can consider these when thinking about making changes in your organization using the Go Slow to Go Fast approach, allowing you to see how simple they are and how they won't require any back-flips by you when deciding to put many, most or some of them into practice **BECAUSE...**

1. You can't lead today's organizations with yesterday's strategies and remain strategically disruptive tomorrow to differentiate yourself from the pack.
2. There really is a difference between leadership and management which means there is a difference between Crisis Leadership—leading out before... and Crisis Management—leading through during! Crisis Leadership is the ways and the means of becoming disruptive to change the future.

3. Leaders need to understand how to build congruence between strategy and execution—then teach the same to others in their organizations.
4. Teamwork can no longer be great; it must be on a trajectory for extraordinary greatness.
5. The weather can be unpredictable, but a leader's performance can never be!
6. Shift happens and happens and happens…how you respond to it matters to the impact you'll make without fail. Either way, an impact will be made. The choice is completely up to you about its importance.
7. Leaders need to *Think Above the Bar* to deliver *Breakthrough Achievable Results.*
8. Leaders must understand the Rule of Three: Many, Most and Some. Many have wanted it, Most think they have it, but Some will actually get it—LEADERSHIP!
9. Leaders must know by now that if leadership were easy, everyone would be doing it. Leadership is hard and has always been, but being better than good at what you do will make it look easy when it is not.
10. Organizational behavior requires 25% interpretation, 25% knowledge and 51% you! It also requires 10% comprehension, 30% listening and 80% eye-balling (tacit knowledge) to ensure people are successful at the end of the day.
11. Leaders must rise to any challenge such as pushing innovation, the application of strategy and the tactical-philosophy to win. Effectively communicating these efforts is where the rubber meets the road to actually matter in the whole thick of things.
12. Transformational leaders assume different kinds of roles and use different management skills with the right tools than most traditional-minded leaders.

13. Conventional wisdom tells you to follow the pack. Unconventional wisdom that's edgy inspires you to chase your dreams. The pursuit must never end, but if it does, you'll have to ask a very important question about how you really think and what you believe... conventional or unconventional?

14. Leaders must understand the rule of SMEAC: They understand their *Situation* that aligns with their *Mission*, to ensure they have what is required to *Execute*, using the right people and resources to *Administer* best practices for the task, in order to *Control* the impacts made on the future to keep momentum moving in the right direction—right-time decision-making.

15. When everyone sees rainstorms in the middle of conflict, Crisis Leaders see rainbows regardless of the fight ahead.

16. Leaders celebrate and encourage contributions made by others to make the environment a better place.

17. Leaders see and understand the direction for where they are headed for others to follow; and know that you'll like what the future holds when you get there.

18. Leaders know the critical importance for keeping up with change and its impact on achieving successful outcomes.

19. Leaders know the importance of integrating the disciplines of Maneuver Warfare to achieve overwhelming results in today's fiercely competitive market environment: targeting critical vulnerabilities, boldness, surprise, focus, decentralized decision-making, tempo and combined arms.

20. Business is a battlefield until true leaders get into the fight. They know how to win without firing as many shots and what's required to tackle the challenges of inattention, interruptions and impatience that every professional faces.

21. Leaders believe and understand the need to systematically transform the leadership culture from a dominating system to a liberating system of reciprocity.

22. Leaders must manage by mind, lead from the heart, change with the feet, and win from the gut with help from others.

23. Leaders synergize, exercise, minimize, stabilize, memorize, categorize, summarize and materialize how to win. They understand the EYES and the lens to see things differently from everyone else.

24. Leaders must master transition to develop the discipline of managing the unexpected.

25. Leaders must know that leadership and teamwork combine to run the race of the Breeder's Cup Championship, and how to communicate the message to the team before the race is won: "You are a great champion. When you ran, the ground shook, the sky opened and mere mortals parted the way to victory, where you'll meet me in the winner's circle, where I'll put a blanket of flowers on your back" — Dreamer.

26. Leaders must hunt for great behavior to become teachers of dignified coaches.

27. Leaders are performance driven thinkers; they see what all see, but think what no other thinks.

28. Leaders LeaderShape; they know leadership as we have known it is dead because most leaders are focused on what they will accomplish and gain rather than on what they are leading for the benefit of others.

29. Leaders must seek first to understand, then to be understood: they execute both strategically and flawlessly… and they do it well!

30. Leaders know the importance of wearing two hats to a meeting; one of a young inner city urban kid and the other of a smart

beautiful woman—one fights for what they want, while the other knows how to achieve (outsmart) what they want.

31. Leaders must never settle for mediocrity when they can attain personal mastery to improve professional commitment.

32. Leaders must understand values are WHY we do and behaviors are WHAT we do to increase understanding of self, others, effective communications and productivity, but decrease tension, conflict, ambiguity and doubt.

33. Leaders must appreciate the viewpoint of others who see life differently; change your lens.

34. Leaders must always be aware of the WHY of their actions—purpose.

35. Leaders must know that to achieve something they've never had, they must be prepared to do what they've never done. Pack your bags; you're about to travel to a place you've never been. Pack well!

36. Leaders must understand the reciprocal relationships between fairness, trust and ethical behavior while in the pursuit of disruption and change for impact.

37. Leaders must know delusion is NOT a part of the creative process.

38. Leaders must know the sweat of a struggling opportunist in disguise from a struggling artist.

39. Leaders must know how to inspire process transformation to change the dynamic of a misguided mission.

40. Leaders must know how to bridge theory (what-is) into practice (how-to) to achieve the best results that overcome the "what-ifs."

41. Leaders must understand that if we can change the view of the future, *people's priorities and objectives,* then we might possibly change the impact on the world.

42. Leaders must understand change and disruption as being two of the most difficult undertakings in our overly sensitive world; a personal questioning of motive and intent.

43. Leaders don't need cue cards to tell the truth!

44. Leaders must know where they stand in life's deck of cards; in the low deck, the high deck or a wild card. If you are smart, you'll know how to be every card for different situations. Only the fool wants to be in a certain deck.

45. Leaders must understand that executives were once in middle management and sometimes needs to be reminded of this fact; they won't mind a challenge in authority when it needs to be challenged.

46. Leaders must know how to avoid the individuals who rent hearts on a day-to-day basis without giving a refund.

47. Experience leaves a limp for life that reminds us about the long hard road and rise to the top. Leaders must know that the road traveled was the easy part; staying there will take true talent.

48. Leaders must have a unique ability to bring themselves to the realization that charisma and success are actually two very different things.

49. The experience of a set-back is only the beginning of a great set-up to come.

50. Leaders must know how to ask the RIGHT questions relative to their Leadership GPS System: WHY are we doing this? This is a descriptor about purpose? WHO will be impacted—benefited, limited or eliminated? WHAT are we applying our energy and resources against? WHERE are we going (this is known as the compass heading)? WHEN do we plan to arrive (this is known as the Future Picture; the 'object' location and desired effect or outcome with 'descriptive memos' for further guidance to make the best decisions for the mission)?

51. Leaders must understand that Crisis Leadership is a conquering of turbulence with a changing of the guard—from the old to the reconstructed, evolutionary process of change through disruptive behavior.

52. Leaders must understand how to approach situations using three focused perspectives: *The Rear-View Mirror*: to observe existing human dimensions and dyadic experiences leading up to a specific point in time. *With Greater Understanding*: to analyze challenges, opportunities, personal vulnerabilities and internal threats that can cause potential derailments leading up to and within the turns of operations, and lastly, *Fulfilling the Promise*: to achieve Future Picture opportunities *(the end result)* by envisioning future possibilities *(the direction to move)*, then executing strategically and flawlessly to finish with finesse.

53. Leaders must think strategically, focus sharply and move quickly to win adverse conditions that had no place in the planning process.

54. Leaders must know that in order to soar above the trees, they must first learn to fly with a different flock.

55. Leaders must take charge, suffer the hardships, assume the risk, share the defeats and victories, and win competitive forces through wise counsel!

56. Leaders must know that true character shows when no one is watching; a successful trait that has somehow lost its way. Everyone will lose their way at some point. The key is realizing the need to find your way back home.

57. Leaders must know the importance of winning with teamwork, collaboration and the innate ability to navigate the path of organizational politics to win TOGETHER. Give and take when the time calls for either.

58. Leaders must understand that the pain and frustration from change is ONLY the mind, body and spirit awakening the soul as an alarm clock to start a new day!

59. Leaders must understand the importance of expressing disciplined-thought as a means of achieving Performance-Driven Execution to create uncontested demand and value innovation while virtually eliminating the bad habits that limit extraordinary greatness used to shape how a society behaves!

60. Smart leaders learn leadership corollary is that when leaders can do the important things in their roles in an exceptional way to command the attention of those they lead, allowing the remainder of the organization to make their influence impactful on the Future Picture *(The Power of Counterintuitive Thinking in Leadership Development)*.

61. Leaders must understand the importance of inspiring others to understand and learn their *philosophy* in order to see the impact of their planned *initiative* and the buy-in to their *methodology* to win the race of a fast galloping horse—the horse knows the track is long, but the patience of knowing when to break away wins every race they are committed to run.

62. Successfirmations are an act of encouraging untapped potential to rise to the top.

63. I can't, says who? Does anything else need to be stated here?

64. Although there are many more leadership reasons for change, leaders must understand the following reason as one that everyone must adhere to regardless of role, position or circumstance...

65. Leaders must understand the importance of establishing RULES as a causation of failure or success: *"Rules overcome the limitations that prevent us from making the right choices. Rules counteract the biases introduced by systematic failure in process. Rules suppress or*

*base our instinct to keep us on a path of righteousness. Rules give us the courage to ignore the fog that obscures the true value of good and great and gives us the resolve to resist the sirens of performance inadequacies and personal limitations. Rules govern many of the important choices that allow us to have a chance at real success. But when faced with challenges, rules should only be followed if they matter in the current time to fit the current circumstances… but there must still be rules to follow…"*—Gen. (Ret) Stanley McChrystal, U.S. ARMY.

If you're determined to achieve a strategic advantage in life, in your career, or in your role as a leader… understanding the importance to Go Slow to Go Fast, you must be able to make a successful mind-shift. The *65 Leadership Reasons for Change* offers the Bootcamp for you to achieve just that. The thought around the *65 Leadership Reasons for Change* is similar to arriving at one of our military Bootcamp's in-processing units whereby it may be difficult to accept a disruptive change at this point in your life and career. But, disruption and change, at any time when it is disciplined and purposeful, is healthy. Try not to think about the entire list of 65, but break them down into small bites of acumen. Focus intently on the task at hand, even if it is just sitting quietly or in the middle of a tough day with hours to go before the day is over.

Nothing easy is worth having and the *65 Leadership Reasons for Change* is the start of becoming a better you to accept a larger journey that waits patiently around the corner—transition and change. They require a strength that you do not know that you possess (in some cases), and will require you to dig deep to find that part of yourself. Completing the *65 Leadership Reasons for Change* requires that you to embrace the Strength of Intuitiveness as a significant concept to use while code switching in leadership.

It requires that you always give your absolute best and you'll find yourself as a graduate of life's leadership Bootcamp that does not allow everyone to enter but a select few. The key to winning in life is the preparation that goes into learning a new way of thinking to experience a 'new way to play;' think differently from others and identify how to shift your mindset that will lead to you becoming different from the pack. A commonly held belief is that the process of developing leaders must begin by finding and inspiring them to improve upon their own weaknesses.

That belief is built on the underlying assumption that their performance is limited by their weakest competencies; simply because the level of the lowest competency sets the bar for any leader's overall success (so the thinking goes). That specific competency needs to be improved and the weakness developed further to become a value and a benefit versus leaving it unattended to linger on to continue being a liability. Likewise, great organizational effort requires a significant undertaking in discovering and communicating these very same concepts to overcome potential weaknesses leaders may be faced with. In turn, leaders are expected to work on these concepts as a way of considering different perspectives to begin improving as a leader of greater purpose. Weakness, if you are dealing with some that are counterintuitive to the *65 Leadership Reasons for Change* and *the Strength of Intuitiveness* concepts, can be fixed with little effort.

Weakness must allow you to engage in a healthy and personal debate between rationalism and empiricism concerns. They each offer a credible argument at different times and for different circumstances. It is true that reason and experience should be the basis of your actions (rationalism), but it is also true that knowledge originates in experience (empiricism). In the end, I believe that it will come down to perspective in your willingness to grow as a leader.

To close on this important topic, I once wrote about the topic of perspective within the debate about a glass being half full or half empty. And the Strength of Intuitiveness concepts makes me think about perspective in our ability to continue growing as leaders. You see, we are programmed in today's world to always look at the positive (everyone gets an award who deserves one). Rationalism has its place and must be considered when thinking about outcomes; hence, the glass should be half full to keep a positive attitude. But in the same right, empiricism must also be considered allowing the glass to be half empty to ensure there is enough room to add more of what is needed later.

Self development becomes apparent when we can see what we are lacking and the areas we must seek to improve. Even in areas where we have become comfortable by having our glass full, there are still times to consider attaining A BIGGER GLASS to work on filling it. We should work on filling our glasses in the good times so we have adequate supplies to get us through the hard times and that's what leadership has always been about—making necessary improvements. Those hard times will usually be defining moments to demonstrate the true character that embodies your work as you lead into the future. You now have a defined mission that lies in front of you on your path of extraordinary growth; do you continue to add to the list of *65 Leadership Reasons for Change* to improve upon your own Strength of Intuitiveness concepts, or do you continue on the path you are now traveling? Action requires a decision, many decisions that only you can make for your own growth and leadership acumen.

The objective here in outlining the *65 Leadership Reasons for Change* was only to push you along the path, further into your journey of becoming an extraordinary coach of leaders who will go out into the world to begin shaping how societies behave. Travel well on your path. A question that you must ask on a periodic basis should be *"why it is important to refocus leadership to change or disrupt existing conditions?"* The answer will be different for everyone because different situations require that question to be asked from different perspectives. But, a common thread runs between all perspectives regardless of circumstance; time and change.

The scale of the complexities across the U.S. financial, political and business sectors in recent years have thwarted attempted leadership reforms to occur because of the devastating issues plaguing the national infrastructure.

Some of the nation's major consulting actors such as Mckinsey & Company, Boston Consulting Group, Deloitte, Booz Allen, KPMG, Accenture, Roland Berger Strategy Consultants, and others in executive education and consulting continue to work to progress the fields of leadership, strategy and execution forward. However, anyone in the field has to be frustrated when they look around and notice the state of things that scream *"we have a mess on our hands!"* With all of this talent and the million others offering consultancy practices to improve upon the existing state of leadership across the nation, the challenges continue to progress in the wrong direction. With the current crisis in leadership we're experiencing across the fabric of leadership, you can't help but wonder if we must abandon our existing efforts out of frustration after acknowledging the lack of progress—if we're honest with ourselves. Now, we're not silly to think that progress must be stalled or stopped all together, but we definitely need a disruptive perspective to bring a common thread of change into the fold.

We MUST slow things down a bit, or a lot, to Go Slow to Go Fast, or we will continue to travel down the road we're currently on at 100 mph and continue to miss the opportunities to actually influence and allow change to happen. Think about the education system across the United States of America.

At one time after WWII, the U.S. celebrated one of the highest high school graduation rates in the world, but today, the U.S. ranks

18th among the top 24 industrialized nations (according to statistics from 2011), with more than 1+ million secondary school students dropping out every year. The alarming fact in this example is that those statistics are now some 3+ years old and with the heroic efforts of countless teachers and administrators, together with billions of dollars in charitable contributions that may have led to important improvements in individual schools and classrooms, system-wide progress seems virtually unobtainable. Against these daunting odds, who wouldn't suggest that something different must be done; something disruptive to eliminate the strife and failings that can no longer be fixed simply by throwing more money behind the problem and challenges that exist in our educational systems.

Go Slow to Go Fast offers a remarkable exception against the existing matrix and although it is not the answer to the crisis in leadership we are experiencing, and will continue to experience, it does represent a significant piece of the puzzle in achieving the solution. And this puzzle screams for *Right-time Decision-making* and disruptive collaborative efforts to join this emerging call to become a solution in the short and long-term. Let us not forget about applying a sense of urgency (important) when coming to grips with learning your role in bridging the gaps between planning to execution to improve your current circumstances.

Do you know why a sense of urgency is important to understand Go Slow to Go Fast strategy? The reason is simple; because it needs to be created and recreated for you, as a leader, to survive in the complex world we have entered into and are now experiencing in the 21st century.

We have short memory of the mid-maps to lead us to a better way or approach to improve our existing conditions. We've become episodic and with change, episodic no longer works; the approach is outdated and pointless. We must move into a continuous and fluid (agile) approach to deal with change to make it both matter and stick in the long-run.

With this shift, urgency to realize Go Slow to Go Fast strategy will move from being an important issue every few years to being a powerful asset *all the time*.

There is good news that waits us. The Go Slow to Go Fast approach is not a hard one to learn nor is it a difficult one to adapt to within your existing conditions. It doesn't matter if you are a leader responsible for leading a start-up or a multinational corporation, with the changing world comes various hazards to successfully navigate. And in doing so, Go Slow to Go Fast offers wonderful opportunities to lead you with an approach that *will* differentiate you and your organization from the pack with shifting methodologies to pivot when needed using disruptive change.

To capitalize on the opportunities requires you to become disciplined in learning the various topics outlined in the Go Slow to Go Fast approach. But, it all begins with you accepting a high aptitude for change, along with a sense of urgency for doing so. Get that right and you are off to a great start. Get that right and you can produce results that you very much want to have within your organization, team and environment. Remember, it's all about doing the right things to get the right things done. You now have a step-wise approach that is poised on making sure you can do the right things. Now, go and get your right things done through change.

### One More Thing!

Here's one last thing to think about as you consider to Go Slow to Go Fast; **"get ready, get set…pause!"** Sometimes, the most valuable action is your ability to use the direct action of the pause to (re)consider your actions before proceeding into the unknown. You'll find questions to become clearer.

You'll find resources to become more abundant. You'll find people to be more willing to help. You'll find outcomes to be more effective.

And, you'll find *effective* to be *extraordinary* given your ability to lead yourself and others to do the right things to get the right things done. As the champion of your Go Slow to Go Fast strategy, you are taking this information into a series of step-wise procedures to create positive outcomes. So with this, I ask you; *"why not?"* What can possibly go wrong? Nothing and much!

# 12

# Preemptive Crisis Analytics
## *Leadership Preparedness and Resilience to Support your Leadership GPS System*

---

*"Perhaps mankind's greatest distinction is his innate ability and utmost capacity to make preemptive and evolutionary decisions to create better or improved choices."*
— Damian D. "Skipper" Pitts


## An Extension Of The Leadership Gps System

Although no one can predict or make bold statements about unforeseen events in the near and long-term future, early forecasting indicates leadership preparedness and resilience efforts are on the rise. When change that causes turbulence threatens, preparedness and resilience are essential for an organization to protect its people, resources and operations. It is critical for decision-makers to capture a full understanding of the dyadic relationships between best practices, Next-Level Decision Practices (NLPDs) and Next-Level Practices (NLPs) in leadership and strategy execution using Preemptive Crisis Analytics within the constructs of the Leadership GPS System. By doing so, decision-makers will be better equipped to establish and interpret the appropriate level of analysis based on the correlation between leader-member exchange quality and commitment in an organizational setting.

## The Leadership GPS System—Extension Process, Preemptive Crisis Analytics: The New Reality

The extension process within the Go Slow to Go Fast' Leadership GPS System evolves from the new reality in business analytics and organizational design. Preemptive Crisis Analytics, *an extension of the Five W's Agenda within the Leadership GPS System,* examines incoming data and decision sciences to increase productivity, efficiency and effectiveness for leaders and organizations to make better informed decisions for their organizations to be more strategically aligned ahead of the competitive landscape.

This effort drives momentum with extraordinary impact and can no longer be dismissive as a right-time decision-making process and organizational behavior. Doing the right things to get the right things done requires a GPS system to achieve high performance-driven execution. Preemptive Crisis Analytics as the new reality answers the call.

With organizations operating in heavily competitive environments, the pressure to make the right decisions at the most opportune time has never been higher for business stakeholders. Leading organizations today are actively using data to go through rapid "decision cycles" to differentiate themselves from the fast running pack.

Starting with the detection of hidden patterns in lessons learned through data to triggering investigations that stimulate explorations in new directions, these decision cycles also involve socializing insights across the enterprise for the implementation of preemptive direct actions and positive organizational behaviors. This will disrupt existing conditions to improve productivity and efficiency. Smart decision-makers are using this approach to keep four preemptive-centric traits and questions at the forefront of all decisions for consideration:

1. **Descriptive Analytics:** What is *going* to happen in the business and organization?
2. **Inquisitive Analytics:** How will our capabilities *allow* it to happen?
3. **Predictive Analytics:** What *must* be done to change the circumstances?
4. **Prescriptive Analytics:** Now what? And, so what? What *do* we do next?

Going through the four decision cycles effectively expresses upon and supports the key drivers for creating a needed strategic advantage that ultimately sustains a more robust and rigorous competitive advantage.

Taking a preemptive approach to solving challenges and problems that require explicit data-driven insights can, by their very nature, be descriptive, inquisitive, predictive or prescriptive. They can be clearly defined or muddy; or ill-defined and shifting. To stay competitive, leaders and decision-makers must be willing to increasingly explore answers to impending crisis scenarios to validate their hypotheses about the day-to-day functioning across the organization. The following information outlines the key challenges that must be overcome by answering the extended Leadership GPS questions.

## Key Challenges for Analytics and Decision Sciences

The question every leader must ask toady is *"what are we doing from an organizational design perspective to scale and maximize ROI using analytics and decision sciences investments for our leaders to be better prepared to close the gaps between today's needs and tomorrow's key requirements?"* Change is happening so fast and has become so unforgiving that leaders and decision-makers must ask better informed questions to affect their organization's design. Here are some to consider:

**At an organizational level (Descriptive),** leaders must begin thinking about:

✓ What *must* we do to better engage business stakeholders to improve the consumption of insights?

✓ What *must* we do to ensure sustainable collaboration and learning across the decision teams?

✓ What *must* we do to improve productivity and accelerate the time to insights?

**On the analytical front (Inquisitive),** they must seek the answers to the following:

✓ What *must* we do to enable better knowledge management practices within the teams?

✓ What *must* we do to capture analytical Next-Level Practices (NLPs) across the teams?

✓ What *must* we do to engage a new 'way to play' and standardization of analytical processes across the organization?

✓ What *must* we do to remain ahead of the trends using emerging techniques and applications to set new trends others have yet to consider and will follow?

**On the human capital and talent (people) front (Predictive),** they'll need to answer:

✓ What *must* we do to get our knowledge professionals to focus more on Next-Level Practices Decisions (NLPDs) that generate Next-Level Practices (NLPs) and insight generation rather than on executing analytics?

✓ What *must* we do to capture, motivate and retain the best industry talent who is already thinking on the path of Next-Level Practices (NLPs) for the organization to be position to respond to change more effectively while delivering more in less time?

**And on the organizational design front (Prescriptive),** they'll need to answer:

✓ What changes *must* we adhere to within our leadership and culture to achieve an increase to the organization's value proposition—and which organizational practices *must* we change to reinforce organizational intent?

✓ What changes *must* we make to identify cost efficiencies across the organization to invest in the critical areas of the enterprise to drive growth—the nip & tuck effect?

✓ What changes *must* we make to define the right strategy for our leaders to put into place the enablers for the organization to be better poised to execute on predictably?

✓ What changes *must* we make to ensure access to resources is available for our leaders to directly deliver on the organizational activities that drives value proposition?

✓ What changes *must* we make to support our leaders when making decisions to eliminate resources and activities the organization can no longer afford to perform that limits opportunities within our strategy—to compete within the organization's emerging markets to further our growth?

Leaders and decision-makers must begin, if they haven't started already, exploring organizational design from a much different perspective. Preemptive Crisis Analytics, an extension of the Five W's Agenda in the Leadership GPS System, offers a different perspective to help organizations further explore new journeys using a step-wise path and approach.

It develops more **PURPOSE** with a different **PERSPECTIVE** that fuels **PROGRESSION** and builds resilience, **PERSEVERANCE** and an extraordinary ability to negotiate an increase in the capability of **PERSUASION** and process competence to achieve greater success and outcomes through your strategic work.

There's no better time to integrate a new step-wise approach to the future than now. In all, the Leadership GPS System, in its entirety, provides the necessary tools to empower knowledge professionals with the right resources and Next-Level Practices (NLPs) to allow a more simplified approach to preemptively solve challenges and problems long before they happen.

Alone, the Leadership GPS System offers accelerated insights to enhance the proliferation (creation and consumption) of analytics across every level of the organization. Thinking deeply through these issues will help leaders navigate the company towards achieving its strategic, operational and tactical objectives for greater impact on its Future Picture.

With arresting insight, vulnerability and having the right tools to empower strategic intent, the Leadership GPS System with its extension, creates a preemptive approach to solving challenges and problems that require explicit data-driven insights using the descriptive, inquisitive, predictive and prescriptive approach. It offers an oversimplification of a disruptive new conception of leadership that utilizes a mix of live interaction for you to capture and fully understand the relationships between best practices, Next-Level Decision Practices (NLPDs) and Next-Level Practices (NLPs) in leadership.

For analytics and decision sciences to become more pervasive within organizations, leaders should focus on moving into a more preemptive approach to ensure they're getting analytics creation, translation and consumption right. This approach will definitely allow them to shape how societies behave around their products and services, making change happen, making change matter and making change stick. Leaders and decision-makers at every level of the organization must have at their availability the right bionics that will both enable and empower other knowledge professionals to function and scale to a wider range of techniques when dealing with business challenges and problems.

In the future, the world will need to consume analytics to strategically compete by more thinking strategically, focusing sharply and moving more quickly to respond to change. Reallocating or relocating needed resources will take too much time causing the organization to fall decisively behind the trends of change... and this could be fatal to most organizations. As a result, the extension to the Leadership GPS System offers a descriptive, inquisitive, predictive or prescriptive approach to making the needed shifts in the organization's design long before they actually be needed. In the end, it will come down to increasing trust through competence and right-time decision-making on capability within the organization's design—and knowing exactly how to execute strategically and flawlessly to ensure the right things are getting done.

# Appendix 1
# Taking a Gemba Walk to Eliminate the Wild Side

Tools to disrupt incumbent strategy and behavior to win your competitive landscape requires a crossing over the bridge between planning and execution. This is a journey where "execution excellence" is both explored and realized using a methodological approach that simply has four independent strategies and stages:

1. A guided system known as the **Leadership GPS System**
2. A disciplined process known as **Lean Leadership** to help achieve a Minimum Viable Product (MVP)
3. A mapping system known as the **Strategy Canvas** to start a simultaneous pursuit of differentiation, growth and impact

4. A process used to achieve execution excellence known as **Performance-Driven Execution**™

This short appendix gives an overview of this material to help you, put this gaming model into perspective to Go Slow to Go Fast. Essentially, it is known as the "gemba walk" in the Lean Leadership model using Go Slow to Go Fast strategy concepts for leaders to change their views about what the future can become for their organizations. It is the main performance measurement framework used to transform the organizational behavior's when executing—strategically and flawlessly—plans of action when directives are decided on about overall performance improvement. Taking a gemba walk in Go Slow to Go Fast positions a leader and organization to make wise decisions, fasts, to ensure deliberate change is both achieved and measured. It provides the framework that not only measures performance, but helps planners identify what should be done, when it should be done, who will be the actors performing each critical task, and how to achieve execution excellence in the end. It enables decision-makers to truly execute their strategy objectives from start to finish.

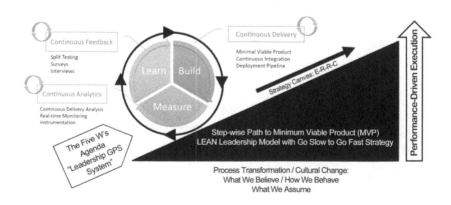

The gemba walk the overall management practice to grasp the situation before taking action on the situation. It should take place where value needs to be increased or created. Value is always created to flow horizontally, yet organizations are organized vertically and **"therein lies the problem!"** How do you take a gemba walk? You select a value stream, gather all the decision-makers (leaders and managers) from all the vertical functions that touch the value stream and walk together for the sole purpose of impacting each of the Centers of Gravity (CoGs). As the saying goes in Go Slow to Go Fast strategy, *"if we all just set-out to take walk together—a gemba walk—we wouldn't have a need to meet just to meet, wasting valuable time and resources that most of the time accomplishes very little (eliminate the frequency for meetings)."* During the walk, everyone *will* focus their efforts and their conversations by asking about the purpose of the value stream and its process, and talk to the one another along the value stream.

There are no substitutes for face time. Ideally, CEOs and COOs *must* participate in a daily or weekly gemba walk, as do customers, suppliers and value-stream leaders. Realistically, it typically falls to whoever is taking responsibility for the value stream, as well as others whose roles directly touch the value stream to create responsibility and improve accountability. Such walks occur, basically before commencing a transformation process regardless of circumstances! Ultimately, a gemba walk should occur as often as necessary to grasp situational awareness to ensure people are doing the right things to get the right things done. **"The gemba walk is the best way to truly grasp the situation so that great *lean* things can happen—from the Lean Leadership model using Go Slow to Go Fast strategy concepts."** It is a practice you learn by doing and improve by practicing the strategy and process. The gemba walk suggests that we view the organization's decisions from four perspectives to develop measures of merit, collect data, analyze and deliver a more purposeful and meaningful outcome relative to each of these perspectives.

At the end of a successful gemba walk, it basically comes down to four outcomes and questions to be answered known as unpacking the "CCBA Thinking Process:" Convert-Create-Build-Accept.

1. Why and What are setting out to convert?
2. What will we create from the initial and final assessment?
3. How are we going to build it—people and resources—and When are we expected to deliver it (continuous integration)?
4. Who will accept the finish *thing* (offering)—product or service—Where will it add value?

This process is in place to make sure decision-makers are setting out on a series of needed tasks with valuable resources to provide actual meaning and purpose to the user experience. Let's take a look at a gemba walk in action relative to the four perspectives:

## P4 Application and Engagement—"People!"

The first step in the Go Slow to Go Fast "gemba walk" is the P4 Engagement & Application improvement process that applies lean thinking to problem solving by starting with the most critical element in a problem—people! It is simply a way to present the best team possible to attack problems and challenges by making sure the right people are in the right seats to do the right things, all working towards the right objectives and for all the right reasons. P4 offers guidance to the decision-makers about who is available and who will be the best choice for the task in a simple and structured way. Some call it P4 thinking and teaming and in light of having brief conversations, the term has been adopted to mean **"aligning your best team to take a walk."** In a gemba walk, there's only one way to think and that is lean, even when choosing the people assigned to accomplish the tasks within the objectives. The P4 perspective offers a waste-free way that ultimately improve communications. It ensures the basics of teaming and maneuvering are at the forefront when starting an approach to do the right things to get the right things done.

It is also a tool that can be helpful to anyone who wants to learn and apply lean thinking to problem-solving around team building to begin a specific project that will be managed to reach a host of other improvement processes. "By standardizing and making visible the process of identifying the right people to assign to the tasks of recognizing problems and formulating solutions that require process improvements," having the right people onboard at the start *(this is still not obviously to some decision-makers)* who are already aligned for the tasks is important to reach the ideal end state.

## Diagram 5. P4 Engagement & Application Chart

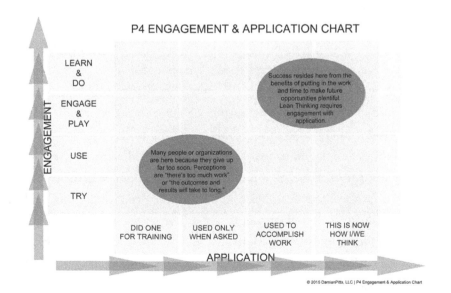

© 2015 DamianPitta, LLC | P4 Engagement & Application Chart

P4 charting identifies four types of people in any given situation within an organizational structure:

1. People who try.
2. People who use.
3. People who engage & play.
4. People who learn & do.

This breakout of the four people types determines the level of engagement an organization will have when taking a gemba walk together. As the chart describes, the people who "try" and "use" do so for one or two reasons. First, is due to them doing something new for training purposes. The next is only because they are asked by another person, normally someone in authority. These are the people who fall in one category: they basically give up on doing something far too early never reaching the end state to celebrate the benefits from the task. This is mainly due to their perspective that what they are doing either takes too long, requires too far too much effort, or is simply too hard. With these people, application and engagement will ultimately be a problem. They are basically your expected resisters to change or doing something different and new to achieve better outcomes. The 'go along to get along' and this is alright as long as you, the decision-maker, have a clear understanding about who these people are on the team.

Then, there's the other two categories types to determine the level of engagement an organization will have when taking a gemba walk together. As the chart describes, the people who "engage & play" and "learn & do" bring another completely different dynamic to the fold. These people are mostly self motivated and are used to accomplishing tasks and objectives regardless of circumstances. When they make up their minds to do something and are compelled to achieve a certain objective after making up their minds, they complete the objective because they believe in its value. These are the people who fall in much different category: they understand the value of putting in the hard work regardless of circumstances—available time and resources (or lack thereof), amount of effort, etc—and they understand the importance of continuous integration, process improvement and providing a more meaningful place with greater purpose to achieve better outcomes for all. These people fully understand the likelihood of doing what's best to get better things done.

What's important for decision-makers to understand is how to quickly assess the people already sitting in a seat within the system. Determining who they are, what level their capabilities are at, where (if at all) they can add value, if they are the right fit for the organization's future state, do they offer any value to an improvement process when striving to achieve an improved future state, and where the performance gaps are to bring in additional people resources if and when needed. P4 provides them with a tool to quickly assess where to place their people resources before embarking on a gemba walk. In some cases, a gemba walk will be required to determine the P4 situation in its own right (more resources may be required, as in performance assessments, emotional intelligence tools, etc). However, it is important to understand where people are as they relate to the four categories.

They each offer a value to the system, but only when it is fully clear when it comes to understanding roles, capabilities and resources. The P4 Engagement & Application Chart provide decision-makers the opportunity to see what they are working with before moving forward. The key is to have more people in the "engage & play" and "learn & do" categories versus the "try" and "use" categories. If the reverse is your current reality, you must do a gemba walk on your people resources before starting a walk in other areas.

Finally, P4 integrates the *12 Requirements for Building Effective Teams* into the fold by making sure the best team possible is formed for the objectives at hand. With all of the uncertainties in today's global marketplace, talk remains centered on the nuances of becoming an effective team. This starts by understanding the differences between a team and a group of people, and how to make them more effective. Even in 2015, people are still searching for the information they need to develop great teams that perform to extraordinary results and outcomes.

The focus of team building using the P4 perspective is focused on improving results, and not simply on improving relationships. This is a process that begins with measuring how clear team members look at their own individual purpose, vision, values and ability to achieve objectives, so when they are working with others, their behaviors will be focused on maneuvering and pivoting with the team to keep momentum moving in the right direction.

To get a full review of the twelve (12) requirements to be used in a P4 environment, you can review the entire article online at:

http://www.drakepulse.com/2013/12/twelve-requirements-for-building-effective-teams/

## The Leadership GPS System

The second step in the Go Slow to Go Fast "gemba walk" is the Leadership GPS System. GPS is a traditional Global Positioning System that provides satellite tracking services to be used in a wide range of commercial and personal applications. Using GPS in business and in leadership however, can carry distinct benefits for leaders and decision-makers, leading to strategically placed competitive advantages, although not every business type can benefit in the same manner. Understanding GPS in the form of a leadership system, and how to apply its applications thoroughly to your business and organizational model, will definitely help to determine whether the advanced thinking is able to take your organization to the next level. Think of your organization having its own unique *Global Positioning System* that directs your leader's decisions and the organization's strategic intent on a more meaningful purpose. That is exactly what the Leadership GPS System offers to any organization, large or small.

During the gemba walk, this global positioning system focuses the organization towards an improved Future Picture, only with greater impact. It require decision-makers to answer what is known as the Five W's Agenda to bring greater clarity to the objectives of the organizational unit:

1. **WHY** are we doing this? …WHY will it be disruptive as a behavior and action? These questions are the descriptors about your purpose.
2. **WHO** will be impacted? …WHO will benefit? …WHO will be eliminated? And, WHO will be limited?
3. **WHAT** are we applying our resources and energy (inertia) against? …WHAT is our compass heading and target (Zulu) time (end point)?
4. **WHERE** are we going? …WHERE are the gaps in our knowledge and experience for the journey?
5. **WHEN** do we plan to arrive? …WHEN should we expect the future, the event horizon and the Future Picture? This includes 'descriptive memos' regarding the decisions to achieve the organization's objectives.

Think of the Leadership GPS System as an organizational check-up in the doctor's office after dealing with significant pains that just won't go away. Unhealthy situations are bound to get worse when they are unattended to over time. This GPS system is the perfect way to identify improvements using a prescriptive approach to rebuild efficiency, direction, effectiveness, control, planning and more critical directives needed to take the organization to the next level. The Leadership GPS

System provides unprecedented mechanisms to address what the future can become for the organization. It will enhance the current suite of services or develop new and innovative one to solve internal and external issues facing the entire culture.

Used on a gemba walk, the Leadership GPS System provides a navigational system to inform on purpose, people, direction, effort, resources, time, location, decisions and objectives—anywhere the organization may be currently and definitely where the organization wants to travel in the future. It bridges the gap between planning and execution anywhere there is a line of sight towards a better future—and there's always a line of sight towards a better future in leadership. It just takes the willingness to want it more than the competition.

## Lean Leadership and the Minimum Viable Product (MVP)

The third step in the Go Slow to Go Fast "gemba walk" is the MVP mechanism to achieve your "Minimum Viable Product." A minimum viable product is the balance between a product with a minimum number of features, but just enough that someone will still want to pay for it. Take too many features out and no one will want it. Leave too many features in and it'll take too long to get to market—longer manufacturing times. In the case of a gemba walk, the traditional three (3) constructs come together to form the MVP, but we add one additional behavior to wrap the MVP in a clearly defined package for others to use the process as well. The traditional approach to arriving at an MVP is to use the Build-Measure-Learn approach. Luckily, this formulation is nothing new at this point and offers enormous information about how to achieve it without fail. The MVP presents the opportunity to spend less time designing and developing. As a result, you'll get a lot of insight early on that allows you to improve the quality of the decisions made for the expected.

It is important that you are given a short tutorial about how to achieve an MVP on your gemba walk using Go Slow to Go Fast strategy and lean thinking together to arrive at a place of improvement. This information will help you understand:

- What's a Minimum Viable Product or MVP...
- How to define your MVP...
- What required to apply your MVP Next-Level Practices (NLPs)...
- What it takes to build an MVP...
- How to launch an MVP using the Six Essential Insights and receiving user feedback...

So, what is a minimum viable product or by its short name, an MVP? This is a product that has *only* enough features to test and see if it will hold up as a viable product in the current market. To achieve this, all unnecessary features are stripped away and the application only contains the features that are look at as the core of the product.

✓ Minimum: This, as described previously, means that the product *only* contains the core features and everything that isn't a must-have is already taken out of the equation—stripped away to make it as minimal as possible.

✓ Viable: This means that the product has the opportunity to get traction and that it creates added value for people who might want it. Value today has become such a broad term when describing something, but it is important in the MVP process because it is where the product is considered worthwhile to generate enough attention that people will want to pay money for it that is much lower than the cost to build and develop it.

✓ Product: Now we get to the meat of the matter, in that you set-out to make the viable aspect a real thing. This is where the production of a needed valuable asset *(thing)* becomes something that people can actually use.

When you have a vision for a product, it's often, in most cases, a complex *thing* that you have in your mind. You want users to achieve a variety of things using your product or service, but the actual *core* is often pretty small and simple. Defining the core of your product is critical. The key is to build the first set of features and test it on the market. Developing every possible feature you have in your mind can take months, while a simple MVP can take only a couple of weeks to create. And although first impressions matter, releasing early has another advantage, **user feedback**. You'll quickly be able to assess early on where the changes need to be made to shape the product into a better offering and product that users will actually want.

The Twitter brand is a great example of a minimum viable product. It has one particular focus that is communicating using only 140 characters in real-time. You can add images to other users, but the images you send take up some of the characters, so it is important to name them wisely. It's a simple product with a social focus. On the initial launch, the company tested the concept and it succeeded. People saw its viability and value, and wanted it; hence the product validation was made and ongoing feedback continues to allow the company to make it better using continuous integration to bring us more feature sets.

What's important to realize when launching an MVP is the opportunity to learn from the feedback. If it doesn't work out and you don't get traction, then it's probably not worth continuing the development of the product. Perhaps a different idea would be more viable. Working on MVPs means taking opportunity cost in account while working on the product. After all, failing early means that it saves you time to build a successful product by stopping product development early when a product fails.

## Defining your MVP

When defining your MVP feature set, you must include the information architecture of your product as well as the technical scope for others to follow. Before you can actually start developing, you need to define your MVP, the product strategy and roadmap to achieve the end result. You must consider which features are must-haves and which ones are nice-to-haves. It's very important to stay as objective as possible during this process to avoid what we call **"Target Fixation on the Important."** This means that you continue to add what you believe to be critically important that the product must have in order to become viable, but without knowing it, you end up outside of the MVP scope. Defining your MVP must avoid the phenomena known as *Target Fixation on the Important*. With this in mind, a feature you might deeply care about might *not* be the core of the product. When this is the case, you'll need to decide if a feature set is a *"must-have"* or a *"nice-to-have."*

A typical nice-to-have is to provide the backgrounds of your development team. Instead, this feature can be added to your website to allow viewers, when they choose, to learn more about the team's functionality. Showing that you have a smart team of people around you is not that important any longer. Everyone today in the development space is smart. Once you have traction, you can find a way to demonstrate why the team's backgrounds are important on the development side to meet respond favorably to the feedback on developing new feature sets to make the product better. At this phase, it's all about limiting the time it takes to get to market—nothing more.

Next, you will want to write down the *feature set* of your product in a document. Basically, you write down all the features of your product in detail. This document is a living, breathing document that continue to gain life over a period of time you deem necessary to keep continuous integration moving in the direction of building and improving on the feature sets. It provides you with an overview of what you will be creating. It's also a useful document to brief designers and investors about the product when asked to provide further information and documentation about the product. It's simply about being able to vision-map your ideas on paper. You can also briefly mention for yourself how you accomplish a feature in a technical sense. Feature sets usually include a technical scope. This is especially useful if you work on a project where multiple developers are need to complete specific tasks.

The next step would be documenting your features in terms of priority. What's the most important feature and which are designed to create the most value in the short term (remember your 90-SRT here). Once you've defined that, you can put the remaining features on a product strategy mapping feature to define the roadmap you'll be using to build on the product once your product takes off.

To better understand your product's feature set is to rate every feature on a scale that outlines your Measures of Merit (MoM). This will allow you to take into account product VUCA: Volatility, Uncertainty, Complexity and Ambiguity to ensure added value is applied to the overall user experience. You can make better decisions in terms of the timeline for your product when you understand the various components of each feature.

### Applying your MVP Next-Level Practices (NLPs)

There are a few reminders to consider here when defining your MVP Next-Level Practices (NLPs) —to arrive at the minimum viable product. When you have an idea, take a look at the incumbent market and ask yourself:

- What similar products are out there *(trust me when I say, there are some out there regardless of how unique you might think an idea is)*?
- What are their real value propositions?
- How would you do it differently or, even more important, better?

This is also where your "CCBA Thinking Process" adds value when considering how to Convert-Create-Build-Accept.

- Why and What are setting out to convert?
- What will we create from the initial and final assessment?
- How are we going to build it—people and resources—and When are we expected to deliver it (continuous integration)?
- Who will accept the finish *thing* (offering)—product or service—Where will it add value?

Once you've finished developing and documenting your unique feature set, you should always review them to ask yourself (and your trusted advisors) if it's truly necessary. Does the user really need what you are offering? Can features be dropped or deleted to avoid building a backend? Second opinions are very valuable when scoping an MVP.

In the case if building our technology offerings at my firm FlexRight Solutions™ to deliver 21st Century Policing and Training throughout the law enforcement community, I had to consider strongly if there were any APIs, SDKs, or frameworks available that can do some of the work for me? For product strategy maps to guide your actions, it's important to plan to release ahead of schedule and try to keep your strategy maps as short-term documents. They'll be strongly influenced by user feedback at some point in the near future. Make sure to conduct the proper technical research once you've finished your feature set. No one likes surprises when they're developing a product. Talk about your idea, but be careful about the people you discuss the idea with to ensure you are receiving the right feedback and support needed to complete your objectives. You'll find there's a lot of value in feedback and when collaborating with designers, ask them to stick as much as possible to iOS, Android and Window's standards. I am saying this for good reason because it was a tough lesson to learn when developing our MVP at FlexRight Solutions™.

## Building an MVP

Every developer or team has different preferences about how to build a product. I'll keep this part brief. Build the product the way you like and don't lose sight of what you initially defined as the minimum viable product. *It's okay to say no.* Just be aware of "feature creep," especially if multiple stakeholders are involved (a known fact). And, make sure that you don't only have people around you waiting on your ideas and not offering any of their own. A lot of suggestions you have for features can be included in a next release. As long as you continue to revisit the feature set and make smart decisions based on the initial product vision and information you might gain along the way. This will definitely keep you on track.

Quality is the whole reason for taking the gemba walk so it cannot be compromised in any fashion, shape or form! Product quality is the most important step of building an MVP. Assure that your product simply works. Spend enough time to do bug fixing. If you're a solo developer, consider a small private beta with friends who will be honest to give valuable feedback. If you have the budget, hiring a QA firm can also be an effective solution to keep your product free of critical bugs that could harm the product's launch.

## Product Launch

Commend yourself now that you finally have a real product to launch. Up to this point, you've put in a serious amount of work to finally hit the market with a strong and viable offering. But, as an author, I always say, the easy part is writing the book (and that's hard for most people). Now that the book has been released, **the real work begins**. Metaphorically speaking, the tents get raised, tickets are sold, the final acts are choreographed, the music is selected, the presentations are developed, the speech is prepared and practiced, the time is set for the showing, all preparations are made about the things forgotten, and the campaign is set to hit the road. Now that all of this is completed, still there's more to do:

- You'll need to get traction for your product.
- You'll need to get feedback on your initial product.
- You'll need to identify flaws, such as market changes, product issues and missing features that are relevant to the market shifts.
- You'll need to identify your product's strengths.

Marketing your new product is not as easy as you might think. Remember, "all best laid plans will change at first contact with the marketplace—guaranteed!" Here's a tutorial to help you if you need help getting that initial traction.

Once you have a first set of users, your priorities will shift once again, but don't fret, you already knew it was going to happen. Now it's all about:

- Identifying and asking for honest feedback from your user base.
- Carefully analyzing user feedback.

- Improving and updating the product strategy map for continuous integration to continue developing.
- Developing and taking the newer version back to the market with confidence.

Don't let anyone tell you that it is easy to garner feedback from your user base. With our MVP at FlexRight Solutions™, I was sitting with the largest police department in the United States in NYPD and found myself in a meeting where we were having our lunch handed to us by the folks on the opposite side of the table. I had already made up my mind that nothing I had planned on was going to happen and come to fruition. So, I looked around the table to assess the situation and made the decision that I was going to ask the questions that would focus on our product receiving feedback from the Deputy Commissioner. The questions I asked infuriated members on our team, but when I told them afterwards why I had taken that approach at that specific time in the meeting, they fully understood. And to me as the owner, it didn't bother me at all that the team was upset. Hell, it's my company and no one was on the hook they way that my name was in the face of the client and marketplace. And that's where confidence in yourself and your abilities must be sound.

**It's not easy to get feedback from users.** The trick is to get some in-depth feedback that you can use to improve your product. It's important to always be available to your users. Have the proper social media accounts—Twitter, Facebook, LinkedIn, etc and include your contact information without being afraid to be proactive by reaching out to your users.

If you've worked with testers for your product, then you already have a list of people you can have a conversation with. Whenever you get feedback, it's important to use your TABLE methodology to properly vet it for the improvement process:

- Time-them.
- Align-them.
- Become-them.
- Lead-them.
- Execute-them.

Be aware that when something is bad, there's a bigger chance people speak up rather than when they like something. The feedback you get might be bad, but that doesn't necessarily mean your product is bad. To evaluate if your product is viable, use the right analytics to keep track of user activity and retention to compare how you'll be able to affect the value stream on the next product iteration. Remember, *statistics define if a product is viable, not user feedback*. Compare the user feedback to your original product vision and product strategy map. The most difficult part is to define how this feedback *should* and *must* shape the product vision and that's a choice every product owner needs to make for h/herself.

So, what does this all mean? The answer to this question is simple. In the Holy Bible (NLT), Matthew 25:23, it says; "...Well done, good and faithful servant! You have been faithful with a few things; I will put you in charge of many things." There's a lot of work you just completed. You've learned about the process of completing a minimum viable product in the gemba walk using Go Slow to Go Fast strategy, and you learned how to make your product development more efficient. More importantly, I hope you learned how to make better choices and decisions about your product before it is launched—and more importantly, about yourself.

I have one final bit of advice to share before we move into the Strategy Canvas in the gemba walk process. **"Know when your MVP is not viable!"** Deciding not to pursue a product idea is probably one of the hardest decisions a leader, entrepreneur, developer and owner must make at some point in the contact sport of business. No one said it would be easy and it is definitely not for the faint at heart, but someone has to do it and why shouldn't that someone be you? Statistics are extremely valuable post-launch and will help you make data driven decisions in the vast information world we are currently living. I'm definitely willing to hear about your experiences building MVP products, so please do not stop and share your stories with me to use your experiences as feedback for others going down our paths later. We're in front of them and should offer any and all guidance from our experiences to help them along their way. I also stated at the beginning of outlining the MVP process that we added one additional behavior to wrap the MVP in a clearly defined package. This final behavior is the use of your Six Essential Insights to ensure others can learn how to complete an MVP product launch. Remember to do the following six steps at some point to help others around you understand how to do the work you just completed. Make sure that you explain how you established your *Six Essential Insights* for the MVP product by doing the following:

1. Declare a Process Transformation is Required. Explain it with your Leadership GPS System.
2. Establish your Strategy—Forward.
3. Train While Working—GODOs (Tacit Knowledge).
4. Develop Master Discipline Trainers (MDTs)—Mentoring
5. Achieve a State of Crisis Leadership & Performance—Driven Execution™
6. Focus Implementation on Flawless Execution—the Art of the Debrief!

Perhaps, you'll want to share your experiences for my next book, Crisis Leadership? Please give it some thought and send me an email. All questions and feedback are welcomed as well.

## The Strategy Canvas "Mapping System"

The fourth step in the Go Slow to Go Fast "gemba walk" is the Strategy Canvas, known by its short name "E-R-R-C." It is one of the key resources used to provide additional insight to the walk by focusing "strategy execution" in the right area within the overall process. Its use is designed to help leaders and decision-makers keep a watchful eye and focus on the bottom-line. It's not only about cost cutting, but more about quality and improving the gaps in performance to ensure quality remains high. Think about it as a mechanism to control quality and to cut costs in a competitive price-sensitive marketplace without ever loosing quality in performance standards.

With this in mind, the Strategy Canvas offers a benchmarking tool on "performance quality," aligning business activities to the vision and strategy of the organization, improving internal and external communications, monitoring organization behaviors and the people involved in the process and performance against strategic objectives, and delivering quality to incumbents that has yet to be considered by others. Using the four dynamics within the system, it remains engaged throughout the overall process to:

- Eliminate things that are outdated.
- Raise factors and performance above their norms.
- Reduce factors, deficiencies and performance levels below their norms.
- Create what has yet to be considered by others to improve buyer utility within the entire value stream.

The Strategy Canvas focuses on removing defects in the workplace, in products and in services, while improving productivity and performance. It is considered when building a coalition of forces to affect both the internal and external systems and "Centers of Gravity" (CoGs). This means the following are all influenced:

- Leadership (decision-makers),
- Processes (strategies and tactics),
- Infrastructure (the organization and emerging markets),
- Populations (people), and
- Action Units (customers and vendors).

It's important to point out that the Strategy Canvas was adopted from the *Blue Ocean Strategy* and its *Four Actions Framework*. It is a tool used to reconstruct buyer value elements in crafting a new value stream curve. To break the trade-off between differentiation and low cost and to create a new value stream curve, the framework poses the four key questions *(the four dynamics within the system)* to challenge incumbent's strategic logic.

More importantly, the Strategy Canvas in a gemba walk using Go Slow to Go Fast Strategy serves two critically important purposes:

1. To capture the current state of play in the known market space that allows users to clearly see the factors that the industry competes on and where the competition currently invests and...
2. To propel users to action by reorienting focus from *competitors* to *alternatives* and from *customers* to *noncustomers* in the industry.

The value stream curve in a gemba walk is the basic component of the Strategy Canvas. It is a graphic depiction of an organization's relative performance across its industry's factors of competition. A strong value curve has *focus, divergence, convergence* and *emergence* opportunities for decision-makers and leaders to create compelling arguments along the walk as they lead up to the final leg in the walk in Performance-Driven Execution™.

## Performance-Driven Execution™

The final step in the Go Slow to Go Fast "gemba walk" is Performance-Driven Execution™. This is where the rubber meets the road. This is also where everything along the journey in a gemba walk combines to complete the transformation process for leaders, decision-makers and organizations alike. Performance-Driven Execution™, known by its short name "PDE" is all about *Managing to Learn the CCBA Management Process*. PDE is used to explore the lessons and insights of acquiring the four perspectives in what is known as the *CCBA Thinking Process*: Convert-Create-Build-Accept.

The CCBA Thinking Process represents four steps that each leader and organization must go through using all of the foundations and insights from the gemba walk to complete the entire Lean Leadership model using the Go Slow to Go Fast strategy concepts. On completion, you will have achieved what is known as the "Pearl Effect" (see diagram in Appendix 2).

The "Pearl Effect" is used to traverse the waves of disruption. It's strategy focuses on disrupting the internal system and enterprise, as well as the external industry or marketplace. It offers a unique and storied design that is inspired from the attack at Pearl Harbor, Hawaii, by the Imperial Japanese Navy on that fateful morning of December 7, 1941.

✓ **Step One: Convert** the Gemba Walk into **"Leading the Possible"** by unpacking Performance-Driven Execution™.

✓ **Step Two: Create** systems to align **"value profit"** and **"people profit"** around differentiation.

✓ **Step Three: Build** new demand for *non customers* to **move into emerging markets**.

✓ **Step Four: Accept** your new realities using the **"Four Action Behaviors"** to pull non customers to your products and services that are both "Functional and Emotional," while **increasing buyer utility and value.** This requires you to shift your productivity frontier using the differences between strategy, implementation and execution to your advantage.

The CCBA Thinking Process creates the "Pearl Effect" and essentially they are used to unpack Performance-Driven Execution™. They align people, process and purpose in understanding **"caused gaps"** versus **"created gaps:"**

✓ **Caused Gaps:** "problem solving" incumbent systems that are not meeting expectations or performance levels; the rat race of the "competitive advantage."

✓ **Created Gaps:** newly introduced "proposals or strategies" requiring a new situation or standard by raising the performance bar to create a "strategic advantage."

## Resources Needed to Understand the "CCBA Management Process"

There are four critical components used to constructs the CCBA Management Process in Go Slow to Go Fast strategy that you *must* be aware:

1. **Leadership Code Switching: the achieved** ability to modify behavior in response to rapidly changing environments using past experiences to manage psychological (limiting) challenges when moving toward the Future Picture.

2. **Four Action Behaviors:** the ability to make the best moral decisions and judgments possible, *in rapidly changing*

*environments,* to not only overcome limitations, but to also create ethical momentum while transitioning toward the Future Picture with impact. The Four Action Behaviors are used to (i) Design the Future, (ii) Target for Success, (iii) Campaign to Win, and (iv) Finish with Finesse to establish forward-motion in the Pearl Effect.

3. **Success TRAPS:** the ability to use disruptive innovation to awaken your realized potential for lasting fulfillment; and to become the "Sleeping Giant" or "Grey Rhino" that everyone fears the most due to Big-bang Disruption.

4. **Big-bang Disruption:** understanding the "Shark Fin" as your strategy in an age of devastating disruption. Essentially, this is facing the inevitable truth that details the death of one incarnation of the industry and its participating enterprises, and the emergence of a new one, driven by new technologies that may not today be ready for prime time but which, everyone knows, are just a few generations of development away from taking over (known as the "Grey Rhinos").

## Considerations used to Execute the "CCBA Management Process"

There are three considerations that you must learn when deciding to execute and begin the *CCBA Thinking Process*:

1. **The Direct Action (DA):** ability to execute a strategic operation for the overall mission objective.

2. **Direct Action Operations (DAOs):** ability to execute several strategic operations for the overall mission objective.

3. **Recon for Risk teams (R4R) or Campaign Teams:** ability to identify the right people assigned to the specific teams to execute—strategic and flawless execution—throughout a

CCBA Management Process objective. This is team building maneuvers at its best; getting the right people onboard to do the right things to get the right things done (the *12 Requirements for Building Effective Teams* is critical here).

## The Four Action Behaviors in the "CCBA Management Process"

1.  **Design the Future**: the first of the action behaviors, Design the Future, is used to identify, create and bring into clarity what the future can become (a very hard, objective and measurable picture) using the three dimensional window and perspective about the future: the "future" (compass heading), the "event horizon" (the place right before the Future Picture), and the "Future Picture" (how you expect the distant future to look prior to arriving).

2.  **Target for Success**: the second of the action behaviors, Target for Success, is used to focus on the leverage points in a system that when affected, have a disproportionate impact on the parent system and on the Future Picture.

3.  **Campaign to Win**: the third of the action behaviors, Campaign to Win, stands before everyone as a clear beacon to guide disciplined actions used to begin the attack against the Centers of Gravity (CoGs) identified within the strategy plan to achieve your **"Shark Fin" as your strategy in an age of devastating disruption.**

4.  **Finish with Finesse**: the fourth of the action behaviors, finish with Finesse, offers the ability to complete the succession process; meaning, once the objective is met or the system has changed from leveraging the Centers of Gravity (GoGs) in the direction that improves effort or increases outcomes, decisions must be made about next steps.

The Four Action Behaviors in the overall "CCBA Management Process" is what, in the end, is used to shift your productivity frontier using the differences between strategy, implementation and execution to your advantage. They allow your Recon for Risk teams (R4R) or Campaign Teams to complete the cycle of "Next-Gen" change to realize a new beginning (Created Gaps). The teams must provide converge on the Four Action Behaviors in the following manner when using the "Pearl Effect:"

- ✓ **Design the Future**: disciplined people (R4RD): the team responsible for executing waves W1-W3.
- ✓ **Target for Success**: disciplined thought (R4RT): the team responsible for executing waves W4-W6.
- ✓ **Campaign to Win**: disciplined action (R4RC): the team responsible for executing waves W7-W9.
- ✓ **Finish with Finesse—Succession**: completion (R4RS): the combined team responsible for executing waves W10.

### Case Study: What to Watch-out for that Causes Trouble

Interim solutions, however, may be enough to stay in the game, so long as those offering them are aware of their limits and keep working toward becoming a true disruptor. Knowing the "inevitable truth" (discussed earlier) is essential for innovators, in other words, but it's not enough or sufficient to formulate a winning strategy. As mountain climbers are always being warned, "Don't mistake a clear view for a short distance."

Consider Square, the well-known start-up that offers a credit card reader in the form of a Smartphone attachment. The company has been through several iterations of both its core technology and its business model since its founding in 2009. After a fast start, the company has been struggling both with scale and profitability, losing about $100 million in FY2013 amid growing talks of a sale to a larger tech company such as Google or PayPal.

Many of the obstacles facing start-up financial services companies like Square have little if anything to do with their technologies. Banking, insurance, securities and finance are all deeply regulated industries. So startups and large tech companies looking for a piece of the action tend to hover around the edges, rather than swallow the time, cost, and constraints of becoming licensed as the incumbents do because doing so would largely limit them to offering today's products and services in any case.

The key to watching out for the trouble spots like those with Square can be found in your ability to close the gaps between planning and execution. The "CCBA Management Process" provides decision-makers the tools to make bold decisions about **value and differentiation**—fast, without being bogged down in "win-lose" politics within a system.

The CCBA Management Process requires that you lead as if you have absolutely no power. The CCBA thinking process: Convert-Create-Build-Accept is neither top-down nor bottom-up when it comes to strategy, implementation and execution. Rather, it is a system in which processes are well-defined and individual responsibility is clear and placed at the lowest possible level, where the work is taking place. As a result, **responsibility** and **power (authority)**, which are generally assumed to be tightly connected, are revealed as separate and distinct. Thus, lean thinkers must focus on responsibility and ownership, which means keying on "doing the right thing," as opposed to power, which deals with who has the right to make certain decisions.

To make the shift from a power-based to a responsibility-based organization, leadership and the management system must shift the focus from a debate about who owns what to a dialogue around what is the right thing to do to move across the finish line. That's why the *CCBA Thinking Process*: Convert-Create-Build-Accept is used to help decision-makers and leaders learn to avoid relying on their powers to instruct others. They strive whenever possible to lead by influence and example (Ductus Exemplo), as if they have no power. This segment in the gemba walk instructs how to lead by example while adding value to internal buyer utility" as well as to the overall process and perspective. It's all about completing the walk with as much value as needed to ensure sustainability in the marketplace regardless of unforeseen circumstances or anything else that might disrupt the organization.

## Summation

Completing a gemba walk takes an enormous amount of discipline, rigor and work. You'll have to take the time to make the time to take the walk with your team to improve outcomes and move away from incumbent strategy and behavior. Value will be added to the customer and user experience in the long-term.

Recent management philosophy has shown an increasing realization of the importance of customer focus and customer satisfaction in any organizational structure or business after taking a gemba walk. These are leading indicators: if customers are not satisfied, they will eventually find other suppliers that will meet their needs. Poor performance from a gemba walk has only the decision-makers and leaders to blame. Poor performance is thus a leading indicator of future decline, even though the current picture may look good. Think about the events that led up to the financial collapse in 2008-2012. No one cared about the unhealthy behaviors going on because everyone was making lots of money. But in the end some years later, we're still reeling from the negative effects and poor performance that placed us on a path of near destruction.

In developing metrics for satisfaction, customers should be analyzed in terms of kinds of customers and the kinds of processes for which you'll be providing a product or service to those customer groups. And unfortunately, the gemba walk using Go Slow to Go Fast strategy is not offered in a software form. This is done on purpose to force users to get their hands dirty to learn more about their organizations and systems as possible. There's no better way to learn than to get on the ground, in the weeds, to do what Jack Welch did at GE—get everyone involved in the improvement process.

The argument will be "this process requires too much time and effort to complete." Well I say, if you don't put the time in to make the time to take the time to pivot and remain relevant, your unwillingness won't matter anyway. Once the after affects from taking a gemba walk has been developed and implemented, performance management issues can be used to get the right performance information to the right people at the right time. Organizational Behavior adds structure and discipline to implementing the steps when taking a gemba walk using Go Slow to Go Fast strategy. It will ultimately help to transform disparate organizational behaviors into information and knowledge to help communicate reasons for driving performance-driven execution at the highest levels for the overall organization. Just remember, the key aspects that will allow a Go Slow to Go Fast transformation to work must include a Leadership Triplicity™ approach:

- ✓ **Lean Leadership** helps to eliminate all forms of deficiencies throughout the process.
- ✓ **Crisis Leadership** helps to avoid risk while leading out from crises before they occur to journey beyond incumbent thinking.
- ✓ **Performance-Driven Execution** takes you beyond best practices, 'Leading the Possible,' for the world to become how you envision it!

# Appendix 2
# Unpacking Performance-Driven Execution: the "Pearl Effect"

Diagram 6. The Pearl Effect

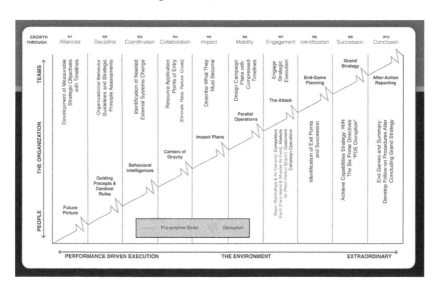

*Learn more about applying the "Pearl Effect" in the Crisis Leadership & Performance-Driven Execution publication.*

# Other Books From the Author

The Art of Detachment: Breakthrough Principles to Transformational
    Leadership
Building Great Teams: Charting the Path of Organizational Politics
Building Great Teams: Charting the Path of Organizational Politics
    *(The Monograph)*
Business Warfighting for Great Teams *(2016 Release)*
Success TRAPS: Awaken your Realized Potential for Lasting
    Fulfillment
Success TRAPS: Awaken your Realized Potential for Lasting
    Fulfillment *(The Concepts Guide)*
Successfirmations: Think, Reveal, Receive—LeaderShaping the
    Formula for Success
Execution Excellence: Strategy in the Continuum—2016 eBook
    Release / 2016 Paperback Release

Ductus Exemplo! ... Lead by Example.

# About the Author

**Damian D. "Skipper" Pitts** is the Founder/CEO at FlexRight Solutions™, *a professional services and technology development consultancy*, specializing in executive education, leadership development, decision sciences, organizational behavior and performance-driven execution. Having authored several books on strategic leadership, team building maneuvers, professional development, Lean and Crisis Leadership, he continues to help leaders and organizations look for ways to avoid risk, lead out from crises *before* they happen and go beyond best practices to impact the Future Picture.